PSYCHOLOGICAL
PERSPECTIVES
ON TRADITIONAL
Jewish Practices

PSYCHOLOGICAL
PERSPECTIVES
ON TRADITIONAL
Jewish Practices

STUART LINKE

JASON ARONSON INC.
Northvale, New Jersey
Jerusalem

This book was set in 11 pt. Galliard by Hightech Data Inc., of Bangalore, India, and printed and bound by Book-mart Press, Inc. of North Bergen, NJ.

Library of Congress Cataloging-in-Publication Data

Linke, Stuart B., 1956–
    Psychological perspectives on traditional Jewish practices /
Stuart B. Linke.
        p.   cm.
    Includes bibliographical references and index.
    ISBN 0-7657-6036-3 (hardcover)
    1. Judaism—Psychological aspects. 2. Judaism and psychology.
    I. Title.
    BF51.L56 1999
    296.4'01'9—dc21   99-13643

Printed in the United States of America on acid-free paper. For information and catalog write to Jason Aronson Inc., 230 Livingston Street, Northvale, NJ 07647-1726, or visit our website: www.aronson.com

To my parents,
Hazel and Phillip Linke,
with love and gratitude

Contents

If religion be a function by which either God's cause or man's [*sic*] cause is to be advanced, then he who lives the life of it, however narrowly, is a better servant than he who merely knows about it, however much. Knowledge about life is one thing; effective occupation of a place in life, with its dynamic currents passing through your being, is another.

—*William James*

Do you know where God resides? . . . I'll tell you. He resides where He is allowed to enter.

—*Rabbi Menahem-Mendel of Kotzk*

Acknowledgments

This book developed out of a series of lectures I gave in London at the Spiro Institute for the study of Jewish history and culture. I am grateful to the students for their insights and, especially, for their many questions which helped me to delve further into the subject matter than I might otherwise have done. The origins of this book, however, go back much further. They lie in my parents' questions—their endeavor to understand the power of the *Yiddishkeit* that they themselves had received and then passed on to me.

My wife, Jenny Goodman, has lovingly supported, challenged, and taught me throughout the lengthy process of writing this book. Some years ago she introduced me to the principles of Kabbalah and the writings of Ken Wilber, and her contribution to this book has been enormous. Jenny read the entire manuscript and many of her extremely valuable comments have been incorporated into the text.

Without the inspiring and groundbreaking work of Rabbi Zalman Schachter and the movement for Jewish spiritual renewal that he founded, this work would have never been begun. Reb Zalman has opened doors into the Jewish tradition for, perhaps, thousands of Jewish people, and I am grateful for his teachings and his personal support. I am also proud to be his student. Reb Zalman's vision far exceeds the parameters of this present book, and I am well aware that my own focus has been constricted to only one small part of the whole.

In the past the mystical side of Judaism has been a closed book to many people. The book was opened to me by Rabbi Zalman Schachter, but also by many teachers from the *Habad* movement in London and Leeds. I am grateful to all of them for teaching the *Tanya* in an atmosphere of warmth, tolerance, and mutual respect. My primary teacher of Kabbalah has been Warren Kenton through his books, workshops, and the Thursday night group.

My teachers in psychology have been my clients. Unwittingly, over a period of more than twenty years, they have taught me what is a useful psychological theory and what is not. One academic teacher, however, stands out. Early in my career Carolyn Kagan taught me how to "think psychologically" and not to be hidebound by political and artificial notions of what psychology is or should be.

Many people have encouraged and assisted the writing along the way. Rabbi Sami Barth directed me toward valuable material. The members of the *Ruach Chavurah* of London, along with many friends and colleagues, constantly asked how the work was going and offered words of support. I am particularly grateful to Aleda Erskine for her expertise and encouragement at an early stage and for setting me on the right track. And to Diane Jamal for transcribing tapes of some of my lectures and reading each draft chapter, almost as soon as it emerged from the printer.

Although I have been helped by many, needless to say, the responsibility for the text is mine alone.

Introduction

The central thesis of this book is that psychology is able to throw light on the inner meanings of Jewish traditions and customs that are hidden when only a theological viewpoint is adopted. The relationship between Jewish belief, identity, and practice is complex and intriguing. This is well illustrated by an old Jewish joke. The setting is a small synagogue where nine men are waiting to begin the afternoon service. They are delayed because they are one man short of the ten required for a *minyan*.[1] The prayer leader turns to one of the others and says "Moishe, why don't you get your son to join us?" Moishe responds, "That's no use, everyone knows that he is an atheist." "What does that matter?" says the prayer leader, "doesn't he still have to *davven minchah*?"[2] Despite the humor, the message behind this story is serious indeed. During the time of the Enlightenment the Jews in Europe became emancipated and, for the first time in centuries, left the ghettos in which they had been previously con-

---

1. The *minyan* is the quorum of ten adult males required before certain prayers can be recited. These prayers are those that must be said in community rather than privately. These include the *Kaddish*, the *Barachu*, the repetition of the *Amidah*, and the reading of the Torah.
2. Recite the statutory afternoon prayers.

fined. Many young Jewish people chose to abandon their faith in favor of the science, arts, and philosophy that they now encountered in the wider world. The response of the older members of the Jewish community was to remind their children of an old Jewish principle. Whereas belief in God is desirable, regular practice and observance of the commandments are essential.

The depth of the dichotomy between faith and practice is further exemplified by a story that emerged from the Holocaust. A group of rabbis found themselves together in a Nazi concentration camp. They had all witnessed terrible destruction and great cruelty, and their faith in God had been sorely tested. Surrounding them were thousands of fellow Jews who asked, "How can God allow this? Is God justified in permitting this terrible slaughter of the Jewish people?" The rabbis responded by forming a *Bet Din*[3] and putting God on trial. In secret they heard testimonies, examined witnesses, and debated the matter according to Jewish law. Their conclusion was to solemnly declare that the court had found God guilty. Having announced their verdict, the rabbis gathered together and recited the afternoon service.

The reverberations of both the Enlightenment and the Holocaust shape the nature of Jewish practice today. In contemporary society the observance of traditional practices is a matter of personal choice and social consensus. Although there has been a resurgence of strict observance in some parts of the Jewish community (particularly in Israel), large numbers of Jews are inconsistent in belief and practice. This raises important questions. Why do people adhere to practices when they no longer believe in the theological precepts on which they are based? Why are some practices observed with vitality and enthusiasm while others are dropped? This work is an attempt to address these questions from the standpoint of modern psychology. Perhaps people practice religious customs they do not believe in because these customs have psychological utility of which they are ordinarily unaware. These functions may have been present when the customs were

---

3. Assembly of three Rabbis empowered to make decisions according to Jewish law.

first introduced or may have been incorporated as the tradition developed over the course of many centuries.

STRUCTURE OF THE BOOK

The book is divided into two parts. The purpose of Part I (Chapters 1–3) is to familiarize the general reader with elements of both Judaism and psychology which are necessary for an understanding of Part II. Chapter 1 considers the development and nature of Jewish traditions, while Chapter 2 outlines some of the trends and movements that have been changing the face of Judaism since the start of the modern era. Chapter 3 introduces some concepts in psychology that will be crucial to our later discussion. Readers who are already well versed in the history and literature of Judaism might wish to skim over Chapters 1 and 2. Whatever the level of previous expertise, however, the psychological perspective may reveal some new dimensions in otherwise familiar material. Similarly psychologists might skim Chapter 3 and attend only to any approaches that are new to them.

Part II (Chapters 4–8) is really the "heart" of the book. Several Jewish customs are examined in detail alongside the work of psychologists relevant to the area. Each chapter follows the same format: a general introduction is followed by a description of psychological work, and the customs are then examined piecemeal.

Some selectivity in a book of this size is inevitable. In addition to the topics chosen, chapters discussing bar and bat mitzvah ceremonies, ritual circumcision, kashrut, divorce, *Shabbat*, festivals, and much else could also have been included. Choices had to be made in the selection of the psychological material presented as well. Although the formal discipline of psychology is only a little over one hundred years old, an imposing amount has already been written. Throughout this volume the principle has been to select subjects that best exemplify the psychological principles inherent in Jewish customs. It is not a comprehensive survey of Jewish tradition.

The essential background of our study is to take a close look at precisely which customs are popularly observed and what people believe about them.

PRACTICE AND BELIEF

The most recent large-scale survey of religious behavior among Jews resulted from concern about the position of British Jewish women in the United Synagogue. The United Synagogue is the largest Jewish organization in Great Britain and represents the centrist Orthodox Jewish community. Its leadership felt that they needed to respond to the concerns of women in the Anglo–Jewish community, many of whom had complained of being marginalized and ignored by the mainstream communal organizations. A review was commissioned in 1992 by the Chief Rabbi, Rabbi Dr. Jonathan Sacks, and the reviewers undertook a major survey of Jewish belief, practice, identity, demography, family and social issues, religious life, and education in 1993.[4] A representative sample of 1,350 British Jewish women, from the Orthodox, non-Orthodox, and secular elements of the community, responded to the survey.[5] Forty-eight percent of the sample told the researchers that they were affiliated to Orthodox communities, 35 percent to non-Orthodox communities (including *Masorti*[6]), and 17 percent had no formal affiliation.[7]

One of the most intriguing findings of the survey was that synagogue affiliation turned out to be a poor predictor of the observance

---

4. Schmool and Miller (1994).

5. It might be argued that as the survey focused on women only, it is not representative of the Jewish community as a whole. Nevertheless, this is not a problem for two reasons. First, focusing solely on women represents a welcome reversal of the trend of considering men to be representative of the community as a whole and ignoring women. Second, as many of the rituals are home-based practices, they are often the prerogative (according to the Jewish tradition) of women, and we can assume that men participate in them as well.

6. The pattern of synagogue affiliation in the United Kingdom is somewhat different from that of the United States and Israel. In the United Kingdom the United Synagogue is by far the largest of the synagogue institutions and is traditionally Orthodox. The *Masorti* movement is roughly theologically equivalent to the Conservative synagogue in the United States and, although small, is growing rapidly and becoming increasingly influential.

7. A survey of both women and men in the United States found that 6.1 percent described their affiliation as Orthodox, 35 percent as Conservative, 38 percent as Reform, and 10 percent as "just Jewish" (*see* Goldstein [1992]).

of key Jewish practices. For example, 30 percent of women affiliated to the United Synagogue did not consistently observe key obligations such as lighting candles every Friday night in honor of the *Shabbat*, or buying only kosher meat, whereas 26 percent of the unaffiliated women did light the *Shabbat* candles every week, and 21 percent bought only kosher meat.[8] As far as religious belief is concerned, the situation is equally as confusing. Although the small group of strictly Orthodox women in the sample held the traditional belief in God that would be expected of religiously observant people, there turned out to be little difference between the mainstream Orthodox and the affiliated non-Orthodox women in regard to their belief in God. For example, 45 percent of traditional women and 35 percent of non-Orthodox women believed that praying to God could help to overcome personal problems, leaving a large majority of these synagogue affiliates who do not believe that praying to God may help. Similarly, 35 percent of traditional women and 26 percent of non-Orthodox women disagree with the statement that "the Universe came about by chance," presumably leaving 65 percent or more who think that creation was due to chance and not the result of a Divine plan.

The picture of faith and practice that emerges from the survey is that even though levels of religious belief might be low, religious practice is quite high, but unconnected with belief. The survey also found that although religious faith was generally weak among respondents, ethnic identification was very high, and that ethnic identity was actually a better predictor of Jewish practice than either synagogue affiliation or belief. In fact, high levels of ethnic identity existed among all the groups surveyed and was not related to either practice or belief.

The authors of the survey concluded that traditional religious belief is weak but stable. Practice, however, has been selectively maintained. A quotation from their conclusions expresses this succinctly:

---

8. The United States study found that whereas 71 percent always attended a Seder and 70 percent lit Chanukah candles, only 19 percent always lit *Shabbat* candles and 15 percent maintained separate dishes for milk and meat as required by the *halacha*.

It would seem that tradition no longer involves a commitment to the precise observance of fundamental home-based rituals, out of habit or out of loyalty. Many do not observe the basic commandment of using ritually slaughtered meat, and almost one third of orthodox synagogue members do not regularly light candles on Friday night. Thus we see the development of a pattern whereby Jews feel it is acceptable simply to buy into both the community structures and religious rituals as and when these are deemed necessary. This trend, combined with a decline in faith, has conspired to transform religious behavior from a strong, value-based, organic whole, into a series of arbitrary customs and mores which are directed toward identification with a group, the Jewish people. If we exclude those who retain genuine religious commitment, for most of our respondents, the tradition, to which their daughters will refer in future life, now consists of personally acceptable practices.[9]

The authors of the "Women in the Community" survey have alluded to the notion that religious behavior is determined by personal preference and directed toward ethnic identification. In this book we will extend this idea to consider how particular Jewish customs and traditions are psychologically attuned to personal needs and spiritual development.

PSYCHOLOGY AND RELIGION

The approach to religious tradition adopted in this book is entirely new in the psychology of religion. The usual approach has been to focus on the religious experience itself (see Chapter 3). This work, however, poses questions that directly address the ways in which we manage the ordinary events of our emotional lives. For example, in Chapter 5, we will take a look at the traditional Jewish customs governing behavior after the loss of a close relative. These customs are extremely detailed and exacting, and they demand a great deal of the mourner. Theologically, they are based on such beliefs as life after

9. Schmool and Miller (1994) p. 133.

death and judgment of the deceased by the heavenly court, beliefs not easily accepted by the modern mind. The mourner is traditionally required to observe a complex series of instructions determined by generations of rabbinical authorities and recorded in the codes of conduct. It is extremely doubtful that many of the Jewish mourners who follow these religious requirements, often down to the final letter, actually believe in the religious precepts that underlie them. It is more likely that they observe them because of an entirely different set of beliefs. Perhaps they believe that it is what their relative would have wanted them to do or, that in fulfilling their religious duties, they are handing on a tradition to the generations that follow. The thesis explored in this book is that, in addition to these important influences, the customs and traditions have survived because they serve other important psychological functions—in this case, the facilitation of the mourning process. So in the chapter on mourning and bereavement we will examine the Jewish mourning customs in the light of cross-cultural data, psychological studies of the bereavement process, and our knowledge and experience of counselling the bereaved.

A similar case can be made with respect to weddings and divorces. Both of these are occasions for elaborate ceremonies and rituals, though they are, of course, quite different. What effects do Jewish weddings have on the process whereby young people individuate and separate from their parents and found a new home? Is this different for an older couple? What messages are there in the Jewish tradition for the development of a healthy and mature sexuality? And what about the divorce ceremony? In contrast to the wedding, this is usually conducted behind closed doors. How does it enable proper separation of the couple, with time for grieving for the relationship that has failed and encouragement for moving on from that relationship?

The rabbinic authorities who formulated the great codes that govern the daily life of the traditional observant Jew were also acquainted with the secret, mystical traditions of Judaism, either through theoretical study, personal experience, or both. We know, for instance, that one of the greatest rabbis of the talmudic era, Rabbi Akivah, engaged in regular meditative practices and spiritual journeys. We also have it on record that one of the greatest religious legal authorities of

I

The Development of Jewish Traditions

Judaism is a rich and complex culture that has evolved over thousands of years.[1] We cannot speak of Jewish tradition as if it is a single, monolithic entity. Instead, we must refer to an extraordinary tapestry of beliefs, customs, rituals, foods, music, liturgy, observances, and literatures spread across centuries, continents, racial groups, and societies. Although a group may argue from time to time that a particular belief is central to Judaism or that certain practices are more important than others, the reality is that we do not have a single Jewish tradition. We do, however, have Jewish traditions. It does not suit our purpose to reduce this complexity to a single set of core beliefs and practices. Rather we shall explore some of this cultural diversity and richness and attempt to understand, from a psychological viewpoint, its meaning.

Perhaps this diversity of expression has had an important part to play in the success story of Jewish survival. Let us use an environmental analogy. Farmers in a mono-crop environment have to guard carefully against diseases that could quickly wipe out the crop if they

---

1. Its origin can be dated variously from the time of Abraham, the Exodus, the establishment of the Kingdom of Judah, or the establishment of the rabbinic era following the dispersion in 70 C.E.

were to gain a hold. Conversely, fields with a wide range of varieties and grains are far more able to survive and resist disease. So too, perhaps, with Judaism. It is not our purpose to endorse a particular approach to Jewish tradition. Rather we seek to focus on the psychological processes that have influenced Jewish tradition and, in so doing, enrich our understanding of its value.

To begin our study we need to look at the sources—the great volumes of texts that record the origins of traditions and customs—and at some of the religious, social, and psychological forces that shaped them.

TALMUD

The classic view of the origins of Jewish tradition is stated clearly in the Mishnah[2] as follows: "Moses received the Torah[3] on Mount Sinai, and handed it down to Joshua; Joshua to the elders; the elders to the prophets; and the prophets handed it down to the Men of the Great Synagogue."[4] In other words, there was a chain of tradition that began with Divine revelation, and this chain ensured the faithful transmission of the revelation to the leaders of the community. The tradition holds that the Oral Law recorded all the details of how the commandments contained in the Written Law (the Pentateuch) were to be carried out in practice. Over the course of time, and often calamitous historical events (notably the great dispersion in 70 C.E.), the Oral Law was consigned to writing in order to preserve the teachings in case they were lost. The result was the creation of the Talmud, which consists of two major constituent works, the Mishnah and the Gemorah, and the written commentaries on both of these.[5] Both the

---

2. The Oral Law, compiled by Judah the Prince around the year 200 C.E.

3. The word Torah is used in Jewish writings in a number of ways. Although it refers, primarily, to the Five Books of Moses, in rabbinic literature it also refers to sacred writings from the time of the Hebrew Bible through to rabbinic commentary, philosophy, homily, study, and practice.

4. *Avot*, 1:1.

5. Completed around the year 400 C.E. The Gemorah is the rabbinic discussion of the Mishnah and some other texts that were contemporaneous with it but not selected for inclusion.

Mishnah and the Gemorah preserve the oral form in that they are written in the form of a conversation and debate between rabbis. These discussions are mainly about *halacha* (Jewish law), but are famous for the way in which the discussions wander from topic to topic before returning to the original point.[6] Because of this the text also contains a category of material called *Aggadah*—stories, customs, moral instructions, and poetry. The Talmud is the classic literature of rabbinic study.

The Talmud was composed over a period of four hundred years following the destruction of the second Temple by the Romans. This military defeat suffered by the Jews precipitated the great dispersion in 70 C.E. and, consequently, two large Jewish communities were established. One, based around those that had remained in Palestine, spawned the Jerusalem Talmud (also called the Palestinian Talmud), and another community, in Babylon, created the Babylonian Talmud. Over the centuries these communities further dispersed. With communications difficult, different traditions were established in different places. These traditions, known as *minhagim,* were based on the rulings of local rabbis who responded to halachic questions posed by their followers. The general rule was that if a person asked a rabbi about what the correct practice should be in a given instance, then the community would follow the ruling of their particular rabbi and would not follow the ruling of another rabbi, in another place, if that was different. Once the practice had been performed on two consecutive occasions, this was considered to be the *minhag* for the region. The influence of these *minhagim* can still be found around the world today in the variety of Jewish customs.

The development of traditions and customs was initially dependent on rabbinic discussion and authority. We can find many examples of the process of forming and refining laws recorded in the Talmud. There are, for example, large sections devoted to laws concerning such things as lost property, land ownership and contracts, the precise way to bring sacrifices to the Temple, and which types of work are allowed on the Sabbath and which are forbidden.

---

6. *Halacha* can be translated literally as "the way to go," but is generally understood to refer to the complex edifice of Jewish law that governs every aspect of daily life.

All of life is to be found in the Talmud; nothing is left out. The arguments between the rabbis swing back and forth and frequently deviate from the topic at hand to cover many disparate subjects before returning to the main theme. There are strict rules of logic about how arguments may be legitimately developed, and many principles and precepts are applied to wide-ranging and diverse topics. For generations the Talmud has been the intellectual stimulation for Jewish scholars. It is a lifetime's work to study it all. The Italian post-war novelist Primo Levi had one of his characters describe it beautifully: " 'The Talmud is like a soup, with all the things a man can eat in it,' Dov said, 'but there's wheat and chaff, fruit and pits, and meat and bones. It isn't very good, but it's nourishing. It's full of mistakes and contradictions, but for that very reason it teaches you how to use your mind . . . . ' "[7]

The Talmud is a very human document that often reflects human, rather than Divine, concerns. For example, the tractate *Berachot* is devoted to a lengthy and detailed discussion of the laws concerning the various blessings and prayers in the Jewish liturgy. In this tractate we find documented some of the most important prayers in Jewish life, and we know from this text that many of the prayers extant today were in daily use 2,000 years ago. We can also infer, to some extent, how these blessings were developed. One such example is when the rabbis responded to a change in political circumstances by developing a new blessing. This concerned the *Minim* (militant secularists/heretics such as the Sadducees). The rabbis instituted an extra (nineteenth) blessing to the main daily prayer (the *Amidah*) requesting that their plans come to nought. The rabbis delegated this task to various colleagues and students, who were sent away to compose a suitable blessing. The various suggestions were considered, and one was selected and added to the standard text and is in use today.

From a Talmudic perspective the rabbis understood their responsibility as interpreting the word of God contained in the Torah and applying it to daily life. The majority of the Talmud is devoted to this task and it is the basis of *halacha* for Orthodox Jews today. The

---

7. Levi (1985) p. 144.

authority for their role is derived from the Torah itself and cannot be gainsaid by any later developments or further revelations. This is well illustrated by a piece of *Aggadah*, a charming story recorded in a tractate of the Talmud otherwise devoted to legal and financial matters.[8]

The story concerns Rabbi Eliezer who had been trying to convince his colleagues that his way was correct in a particular legal matter. "If the *halacha* agrees with me," he said, "let this carob tree prove it." Whereupon a neighboring carob tree was uprooted from the ground and thrown a hundred cubits. This, however, did not convince his opponents. "If the *halacha* agrees with me," he continued, "let this stream of water prove it." The stream flowed backward, but they remained unmoved. Again he urged; "If the *halacha* agrees with me, let the walls of this studyhouse prove it," and this time the walls began to lean inward. However, Rabbi Joshua rebuked the walls saying, "When scholars are engaged in halachic dispute, what right do you have to interfere?" At this the walls stopped falling in honor of Rabbi Joshua, but remained leaning in honor of Rabbi Eliezer. Finally Rabbi Eliezer declared, "If the *halacha* agrees with me, let it be proved from heaven!" Whereupon a Heavenly Voice cried out, "Why do you dispute with Rabbi Eliezer, seeing that in all matters the *halacha* agrees with him?" At this Rabbi Joshua arose and quoted from the book of Deuteronomy saying, "It is not in heaven." Another scholar, Rabbi Jeremiah, explained what he meant. "The Torah had already been given at Mount Sinai." We pay no attention to a Heavenly Voice because it is written that the decision-making is now in the hands of the majority of the rabbis.

The story has a postscript. Rabbi Nathan met Elijah (the prophet) and asked him, "What did the Holy One do in that hour?" Elijah responded, "He laughed with joy saying, 'My sons have defeated me, my sons have defeated me.'"

There is a rabbinic dictum that Jewish law should not be impossible or, for that matter, even difficult, to practice. And it is under-

---

8. *Baba Metziah* 59b.

stood that the early rabbis took care to interpret the law in such a way as to be mindful of the needs and capacities of ordinary people. Furthermore, it seems that the rabbis were not beyond incorporating folk customs into the standard rituals. For example, Chanukah (the midwinter festival of lights) receives very little attention in the Talmud. It is mentioned specifically in only two places and in one of these the Gemorah describes the rabbis asking the question, "What is Chanukah?"[9] Apparently it was not a custom they were familiar with. They received the response that *Chanukah* is a festival of candle lighting that the people observe to commemorate a miracle in the Temple during the time of the Greek occupation. Nowadays Chanukah is a popular and widely observed minor festival. On another occasion the rabbis were uncertain about what the correct practice of a custom should be, so they decided to go out into the street to see what the people were doing and they made their ruling based on what they observed the custom to have been.[10]

These examples all point to an important point. On the one hand, the rabbis of the Talmud were concerned to interpret the Bible to understand accurately the word of God, but they were also interested in applying the law in humane and acceptable ways. This is a point made forcefully by Rabbi Louis Jacobs, an Orthodox scholar who has, controversially, questioned some of the received assumptions about both the origins of Torah and the process whereby *halacha* was determined. As far as *halacha* is concerned he expresses his main idea as follows: " . . . . the *halacha* . . . . far from being entirely self-sufficient and self-authenticating, is influenced by the attitudes, conscious or unconscious, of its practitioners toward the wider demands and ideals of Judaism and by social, economic, theological and political conditions . . . . "[11] Rabbi Jacobs suggested that these extrahalachic considerations are most evident in the rabbinic literature that came after the Talmud, but his general thesis applies throughout.

---

9. *Shabbat* 21a.
10. *Eruvin* 14b.
11. Jacobs (1984) p. 9.

MIDRASH

For one thousand years after the composition of the Talmud another category of literature, *midrash*, was developed. It is a literary form that could not be more different from the legal discussions of the *halachists*, yet it exists alongside their dialogues and amplifies their debates. The *midrash* includes *Aggadic* material contained in the Talmud as well as volumes of independent material and is usually organized around a particular book of the Bible. Hence we have collections of *midrashim* based on most of books of the *Tenach*. In them we find fantastic tales of mythic creatures, along with lengthy narratives involving familiar characters from the Bible, yet relating tales that do not appear in the biblical text itself. We have already encountered the story of Rabbi Eliezer in the Talmud. A few additional examples will give us a fuller flavor.

The *midrash* expands greatly on the miracle of the waters parting as the Israelites crossed the Red Sea.[12] It tells us that the waters formed a roof-like protection over their heads, that it split into twelve individual pathways (one for each tribe) with transparent walls of solid water, that the ground was perfectly dry beneath their feet, but it was like clay for the Egyptians, and that if a Jew became thirsty, he had only to reach out his hand and the wall melted, yielding sweet drinking water, and then returned to a solid wall once again.[13]

Another example: on the occasion of the revelation of Torah at Mount Sinai, The Children of Israel not only heard God's voice but actually saw the sound waves as they emerged from his mouth. They visualized them as a fiery substance. Each commandment traveled around the entire camp and then came back to each Jew individually asking, "Do you accept on your self this commandment with all its details?" Every Jew responded "Yes" after which the fiery substance engraved itself on the tablets of stone.[14]

The Hebrew word *midrash* means "to seek out," and this tells us its primary purpose. The Hebrew text of the Bible does not spell out

---

12. Exodus 14:21–23.
13. Weissman (1980) p. 129.
14. Ibid p. 182.

all the details of all the narratives contained within it. The authors of the *midrash* provide us with the details we require to fill in the gaps. And it is not simply a matter of completing the stories. The *midrash* sometimes raises new questions about a text and will also instruct us about deeper meanings that we might otherwise have missed. The two examples given above, by embellishing the original account, take us more directly into the experience itself.

At times the *midrash* can be psychologically sophisticated and direct. The Bible explains that the second patriarch, Isaac, is blind in his old age.[15] We are, however, given no adequate explanation for his loss of sight in the text. The *midrash* helps us out. It tells us that when, many years earlier, Isaac was bound by his Father ready to be sacrificed,[16] the sun flashed on his father's raised knife and this flash of light blinded him. This is surely a simple and brilliant statement about the effects of early trauma on development and about the mechanism of psychological denial.

The nature and style of *midrashic* literature are very familiar to the psychologist. It has all the qualities of a dream. The characters and tales that arise are rarely intended to be taken literally; their meanings are disguised in symbols. In the *midrash,* as in our dreams, we frequently find that characters from later stories are transposed into earlier narratives and that figures are transported across time and space in improbable ways. Thus we find in one classic example, recorded in the Talmud, that Moses is sent forward in time secretly to observe the Talmudic sage Rabbi Akivah teaching his students the very material that Moses had himself received at Mount Sinai. Midrashic material provides us with a key to the unconscious aspects of the Jewish mind. It both expresses the unconscious and, importantly for our purpose, helps to shape and mold the unconscious. So, when examining Jewish traditions, we will need to look at *midrashim* that relate to the topic we are discussing.

The main corpus of *midrashim* was composed during the first thousand years of the Common Era. A great deal of the literature was

---

15. Genesis 27:1.
16. Genesis 22.

based on the texts attributed to the early sages and recorded in the Talmud. The relative importance of this original material is controversial, as it has usually been seen as secondary to the halachic discussions. Nevertheless, its significance may have been greater than we realize. It was sufficiently important to include in the Talmud, whereas a great deal of other original material was left out. It is part of Louis Jacobs's argument that this *aggadic* and *midrashic* material had an important influence on the legal discussions within the Talmud. Furthermore, these *midrashim* were later expanded upon, reworked, and collected into large anthologies in the form of exegetical and homiletic commentaries on the biblical text.

"Turn unto me ye unlearned, and lodge in my *Bet Midrash*" (*House of Midrash*). This quotation from an early homiletic text discloses the true purpose of *midrash*. It is not necessary to be a scholar or an academician to understand the essence of Jewish tradition. The *midrashim* convey the atmosphere and culture of Jewish law in a way that is immediate and directly accessible. It is so successful a device that for many people midrashic material, Talmudic material, and biblical texts have become confused and interwoven. A familiar example of this is the Passover Haggadah.

The Haggadah is the text relating the story of the Exodus that is read in the home on the first and second nights of Passover. It is an extremely popular ritual that takes the form of a highly dramatized reading, punctuated by song, poetry, and ceremony.[17] The text interweaves biblical verses, *aggadic* passages from the Talmud,[18] and *midrash*.[19] The effect is that the Passover meal has become a superb pedagogic and communal occasion. Many people are unable to distinguish between the parts of the story that are true to the biblical

---

17. The "Women in the Community" review reported that ninety-six percent of traditional women, seventy-five percent of non-Orthodox women, and thirty-two percent of secular women attend a Seder (Passover meal) every year. This makes the Seder the most widely observed of all the Jewish traditions surveyed.

18. For example, the story of the rabbis of *B'nai Brak* can be found in the *Tosefta* on *Ketuvot* 10a.

19. For example, that God rebuked the angels for celebrating when the Egyptians were killed by the plagues and drowned in the Red Sea.

text and those parts that are embellishments added by the sages over the centuries for homiletic purposes or simply to add drama to the occasion.

THE CODES AND RESPONSA

We have already seen how the *halacha* ranges over all aspects of life. It must have been inevitable that different halachic authorities, in different communities and countries, would have reached different conclusions at different times. Sometimes this may have been because they addressed issues in slightly different ways and sometimes it was because they based their decisions on different source texts. In pursuit of consistency, great codes of Jewish law were established. These codes sought to perform two functions: first to standardize the *halacha* in areas where there may have been uncertainty, and second to summarize the conclusions of halachic authorities for easy reference. The codifiers would often state that their intention had been to produce a code that was both definitive and comprehensive. However, new authorities would come along and proclaim that their code was superior to previous efforts and dealt with situations that had not previously been covered. In consequence the codes proliferated.

The process of codification began with the Mishnah and continues until the present day. The literature, however, is dominated by two landmark texts and, for the most part, we shall restrict ourselves to these. The earlier of these is the *Mishnah* Torah[20] by Rabbi Moses ben Maimon, who is known popularly either as Maimonides or by the acronym *RaMBaM*. The second text is the *Shulchan Aruch*, attributed to Rabbi Joseph Caro.

From the outset Maimonides's work was controversial and reactions to his approach, both positive and negative, dominated the halachic literature from the twelfth century onward. Maimonides's explicit claim, made in the introduction to the *Mishnah* Torah and elsewhere, was that from then on no one need ever refer to the dis-

---

20. Also known as the *Yad Hazakah* (*The Strong Hand*) or *Yad* because the numerical value of *yad* is fourteen, which corresponds to the number of sections in the work.

cussions in the Talmud for a legal ruling. Maimonides believed that his review of the previous legal discussions was so complete that there would never be variance between his code and the accepted conclusions by previous *halachists*. In fact, Maimonides went so far as to publish the conclusions of halachic debate without providing the names of the authors of the different opinions that had gone to produce the final ruling. Neither did he give references to where a matter had been previously debated in the Talmud. This was an innovation in halachic literature and was the cause of much of the later controversy.

Maimonides (1135–1204), was a giant of the Jewish world of his time, and has remained a dominant figure in Jewish thought. He was born in Cordova, during the Golden Age in Spain, but from the age of about 30 lived in Egypt, where he flourished. He was a scholar of outstanding brilliance, the head of the Cairo Jewish community, and also, for many years, the physician to the viceroy of Egypt. His published works include *The Guide to the Perplexed,* which was a philosophical defense of Jewish, indeed religious, theology against the Aristotelian critique that was almost universally accepted by the intelligentsia of the time. This intelligentsia included many Jews, and it is significant that Maimonides devoted so much intellectual effort to addressing their concerns. In so doing, he came close to arguing that an understanding of Aristotle was necessary before the Jewish view of God could be properly understood. This caused considerable furor and a somewhat violent reaction from traditionalists within the community.

The arguments surrounding his code, the *Mishnah* Torah, were of a different nature. Later authors criticized Maimonides, arguing that a *dayan* should not make legal decisions without reference to the various opinions stated in the Talmud.[21] In their view this could lead to bad practice and bad decisions. Although they were critical of the *RaMBaM's* approach, for the most part they did not criticize his conclusions, and his code was eventually widely accepted. Even his fore-

---

21. A *dayan* is a senior rabbi appointed to make decisions according to Jewish law, usually as a member of a *Bet Din.*

Samson Raphael Hirsch set out to defend Orthodox Jewish life in the face of some dramatic changes that had occurred in the Jewish community. These were primarily the political emancipation from the ghettos of medieval Europe, the intellectual challenge from the enlightenment, and the growing reform movement (see Chapter 2) of the period.[32] His basic notion, like that of the reformers, was that the modern world was to be embraced and not shunned. However, he saw it as the responsibility of Orthodox scholars to show how Orthodox belief was in fact compatible with modern life. In so doing he followed the path of his illustrious predecessor, Maimonides, and encouraged his students to take up serious study of secular subjects and to do so as part of their Jewish education.

As one of his innovations Hirsch introduced new styles of worship without compromising his orthodoxy. He transformed services from the informal, rather anarchic style associated with small communities and lay leadership and introduced a considerable degree of formality and ceremony. There were now trained choirs and the ministers wore canonical robes like their gentile counterparts. Hirsch preached in High German rather than the homely Yiddish that had been more customary."[33] He even went so far as to delete the famous *Kol Nidre* prayer from the service on Yom Kippur (Day of Atonement), declaring it inappropriate for modern times.[34] Another innovation was to hold wedding ceremonies inside synagogue buildings, rather than in the open air, which had been the usual practice.

Hirsch recognized that each individual Jew now had to develop a dual personality: that of the Jew and that of the citizen; that of Torah and that of the secular. To the extent that occupation with secular activities was compatible with Jewish religious principles, Hirsch was content. If there was a conflict, then it was the path of Torah that

---

32. Hirsch published his arguments in "The Nineteen Letters on Judaism" (1836).

33. It is interesting to observe the reversal of this trend in modern times with the development of small alternative services in synagogues, *chavurot* (small, informal groups), and *Shtibles* (small highly Orthodox synagogues).

34. Prayer for forgiveness for broken vows recited on the evening of Yom Kippur.

should predominate. Hence, the maintenance of Jewish practice became a matter of individual conscience, rather than simply a result of a habit reflecting the community in which one was raised. Intellectual conflict, however, was inevitable. The debate between religion and science was the hallmark of the age and, of course, this produced an internal psychological conflict within the individual.

The situation that Rav Joseph Soloveitchik encountered in the middle of the twentieth century was even more complex. Science and religion had grown further apart and it now seemed to many that they were philosophically incompatible. Furthermore, Soloveitchik perceived that modern American Jews had little interest in fidelity to Jewish tradition for its own sake, but were more concerned with participating in, and experiencing, a Jewish culture. His solution, however, was stark and startling. The individual is not to retreat into the intellectual ghetto of fundamentalism and turn away from modern secular life and thought. Rather, he or she is to embrace the inherent existential conflict as an inevitable facet of being an Orthodox Jew. His major philosophical work, *Halachic Man*, set this out most clearly.[35] In this essay he explains how the events of ordinary life provide opportunities for halachic observance. When the halachic course is chosen, this may separate the individual from the wider secular culture and set them apart. His image is that of "the lonely man of faith" who sets observance of Jewish Law above personal and emotional needs, in the service of spiritual life and obedience to God.[36] It follows that the religious individual is required to participate in all aspects of secular society and to study secular subjects alongside Jewish ones. However, as one does so, the question in front of the individual is, "What does the *halacha* require of me?" This does not make for an easy or harmonious existence, but for Soloveitchik, it is the only path of integrity.

Before concluding our survey of the development of Jewish tradition, there are four other important influences that we must give full weight to. These are the *Musar* or ethical movement of Rabbi

---

35. Soloveitchik (1944).
36. Soloveitchik (1965).

Israel Salanter, the hasidic movement founded in the eighteenth century in Eastern Europe, non-Orthodox or progressive forms of Judaism, and the Jewish feminist movement. Together, they provide the intellectual backdrop and starting point for our psychological analysis of Jewish tradition. We will encounter them in the next chapter.

2

Judaism and Modernity

We are not the first to search for psychological insight within Jewish tradition. Throughout this book we will encounter individuals, schools, and entire movements that have engaged with the difficulties of understanding human motivation, behavior, and consciousness from a Jewish point of view. In this chapter I have selected four groups that have been pillars on which my understanding has stood. *Musar*, hasidism, progressive Judaism, and Jewish feminism have all addressed different aspects of tradition. Each is needed to reach a whole.

The *Musar* school recognizes the struggle that each of us has when we come to align our lives with our highest ethical aspirations, and it has given us tools to help us overcome the psychological and emotional barriers that we face. In hasidism we encounter those who seek to directly experience the spiritual aspect of life and make it manifest in the material world. Progressive Judaism teaches about the prophetic capacity to transform our society and the struggle between individual autonomy, tradition, and the covenental relationship with God. Jewish feminism exposes aspects of the deep structure of Jewish consciousness and profoundly challenges us to rethink the basis and nature of Jewish tradition. Each of these has had, often in overlapping ways, an enormous impact on our psychological understanding of the inner meaning of Jewish traditions.

THE *MUSAR* MOVEMENT[1]

The *Musar* movement, however was founded in the 1840s by Rabbi Israel Salanter (1810–1883).[2] Salanter's original aim was to encourage the moral and ethical development of young Torah students by introducing a large selection of *Musar* material into their curriculum of studies. It became, however, through the indefatigable efforts of Rabbi Salanter and his students, an enormous influence on the spiritual life of large sections of the Jewish community—at first in the Eastern European Pale of Settlement[3] and later in Germany and France. As we shall see, the *Musar* perspective was truly psychological. It concerned itself with the structure of the psyche and the soul,[4]

---

1. *Musar*, the Hebrew term meaning "ethics", generally connotes literature directed toward moral development and self-improvement. Of course, in one sense, all religious writings have this aim; however, *Musar* is generally considered a distinct category of Jewish literature. In the biblical context the books of the prophets, in which the Jewish people are rebuked for their wrongdoing, are considered *Musar*, along with the book of Ecclesiastes (Kohelet). In later periods the category included specific books of moral instruction by respected and influential rabbis and also works of moral philosophy. This latter category includes texts discussing the structure of, the character from a rabbinic perspective.

2. Rabbi Israel Lipkin took the name Salanter to denote his association with the town of Salant where he had studied during his youth. As a young man he had moved to the city of Vilna and established a reputation for himself as a brilliant and original talmudic scholar. Within a few years he had founded his own yeshiva (advanced rabbinic academy) and a distinctive style of talmudic discourse. This style owed much to the training he had received from his teachers in Salant.

3. The Pale of Settlement refers to the areas where Jews were legally permitted to live on a permanent basis by the Czarist authorities (1791–1917). These areas were principally in Poland, Lithuania, the Ukraine, and White Russia.

4. The terms *psyche* and *soul* are often used interchangeably, although the term soul is usually reserved for use in a religious context. Soul is very similar to psyche, which itself originates in Greek myth. (Psyche descends into the underworld, sent on a dangerous journey by Venus to retrieve caskets. Venus tries to kill Psyche because of her love for Venus's son Amor.) In Kabbalah, the soul refers to a level of spiritual awareness that mediates between the physical, psychological, and spiritual

the nature of the human character and human desire and, as its ultimate goal, methods of characterological and behavioral change. Rabbi Salanter's concerns were quite simple. From his perspective as a Rosh Yeshiva,[5] if Torah study didn't lead to high standards of ethical behavior and personal fulfillment, then something had to be wrong. He set out to make a *Tikkun*[6]—to put it right—through his teachings and by his personal example.

Many legends have come down to us about the life of Rabbi Israel Salanter and, as with all legends, their historical basis is difficult to verify. Stories about his life have become one of the main pedagogic instruments of his followers. They are responsible for the popularity of his ideas outside the yeshiva world. From this perspective, the accuracy of the details is unimportant. Two such legends will suffice to set the scene and give a flavor of his teachings. They are both illustrations of the way in which strict interpretations of the *halacha* need to be softened by a concern for the welfare of ordinary people and the imperative of ethical behavior.[7]

The first story is taken from a time when Rabbi Salanter occupied an official rabbinic position in the community. He was called upon by the owner of a *matzah* factory to inspect the premises and issue a certificate of kashrut.[8] Rabbi Salanter inspected the factory but

---

worlds. Conversely, psychoanalysts often make a great play of Freud's identification of the soul with the mind and discount any other form of influence or awareness. However, Bruno Bettelheim has sharply challenged this psychoanalytic orthodoxy. He was a native German speaker and has argued that the German terms used by Freud (*Seele* and *Seelische*) have been erroneously translated as "mind" or "mental apparatus" and that these terms really refer to "soul" which, in German, has an avowedly spiritual meaning and that this had been Freud's original intended meaning (Bettelheim [1982] pp. 71–78).

5. Head of the academy.

6. The term used in *Musar* literature for making a correction. It is connected with the kabbalistic conception of the task of the human being in the world.

7. Both of these tales were told to me by personal acquaintances. I have not seen them recorded anywhere in print.

8. *Matzah* is unleavened bread eaten during the festival of *Pesach* (Passover). Great care is taken to ensure that *matzah* is not allowed to rise, and it is the custom for the premises to be inspected by a *mashgiah* (authorized inspector), who will issue a certificate of kashrut declaring that *matzah* is fit to eat during Pesach.

refused to issue the certificate. The owner of the factory was incensed with anger. "What did you find wrong?" he exclaimed. "Surely everything is in order?" Rabbi Salanter replied that he had found everything to be correct according to the strict interpretation of the law. "Then why won't you issue the certificate?" said the owner. "I will not issue a certificate authenticating the *matzah* produced in this factory," he said, "while the workers who produce the *matzah* are so poorly paid and badly treated." For Rabbi Salanter, the exploitation of the workforce invalidated the kashrut.

The second story is known in two versions. In both versions Rabbi Salanter is traveling and happens upon a small community shortly before *Shabbat*. The richest men of the community compete with each other to invite the great sage to their houses for a *Shabbat* meal after the Friday night service in the synagogue. Rabbi Salanter accepts one of the invitations and enters the home, which has been specially prepared to honor the illustrious guest. The master of the house, however, behaves pompously and orders his wife around, criticizing her loudly and demanding that she make a fuss over Rabbi Salanter. In one version of the story, before the meal was eaten, the master of the house pronounced the *Kiddush*[9] slowly and at great length, evidently keen to show his guest how piously he had fulfilled his religious obligations. When he had finished, the Rabbi turned to him and asked, "Why is it our custom to cover the bread with a cloth while we make the blessing over the wine?"[10] "The *baal habayit*[11] was quick with his reply. "Rabbi," he said, "it is well known, even to little children, that if the bread could see what was happening it would be jealous of the wine being blessed first. So we cover the bread to protect it from this embarrassment." Rabbi Salanter rebuked his host

---

9. Sanctification and blessing of the wine in honor of *Shabbat* before the meal.

10. Two loaves of special bread (*challah*) are blessed after the wine has been sanctified and drunk. The custom to cover the loaves has several explanations in addition to the one given in this story. The most popular is that, as the bread represents the manna that was eaten by the Israelites while they wandered for forty years in the desert, the cloth represents the layer of dew that covered and protected the manna and prevented it from going moldy.

11. Master of the house.

sternly. "You show concern for the bread, yet you are willing to publicly embarrass your wife in front of all this company."

The second version of the story provides a different ending and a slightly different lesson in *Musar*. Before blessing and eating the bread, each of the diners is required, according to the *halacha*, to wash hands and pronounce a blessing. The *baal habayit* made a great show of pouring water over his hands, but when Rabbi Salanter came to wash he used only a little water. The *baal habayit* questioned his behavior and invited him to wash more elaborately. Rabbi Salanter refused, however, explaining that he had seen how far the servants had to go to fetch the water and that, as water is so heavy to carry, he had no wish to make their burden greater.

Stories such as these, although inspiring and instructive, were not the main basis of *Musar* doctrine—this was more scholarly. A great intellectual, Rabbi Salanter was frequently referred to as a Gaon and was held by many to be the supreme halachic authority of his era.[12] The intellectual origins of the *Musar* movement are disputed,[13] but the general view held by the students and followers of Rabbi Salanter is that they derive from the legacy of the great Rabbi Elijah ben Solomon of Vilna (1720–1797) known as the Vilna Gaon. The Vilna Gaon was the outstanding scholar and spiritual leader of Eastern European Jewry of the period. He was also the founder of the Mitnagdic movement, which stood in profound and militant opposition to the hasidim.[14] The Vilna Gaon was both a halachist and a

---

12. Gaon (meaning "eminence") originally was the name given in the Babylonian community (sixth to eleventh centuries) to the greatest Talmud scholars of the generation who exercised considerable political power and were the halachic authorities of their day. The term was later used as a title of honor for outstanding Torah authorities.

13. *See* Etkes (1993), Chapters 1–3, for a scholarly discussion of this topic.

14. *Mitnagdic* is a Hebrew term meaning "opposition." The Mitnagdic movement was formed in opposition to the hasidim who they severely criticized because they considered them to have deviated significantly from the proper path of rabbinic Judaism. Although the hasidim kept to the *halacha*, the Mitnagdim took exception to some of their theological doctrines and to the adoption of the Sephardic mode of prayer (*nusach sepharad—see* Chapter 1). In particular they objected to their reverential attachment to their *Rebbes* or *Tzaddikim* who were the charismatic spiritual leaders of the various hasidic groups, no doubt fearing a return to the cult of

kabbalist, but his main concern was with commitment to a life embodying the principles of Torah and of *yir'ah* (the fear of heaven). The followers of the Vilna Gaon respected both his learning and his way of life, which included lengthy periods of seclusion and asceticism (especially during his youth). The Vilna Gaon commended this path to his students as the principal way of acquiring *yir'ah*, which he deemed necessary for the refinement of the character traits or *midot*.

The Vilna Gaon had concerned himself with explaining the nature of the soul to his followers and, in so doing, clearly articulated a psychological perspective. He distinguished between the conscious intellectual soul and the vital soul that contained character traits and appetites that inhabited the body. These appetites had both positive attributes (derived from heaven) and negative attributes (derived from the *sitra achra*—"the other side"). The task of the individual was to tame the appetites by means of restraining the negative aspects and developing the positive ones. This could be achieved, over time, by ascetic practices and immersion in Torah study. Such Torah study had to be self-motivated, for its own sake, and not for any other purpose (such as teaching for payment or gaining honor among peers).[15]

The teachings of the Vilna Gaon were widespread. A center of learning had been established in the Lithuanian town of Salant where Israel Lipkin (later Israel Salanter) was sent to study by his father. It was here that the young Israel encountered *Musar* for the first time. Israel was attracted to the personal qualities of the teachers, which he perceived as demonstrating great *yir'ah*, and he began following the recommended daily practice of self-examination and self-rebuke in order to ward off the influence of the evil impulse. He was a talented Talmudist and became known as an *illuy*, a great prodigy of Torah. At the age of 30 he moved, with his family, to Vilna. Once in Vilna he quickly established himself as an outstanding and original teacher

---

Shabbetai Tzvi (see main text below). In 1772 the Vilna Gaon issued a *herem* (a ban of excommunication) on the hasidim, which culminated in the arrest of one of their leaders (Rabbi Schneur Zalman of Liadi, the founder of Lubavitch or Habad hasidism) and his temporary imprisonment in St. Petersburg in 1798.

15. Known in rabbinic literature at *Torah Lishma*.

and established his own academy. Vilna was the center of rabbinic study of the period, and at that time the Jews of Vilna had not yet been greatly influenced by the forces of the Haskalah (Enlightenment).[16]

Rabbi Salanter traveled a great deal, working furiously to promote his methods. In later life he moved to Western Europe, particularly Germany, where he encountered the Maskilim, the teachings of Rabbi Hirsch (see Chapter 1) and the Reformers (see below).

In the sixth decade of his life Rabbi Salanter's thinking entered a deeper and, in many ways, more modern phase. He became increasingly aware that the old methods of *Musar* were a necessary but insufficient condition for character development and refinement. He had already realized that to fully grasp the truth of Torah a student's mind had to be both pure, that is, freed from the influence of the evil impulse (negative aspects of the appetites), and also sharpened to a keen edge by the intellectual training acquired through rigorous study of the Talmud.[17] But more was needed. In Germany and France, Rabbi Salanter had contact with some of the central ideas of Western philosophy. In particular he read the works of those who became the intellectual precursors of Freud and modern psychoanalysis such as Immanuel Kant.[18] Through this influence he discovered the role of what would later be called the unconscious, and as a consequence of this began to refine and further develop his approach to *Musar*. Al-

---

16. The term *Haskalah* (Enlightenment) refers to the movement dedicated to spreading modern European culture among the Jews between the 1750s and 1880s. The followers of the Haskalah were known as Maskilim. The Haskalah was an attempt both to modernize Jewish religious culture and also to establish a Jewish literary culture (including the use of literary Hebrew) capable of participating in the non-Jewish world. It was at its strongest in the western European communities and slowly spread east into Lithuania, where it came under the influence of those Russian monarchs who sought to improve the position of the Jewish communities. In supporting the Haskalah they succeeded in establishing, for the first time, rabbinic schools whose primary aim was to train rabbis rather than teach Torah "for its own sake." As such they succeeded in strengthening the Jewish communities but threatened to weaken pure scholarship, and for this reason were opposed by Israel Salanter.

17. Utilizing a technique of stylized argument and disputation known as *pilpul*.

18. Etkes (1993) p. 304.

though in many ways Rabbi Salanter had throughout his life remained firmly within the traditional yeshiva world and had been wary of the approach of *Torah im Derech Eretz* advocated by Rabbi Samson Raphael Hirsch (see Chapter 1), his later involvement with Western thought was actually a prime example of the integration of tradition and modernity.

We now turn to an examination of the *Musar* doctrine itself and the psychological principles it embodies. Rabbi Salanter articulated his concerns in the form of an extended discussion of the best methods of *Tikkun ha-midot*—character training.[19] Salanter thought that bad character traits could be reformed by perseverance and also that repeatedly enacting the preferred behavior would subdue the appetites. This technique is similar to the principle of "overcorrection" adopted today by behavioral psychologists. In so doing a significant change in personality could be achieved. The personality would then be in perfect harmony with the *mitzvot*, and all psychological barriers between an individual and God would have been removed. No particular *mitzvah* or injunction was implied by Salanter; rather, he was referring to a lifestyle attuned to the performance of God's will.

This approach to character training was not particularly innovative, but Salanter differed from some of his distinguished predecessors in important ways. Maimonides, for example, had stipulated that it was possible for all evil impulses to be subjugated by the individual, whereas Salanter extended the idea and believed that it was possible to not merely subjugate the impulses (*kibbiz hayetzer*), but also to correct or transmute them altogether (*tikkun hayetzer*). The early kabbalists had adopted a comparable approach to the issue and had spoken of two kinds of soul: the soul that experiences evil desires, but does not act upon them, and the soul that has negated all evil desires.[20] Consequently, the character is naturally inclined toward the

---

19. *See* Etkes (1993) Chapter 18.
20. For example *sha'arei kedusha* by Chaim Vital. Vital was the foremost follower and student of Isaac Luria in Safed and recorded and published his teachings.

mitzvot and, for such individuals, character training is not necessary.[21]

Salanter spoke of "dark" and "light" forces in the psyche, paralleling the ideas of the unconscious and the conscious in modern psychology.[22] The "dark" forces exercised an influence on behavior in ways of which the individual was not usually aware. He saw the dark forces as being more powerful than the light forces. He pointed out that the dark forces were only removed from concealment and brought into awareness by the way in which they responded to external stimuli. Such responses were often disproportionately large and exerted an influence on behavior that could not be controlled by the usual *Musar* methods of self-rebuke and moral education. In fact, because of their hidden nature, they could not be revealed by self-analysis. Even those who had otherwise managed to train their external character and had achieved good control over their appetites could be thrown off course if they came across a stimulus that provoked a response from the dark forces.

The unconscious in Salanter's descriptions has some resemblance to the unconscious later depicted by Freud. However, unlike Freud, Salanter did not go on to fully develop a model of the way in which the contents of the unconscious could become known to a person. He assumed that this was not possible. Instead, Salanter returned to the basic *Musar* approach and recommended that although self-analysis and contemplation were limited, they were still useful tools. One could become adept at recognizing occasions and circumstances when the dark forces had broken through and use this knowledge to curb their influence and better control behavior. A similar approach is adopted in modern psychology in the form of cognitive behavior therapy where one is encouraged to become aware of the stream of automatic negative thoughts and, having identified them, learns to challenge them or distract oneself from them. More radically, however, Salanter also

---

21. This characterization is taken up and extended by the hasidic leader Reb Schneur Zalman of Liadi in his principal work "Tanya."

22. In Salanter's approach "dark" and "light" do not connote the nature of these forces or imply value judgments about them. His terms were chosen to emphasize the notion that some influences on behavior were not perceived by the individual.

introduced a new element into his program—the development of techniques that utilized conscious behavior to influence the dark forces indirectly.

Chief among these new techniques was the use of *hitpa'alut* (intense emotional excitement) to enhance the *Musar* training method.[23] By combining *hitpa'alut* with studying appropriate *Musar* texts, the influence of the teachings contained within the texts could increase, albeit gradually, so that the dark forces would have less influence. For example, if one wanted to diminish the influence of pride, then the student would be encouraged to repeat suitable rabbinic sayings about the evil of pride, its harmful effects, and so forth and, at the same time, raise the voice and use a particular rousing melody.[24]

Rabbi Israel Salanter had sought, through his writings, his teaching, his sermons, and his personal example, to raise the ethical and religious level of the traditional Jewish communities in Lithuania and then, toward the end of his life, Western Europe. He was the greatest exponent of *Musar*, but he also understood the limitations imposed on it by the narrowness of outlook he sometimes encountered and by psychological barriers inherent within the human condition. This could have led to a destructive pessimism on his part, but instead he concentrated on developing pedagogic and behavioral devices to overcome the detrimental influence of these unconscious forces. In so doing he no doubt drew on ideas from the philosophical milieu of Western Europe, but only to refine and sharpen those already present in his original doctrine.

Salanter's influence continued to be felt in the Lithuanian-influenced yeshivot right up until the middle of the present century. The

---

23. The use of *hitpa'alut* has something in common with the experience of *hitlahavut* (ecstasy) sought by the hasidim (*see* below). The differences between the followers of *Musar* and those of the hasidim, however, should be noted. The hasidic followers sought to abnegate their bodily existence through *hitlahavut* and cleave to the Divine, whereas the adherents to *Musar* were concerned with bodily existence and concentrated on purifying their bodies from sin.

24. Melody and rhythm to aid learning are used in traditional yeshivot and would have been familiar to *Musar* students. There are different melodies for Mishnah, Gemorah, and so forth.

great yeshivot of Eastern Europe were then destroyed by the Nazis and the students transported and murdered. Only a few of the teachers and students escaped and were able to reestablish themselves in Western Europe, North America, and Israel. The influence of his ideas, however, has also been diminished by the growing sophistication in psychological knowledge of some yeshiva students who nowadays may have also benefited from a Western education.[25] Nevertheless, his approach is one of the cornerstones on which a psychological analysis of Jewish tradition rests.

At the same time that Rabbi Salanter was developing *Musar* in the yeshivot, hasidism was sweeping the Pale of Settlement with its own distinctive psychological approach.

THE HASIDIC PERSPECTIVE[26]

Mitzvah g'dolah l'chiyos b'simchah tamid.
The greatest commandment is to be joyful all of the time.
                                        —traditional hasidic song

---

25. This is not necessarily true of *Musar* principles in other ways. There are numerous popular books on Jewish ethical behavior. In particular, the thinking of Reb Yisrael Meir Kahan, known popularly as the Chafetz Chaim (after the title of one of his books), has become extremely popular in Orthodox circles. The Chafetz Chaim has written revealingly on the evils of *loshen hara* ("gossip" or, literally, "evil language") and human relationships. *See*, for example, *Ahavath Chesed* Kahan (1967).

26. There are numerous accounts, both scholarly and literary, of the development of the hasidic movement and its doctrines. It is beyond the scope of this book to attempt another such account and, furthermore, I could hardly do the subject justice. My purpose here is to acquaint the reader with sufficient detail to transmit a flavor of the movement's teachings. Inevitably my descriptions will be partial and incomplete. The sophisticated reader may be expected to take exception to the fact that some important point or other has been excluded from my summary. My particular perspective on the hasidic world comes from my contact with hasidic teachers who have generously shared their teachings with me, especially Rabbi Zalman Schachter and the numerous teachers from the Lubavitch movement in London, Leeds, and elsewhere. I have also gleaned a great deal from the writings of Martin Buber, Elie Wiesel, Gershom Scholem, and others. The thoughts of all these are scattered liberally throughout this section and, indeed, throughout this book. I hope I have represented them faithfully. If I have failed to do so, then it was not my intention to mislead; rather, my mistakes derive from limitations in my ability to grasp the subtlety of their thinking and perception.

The hasidic movement was founded early in the eighteenth century and continues as a vibrant force today. According to the famous scholar of Jewish mysticism Gershom Scholem, the origins of hasidism lay in the communities' response to great cultural and social upheaval, especially the devastation of the Chmielniki massacres[27] and the profound spiritual disillusion following the catastrophic failure of the extraordinary messianic movement led by Shabbetai Tzvi.[28] The rabbinic leadership was in disarray, and there could be no return to old formulas and lifestyles to provide comfort and meaning to the people. New leaders emerged who were intelligent, charismatic, and capable of responding to the needs of their followers. Martin Buber, the renowned philosopher of hasidism, described the situation like this:

> Stirred in his innermost core by the Sabbatian revolution, shaken to his foundations by the outcome, the Polish Jew longed passionately for leadership, for a man who would take him under his wing, give certainty to his bewildered soul, give order and shape to his chaotic existence, who would make it possible for him again to both believe and live. The hasidic movement educated such leaders. Rabbis who only bestowed advice as to how the prescriptions of the law should be applied could no longer satisfy the new longing, but sermons on the meaning of the teachings also did not help. In a world in which one could no longer muster the strength for reflection and decision, a man was needed to show how to believe and to say what was to be done.[29]

---

27. In 1648 Bogdan Chmielniki led Cossack and Ukrainian peasants in a violent rebellion against the Polish landowners, the Catholic clergy, and the Jews, resulting in the extinction of over seven hundred Jewish communities.

28. Sbabbetai Tzvi (1626–1676) was a false messiah who attracted thousands of Jews to his doctrines. These doctrines included mystical practices involving fasting and deliberately reversing the practice of many of the mitzvot in the belief that it was necessary for him to descend to the lowest levels of sin in order to bring about the redemption. In 1666 Shabbetai Tzvi traveled to Constantinople intending to convert the Sultan. Contrary to his expectations, Tzvi was arrested and imprisoned in Gallipoli. For a while he continued to proclaim his messiaship, but eventually, under the threat of death, he converted to Islam. As a result, a great spiritual depression beset the communities.

29. Buber (1988) p. 42.

The individual who arose was the legendary Rabbi Israel ben Eliezer (1699–1761), known as the Baal Shem Tov.[30] Fact and legend about the BeShT are hopelessly intertwined. Gershom Scholem prefers the notion that most of the stories about him are composites of accounts about other similar personalities of the same era.[31] Buber, however, considers the Baal Shem himself, the particular individual and personality, as crucial, and he dismisses accounts that focus only on the social or economic factors that gave rise to the birth of hasidism. "The economic development supplies . . . only the fertilizing forces; the spirit supplies the forces of the seed."[32] Nevertheless, it is the stories about the BeShT, his followers, and the leaders that came after him that best convey the flavor of hasidic teachings and life, and there are numerous volumes devoted to this task.

The factual basis of the tales is, at least for our purpose, irrelevant. According to Elie Wiesel, " . . . events . . . may or may not have happened, and if they did, may or may not have happened in quite the way they are told. Viewed from the outside, all of these tales are incomprehensible; one must enter them, for their truth can only be measured from the inside."[33] The tales are incomprehensible indeed. They tell of miracle-working rabbis who are capable of reading a person's soul and all its incarnations as easily as they might read a book, and rabbis who travel mysteriously across vast distances in a chariot drawn by horses from another realm. There are also accounts of those who storm heaven and make demands of the heavenly court, or who have encounters with the prophet Elijah, who perform healing, who intercede successfully with heaven on a follower's behalf, who enter into deep trance during prayer, and who compose

---

30. "Master of the Good Name." At this time there were a number of individuals known by the title "Baal Shem" as this was the name ascribed to preachers who were masters of Kabbalah, who performed healing, and who told wondrous stories. The most notable predecessor of the Baal Shem Tov was Rabbi Adam about whom there are many similar tales. The Baal Shem Tov is known in rabbinic literature by the acronym "BeShT."

31. Buber (1988) p. 331.

32. Ibid p. 62.

33. Wiesel (1972) p. 16.

The BeShT taught that simplicity and purity of heart were to be valued above status and power. Reb Dov Ber went on to systematize the teachings, and he brought them into line with central themes from the later Kabbalah.[38] However, the focus of hasidism was not on discussion of abstract metaphysics, but on the human condition itself and its role in bringing about the redemption of the world. Hence, a deep understanding of one's psychological state was of paramount importance. Personal refinement and psychological awareness were almost a religious obligation.

Through the influence of Dov Ber and the charismatic and influential individuals he gathered around him in Mezeritch, the role of the *tzaddik* or *rebbe* was emphasized.[39] The *tzaddik* was venerated by his followers, and communities were established around the households of the various *tzaddikim*. Individuals would attach themselves to a particular *rebbe* in the belief that by so doing and by following their master's teachings and traditions they would be raised to a higher spiritual level.[40]

Not only were the teachings of a *rebbe* holy but so was his food, his clothing, and even the manner in which he danced. There is a famous legend of a follower who said that he didn't come to the court

---

38. Dov Ber took over the main concepts of Lurianic Kabbalah and introduced them into hasidic thought. The concepts were primarily those of *Tszimtszum* (contraction), the raising of the sparks and the use of kabbalistic *kavannot* (intentions) and unifications.

39. Literally "the righteous one," but in hasidic parlance the head of a dynasty who is separate from the others, is endowed with "saintly" qualities, and is at a higher spiritual level. The *tzaddik* is considered to have the power to read an individual's destiny and is, therefore, in a position to lead and direct his followers.

40. The idea of attachment (*devekut*) is of central importance in hasidism. *Devekut* refers to the aim of attaching oneself to God, so that one can become closer to God and, ideally, achieve *yihud* (unification) with God. In hasidic thought the state of *yihud* had been attained by the *tzaddik*. By attaching oneself to the *tzaddik*, the Hasid could become closer to that state himself. The state of *yihud* does not involve the *tzaddik* in removing himself from the material world; rather, it is the act of revealing the holiness already inherent in the world because "God's presence fills the world." The state of unification achieved by the *tzaddik* was not a result of his spiritual efforts alone, but something bestowed on him by God—an act of divine will.

of the *rebbe* to hear him say words of Torah, but to watch the way in which he tied his shoe laces. In the hasidic communities the *tzaddik* was seen as the total embodiment of Torah, and he was capable of redeeming the sparks of holiness that existed in even the most evil of people and situations.

In the presence of the *tzaddik* the follower could expect to experience *hitlahavut* (ecstasy).[41] But the Hasid was also prepared for *avoda*: service to God and a lifetime dedicated to self-improvement and development. Great emphasis was placed on the prayer life of the individual and its role in overcoming evil. "Alien thoughts" that arise in prayer were acknowledged and dealt with in a special manner.[42] They were not to be sublimated or turned away, because in these thoughts sparks of God were to be found. Instead the thoughts were to be turned around and transformed and returned to God purified.[43] Beyond the prayer life, although also including it, every single action contains the potential of redemption—the possibility of further revealing the divine light in the world.

The hasidic masters read the classical Jewish texts in a unique, psychological way. They saw them as allegorical references to the inner life of the individual.[44] In their hands the biblical stories became psychological maps of an individual's spiritual journey and the festivals became stations en route, each offering the possibility of spiritual transformation and growth. The mystical literature they studied was also subjected to a psychological interpretation. When names and attributes of God were mentioned, the hasidim identified the manner in which these qualities were revealed in the soul of the individual and the influence they had in determining the qualities of intellect and emotion. The act of transforming oneself, therefore, was an act that brought with it an intimate interaction with God.

---

41. Particularly at the time of the third meal on *Shabbat* when the *rebbe* would teach and there might be much singing, dancing, and drinking.

42. *See* Chapter 7.

43. *See* Chapter 7 for an extended discussion of this practice.

44. For a detailed discussion *see* Idel (1995), especially the beginning of Chapter 5 (pp. 171–176) and Appendix A (pp. 227–238).

For the hasidim there is no great uncrossable divide between ourselves and God. Each penetrates the other, and knowing God requires one to know oneself. The revealed Torah, the Oral Law, the *midrash*, the rabbinic codes, and the mystical literature all provide tools for self-refinement and, as we shall discover, this insight resulted in a unique psychological perspective on Jewish tradition.

In the course of my account of hasidism I have said little of the great *rebbes* themselves. Although it is beyond the scope of this book to discuss their individual contributions, it would not be fitting to pass them over completely. So I now make brief mention of the generosity and humility of Reb Zusia, the dialogues and openheartedness of Reb Levi Yitzchak of Berditchev, the intellect and light of Reb Schneur Zalman of Liadi, the depressions and ecstasies of Reb Nachman of Breslov, the perceptiveness of the Seer of Lublin, the silence and existential conflict of the Kotzker Rebbe, the dignity and power of the Rizshiner, the educational methods of the Piazetzner, and so on, for there were many who led and inspired generations of seekers. Each of us will have our own favorites, individuals capable of speaking directly to us across the years, and we are all the beneficiaries of their legacy.

PROGRESSIVE JUDAISM[45]

Progressive Judaism arose in Germany as the Reform movement, in the middle of the nineteenth century, as a direct response to the emancipation.[46] At first the reformers were concerned with external aspects of Jewish practice such as shortening services, introducing the use of the vernacular in both prayer and sermons, and using an organ during *Shabbat* services (prohibited according to most halachic authorities). However, they quickly established a far more radical strand

---

45. The term *progressive Judaism* has been chosen in order to denote a genre of ideas and approaches, rather the doctrines of any particular denomination or group.

46. *See* Chapter 1 for a discussion of the rabbinic response to the emancipation and the development of Orthodox responses in the form of *Torah im Derech Eretz* by R. Samson Raphael Hirsch.

within Judaism. The early leaders, such as Rabbi Samuel Holdheim (1806–1860)[47] and Rabbi Avraham Geiger (1810–1884),[48] broke away from previous rabbinic authority and allowed themselves to deviate significantly from the strictures of *halacha* and talmudic argument.[49] They also broke with the principle, established initially in the Mishnah and supported by Maimonides (see Chapter 1), that both the Written Law (Pentateuch) and the Oral Law (Talmud) were the literal word of God. For the Reformers, only the biblical scriptures were of divine origin; the rabbinic literature, although important and highly valued, was considered to be the work entirely of human beings.

The founders of Reform strongly promoted the view that Judaism needed to be adapted for modern times. This was not only so that it would be better able to survive, but also, and perhaps most importantly, so that it could make its specific contribution to the improvement of the wider society.[50] Reform Judaism commenced a journey away from concerns with Jewish particularism and ritual observance and moved toward a vision of Jewish prophetic universalism and ethics. This perspective found favor in the new Jewish communities of North America. Initially small numbers of German Jews moved to the United States in the early nineteenth century, bringing with them the principles of Reform and seeing themselves as the inheritors of the intellectual traditions of Mendelssohn, Spinoza, and Kant.[51] The liberalism and individualism of North America proved

---

47. Holdheim was the first to justify Reform on the basis of the precedent of the great sage Rabbi Yochanan Ben Zakkai. Yochanan Ben Zakkai had escaped from the Temple as it was being destroyed by the Romans and negotiated with the Romans to establish a community of scholars at Yavneh. At Yavneh a new adaptation of Judaism was consciously devised to fit the new circumstances. The new form replaced animal sacrifices with verbal prayer and replaced priestly Judaism with rabbinic Judaism.

48. Geiger was the convener of the first convention of Reform rabbis. He was a scholar who emphasized the prophetic nature of Jewish teachings.

49. *See* Meyer (1988) Chapter 3.

50. The issue of Israel's "chosenness" was dealt with by suggesting that Israel had a unique role both in preserving the scriptural heritage and in creating a fairer society in accordance with the vision of the Hebrew prophets.

51. All critics of institutional "Orthodox" religion and belief.

to be fertile soil for the ideas of reform among the new immigrants that arrived at the turn of the century and, over the course of the last one hundred years, Reform Judaism has become the largest single denomination (with over 1,250,000 members) in the country.

Unlike those of the *Musar* movement and hasidism, the doctrines of Reform Judaism have been clearly spelled out in the form of Rabbinic conferences and platforms.[52] The position statements issued by these groups dealt with such issues as Reform's view of the role of God in history, Torah, Israel, and religious life and practice. On Torah, Reform Judaism broke significantly with the past as it taught that while the Torah may be an inspired and inspiring document, it no longer had the power to totally determine religious practice and belief. The Columbus Platform states that " . . . as a depository of permanent religious ideals, the Torah remains the dynamic source of the life of Israel. Each age has the obligation to adapt the teachings of the Torah to its basic needs in consonance with the genius of Judaism." Consistent with its emphasis on the universalist teachings contained within the biblical books of the Prophets, the Reform movement took up the theme of *Tikkun Olam*[53] and created strong social issues and social justice platforms that remain an important part of progressive Judaism's message across the world.

The Reconstructionist movement, another strand of progressive Judaism, also challenged the Orthodox view of religious faith and practice. Its founder, Mordechai Kaplan,[54] construed Judaism in terms of "Jewish peoplehood" and he spoke passionately of "Jewish civilization." His famous statement about the role of tradition in Judaism, that it " . . . has a vote, but not a veto," summarizes the approach progressive Judaism has adopted toward the *mitzvot* and ritual observance in general. Kaplan also spoke about the *mitzvot* as "Jewish folkways."

---

52. For example The Pittsburgh Platform (1885), The Columbus Platform (1937), and The San Francisco Platform (1976).

53. Repair or fixing of the world. In Reform Judaism this was seen as a political-social imperative, rather than the more mystical view adopted by kabbalists and hasidim.

54. 1881–1983. Founder of the Reconstructionist movement and former lecturer at the Jewish Theological Seminary in New York City.

For him the *mitzvot* are beautiful and life-enhancing and this is sufficient reason for us to follow them. In formulating them in this manner, however, he further reduced the transcendental nature of the divine influence and located the sacredness of the customs in the immanence of God, manifested through the Jewish people themselves.[55]

The devastation of the European Jewish communities by the Nazis during World War II and the nuclear destruction at Hiroshima and Nagasaki presented an uncompromising challenge to Reform doctrine.[56] The prophetic vision of a world moving toward a better age, a messianic age, guided by a powerful benevolent God, no longer seemed viable to many American Jews. Instead the Reform movement fell back on a theology that relied more on human and less on divine action. This theology had originally been developed in response to an earlier crisis in faith. Christian scholarship in nineteenth-century Germany, and indeed across Europe, had developed a critical stance toward the authorship of the Bible, including the Pentateuch itself. The Documentary Hypothesis and the Higher Criticism had shown, to the satisfaction of most scholars, that the biblical text was a composite of a number of preexisting texts by different authors. This challenge had been most adequately met by the Covenental theologies of Martin Buber (1878–1965) and Franz Rosenzweig (1886–1929), and it was to this that non-Orthodox theologians now turned.[57]

---

55. The influence of the Reconstructionist movement, and Mordechai Kaplan in particular, has never been restricted to the movement's own rabbis and synagogues. It provided the theological basis for the broadening of activity within American synagogues of all denominations to include cultural, sporting, and recreational facilities along with radical social activism (it was among the first groups to ordain women rabbis). In more recent years Reconstructionism has further developed its theological basis to include ideas from Jewish mysticism and *kabbalah* (*see* Green [1992], and students from its rabbinic college in Philadelphia continue to have a strong influence on Jewish life across America.

56. *See* Meyer (1988) pp. 360–364.

57. Neither Buber nor Rosenzweig was a Reform Jew, and both held more traditional views than the German Reformers. Buber did not accept any form of organized religion, whereas Rosenzweig at one point in his life came close to converting to Christianity but later became quite traditionally observant. Their views on theology have influenced generations of Jewish thinkers.

Revelation, for progressive Jews, had not been a "one-off" event. God was understood as providing enough clues about the nature of spiritual truth to satisfy each generation. As each successive generation grew in understanding, more of the truth was revealed and previous visions (even if found in rabbinic or biblical literature) were discarded or modified. Revelation was progressive.

The implication of this perspective, as with the traditional view of revelation occurring only at Sinai, is that God is placed in the position of revealing propositions to the people. The alternative, proposed by Buber and Rosenzweig, is that God enables us to have a special intense encounter with the Divine and that by means of this encounter it is God (rather than specific texts) who is disclosed in the revelation.[58] The biblical account is the record of such encounters.

Buber and Rosenzweig undertook a joint translation of the Bible into the German language. As translators they were well aware of the textual difficulties that had been identified by the biblical scholars, yet they chose to present the text as if it had been written by only one author or, as Rosenzweig preferred, one spirit. They called this spirit "R," just as the biblical critics had referred to the Redactor as "R," only they used "R" to refer to "Rabbenu"—"our teacher."[59] This view had implications for Jewish practice, for if the biblical and rabbinic literature is no longer considered the literal word of God, then the mitzvot can no longer be considered binding and for all time. The Reform movement spoke of an ongoing covenental relationship between God and Israel. The covenant required constant renewal. All Jews were entitled to question the terms of the agreement and interpret the mitzvot according to their own perspective of what was required in the present situation. Some Reform Jews understood this as an impetus to reinterpret the original rabbinic texts and to try to

---

58. *See* Jacobs, L, 1973 (Chapters 14 and 15) for a discussion of traditional and progressive views of revelation.

59. There is an intended pun here. In rabbinic literature the traditional author of the Pentateuch, Moses, is often referred to as Moshe Rabbenu—"Moses our Teacher."

understand their import for the modern age. More conservative Jews, however, were less willing to abandon the authority of *halacha* and extended Rosenzweig's approach to include the rabbinic literature. For them the rabbis were also recording encounters with God, and the *mitzvot* are the product of such encounters. They are the guidelines for living a life close to God's will. Rabbi Louis Jacobs gives an example:

> Search the Bible from beginning to end and you will find there no command for Jews to build synagogues. And yet Jews do build synagogues and pray in them in their conviction that this is the will of God, since this is how Jews have expressed their religious strivings. We need a vocabulary of worship and this is provided by the *mitzvot*. That is their sanction.[60]

Progressive Judaism, perhaps more than any other Jewish group, values the autonomy of the individual. It is the individual's responsibility to foster faith, encounter God, and live an ethical life. No wonder then, that psychology has an explicit role to play.

Initially the Reform movement developed an interest in psychology because it needed to respond to the vast numbers of Jews who had taken up an interest in Christian Science.[61] Clearly these Jews had been looking for something that had been unavailable to them in the rather intellectual, rationalist approach of the reformers. Reform rabbis began to explicitly address themselves to the emotional needs of their congregants, and in 1937 the Hebrew Union College offered a course in pastoral psychology to its rabbinic students. From a theological perspective the rabbis were wary of psychology, with the determinism of behaviorism on one hand and the antagonism to religion and pessimism of Freud on the other.[62] One rabbi in particular, however, Joshua Liebman, took up the challenge of combining the religious perspective with the psychological. He himself had had psychoanalysis. He promulgated the value of a psychological approach

---

60. Jacobs (1984) p. 225.
61. In 1925 the New York area had 50,000 Jews in Christian Science.
62. *See* Chapter 3 for a fuller discussion of Freud's views on religion.

to the problems of life by means of regular national radio broadcasts and the publication of his volume *Peace of Mind* (1946), which sold over a million copies. Liebman explained that psychotherapy could assist in removing obsessive guilt, irrational fear, and suppressed emotion.[63]

There is almost no area of modern Jewish life that has not been influenced by such psychological perspectives. This is unsurprising given the number of Jews to be found among the founders and practitioners of the various schools of psychotherapy. Yet it is progressive Judaism that has been most concerned to integrate the different strands. One example will suffice. In 1985–1986 at Leo Baeck College in London, the center for training Reform and Liberal rabbis in Europe, a series of lectures were given by rabbis and psychotherapists on the relationship between religious values and psychotherapy. The proceedings, twenty-one lectures in all, were published in a single volume.[64] Similar series of lectures have been held every year since, and such activities are replicated in rabbinic colleges and Jewish therapy centers across the globe.

JEWISH FEMINISM[65]

> ... my (former) husband and I were standing outside the Yale chapel on a Sabbath morning, chatting with a friend before going in for services. While we were talking, a member of the congregation came and asked my husband to come in right away because they needed a *minyan*. I suddenly realized that, while I had attended services regularly for a year and a half and my husband was a relative newcomer, I could stay outside all day; my presence was irrelevant for the purposes for which we had gathered.[66]

---

63. *See* Meyer (1988) p. 316.

64. Cooper (1988)

65. An important aspect of Jewish feminism is that throughout Jewish history the voices of women have not been heard. There has been a silence. For this reason I have chosen to describe the Jewish feminist contribution by including extensive quotations from their writings as a balance to my own words. The selection of quotations, however, is inevitably my own.

66. Plaskow (1990) p. xi.

Concern for the position of women within Judaism is not new. The Talmud, for example, contains volumes of material devoted to laws defining the status and role of Jewish women. It is precisely such definitions that modern Jewish feminists have challenged and wish to overthrow. The reforms of the nineteenth century, Jewish secularism, and Zionism all did little to challenge these laws in themselves; rather, these movements gave women the opportunity and support to ignore them. Jewish feminism is considerably more far-reaching; it goes to the heart of the issue of divine authority and the very nature of Jewish tradition and practice. Hence it challenges the basic assumptions associated with Jewish tradition in the first place. The feminist critique, however, does not come from outside the Jewish religious community, but from within it. Susannah Heschel has written that "the most recent wave of Jewish feminism, beginning during the 1960s, is . . . not breaking away from the community, but struggling to become full members of it."[67] While Jewish feminists, by and large, have felt marginalized from Jewish religious practice, they have no wish to exclude themselves from the community.

The problem presented by the tradition, and most overtly by the *halacha*, is that women do not have comparable status with men. The halachic category women occupy also includes children and Canaanite slaves and as such they are excluded from various religious obligations and precepts, many of which are traditions highly valued in Jewish life.[68] Furthermore, a close reading of the biblical text describing the revelation of the Torah reveals an account in which only the men are addressed. The women are not included in those spoken to at Sinai at all. The biblical record is explicit: "Do not go near a woman."[69]

There have been a range of feminist responses to these concerns. Some women have been more optimistic than others about the capacity of rabbinic law to reform itself from within. Blu Greenberg, for example, has argued that many of the most oppressive and offen-

67. Heschel (1983) p. xv.
68. *See* Adler (1983).
69. Exodus 19:15. *See* Plaskow (1990) for a feminist analysis of this text.

sive aspects of *halacha* can be changed without radically undermining the corpus of Jewish law in other ways. For her it is simply a matter of rabbinic ingenuity and interest. Her well-known dictum that "where there is a rabbinic will, there is a halachic way" makes this clear.[70] Most Jewish feminist writers, however, agree with Susannah Heschel that the rabbinic view of women cannot simply be adjusted to include a more favorable attitude toward women: "Once we acknowledge the laws regarding women as products of a particular historical period and outlook, what is to keep us from considering other Jewish practices—such as the synagogue service—as a comparable historical outgrowth that has outlived its meaning and relevance?"[71]

The starting point for the feminist approach to Judaism is feminism itself. This involves far more than an argument for women's liberation or for equality in the religious sphere, although these concerns are certainly part of it. Rather, Jewish feminists have pointed out that Judaism as a religion (although no more so than many other religions) reflects the patriarchal nature of society as a whole and is addressed only to men and to the concerns of men. Because of this, women are perceived as "other" and, apart from rare exceptions, women's influence and significance are invisible. Both Susannah Heschel and Judith Plaskow cite Simone De Beauvoir's *The Second Sex* as one of the most influential feminist works. Their approach is based on De Beauvoir's analysis of the position of the female as "other" compared to that of the male who is "subject." Judith Plaskow puts it clearly:

> Half of Jews have been women, but men have been defined as
> normative Jews, while women's voices and experiences are largely
> invisible in the record of Jewish belief and experience that has
> come down to us. Women have lived Jewish history and carried
> its burdens, but women's perceptions and questions have not
> given form to scripture, shaped the direction of Jewish law, or
> found expression in liturgy.[72]

---

70. Greenberg (1981).
71. Heschel (1983) p. xxi.
72. Plaskow (1990) p. 1.

Women do not name reality, but rather are named as part of a reality that is male constructed. Where women are Other, they can be present and silent simultaneously; for the language and thought-forms of culture do not express their meaning.[73]

Susannah Heschel has identified three general approaches within Jewish feminism.[74] "The first approach . . . has been principally concerned with the recent efforts to make changes in the roles of women and men within Jewish religious communities in the United States." This has been the approach adopted by Blu Greenberg and others who have argued that the sexism within Judaism is unjust and that there is a theological basis for altering those rulings that are discriminatory against women by appealing to the "overarching, immutable Jewish principles of justice and equality."

The second group has focused less on arguing about equality and more on exploring the differences between women and men. They say "that it may not be an accident that *halacha* was developed exclusively by men; it may express an innately male concern with establishing rules." These Jewish feminists have focused on creating new observances, composing new prayers,[75] reinterpreting the use of the *mikvah*,[76] and writing new biblical interpretations. Rosh Chodesh (the celebration of the new moon each month), for example, has become a special festival for women's groups.

The third group of Jewish feminists "draw on archeological evidence for the worship of the Goddess . . . (and contrast) such evidence with biblical references to the suppression and condemnation of such worship." Heschel suggests that such women are rejecting Judaism, whereas others might argue that they are returning to a form of

---

73. Plaskow (1990) p. 2.

74. Heschel (1986). In this article Susannah Heschel describes the similarities between Christian feminist theology and the Jewish version. She suggests that feminists may have been less than successful in truly developing an independent theology as sexism is subtle, pervasive, and destructive.

75. *See* for example the poetry of Marge Piercy and others based on traditional prayers such as *Nishmat* and the *Amidah* published by the *P'nai Or* Religious Fellowship in *Siddur Or Chadash* (1989).

76. Ritual bath.

prebiblical Judaism in which Canaanite Goddesses were revered. Intermixed with this kind of discussion are varying perspectives on the concept of monotheism. Judaism, undoubtedly a monotheistic religion, is also opposed to any form of idol worship. From this point of view it would seem that any involvement with the Goddess is antagonistic to Judaism. However, an opposing position is that the Goddess only represents different aspects of the single indivisible source and that the Goddess herself isn't to be worshiped at all, in much the same way as the kabbalists worshiped God as manifested in the Shechinah (feminine presence of God), or contemplated the attributes of God (the *sephirot*) without compromising their monotheism.[77]

Susannah Heschel also has a more positive view of this third group:

> Hand in hand with Goddess spirituality has been the effort to resurrect, from within Judaism . . . long-forgotten women's spiritual traditions that were denounced as witchcraft. Preliminary research within Judaism seems to indicate that women were sometimes recognized by Jewish communities as having special spiritual gifts and that their secret prayers, rituals and incantations were sometimes thought to be more effective than those of the male rabbinic leaders.

In the light of a feminist analysis of Jewish history, tradition, and custom, one might expect that all aspects of traditional Judaism would be abandoned altogether. However, this has not been the response at all. The recognition that "normative" Judaism is socially constructed has resulted in the production of new traditions, rituals, ceremonies, and theology that include women and women's experience, but do not totally abandon the past. Psychologically this involves the reconciliation of what would otherwise be a split in identity: the Woman and the Jew. Rabbi Sheila Shulman describes her relationship with Judaism like this:

---

77. *See* Postscript for a further discussion of this issue.

My relation to my own tradition is necessarily both critical and loving, or, as the Christian feminist Elizabeth Schussler-Fiorenza once put it, I and others like me operate with a double perspective, a "hermeneutics [interpretation] of suspicion and a hermeneutics of reverence." While on the one hand we live within the parameters of our tradition, on the other hand we claim the right and the necessity to participate fully, centrally, in the creative work, inherent in any living tradition, of its continuity and development.[78]

The position of women within the Jewish community is changing rapidly across the entire spectrum of religious observance. In Orthodox communities women are to be found studying Gemorah (a subject previously forbidden to them by Orthodox rabbis), participating in women-only *tephillah* (prayer) groups, and *leyning* (chanting) the weekly *Parsha* (portion) directly from the Torah scrolls (again a practice that was frowned upon and sometimes forbidden). In egalitarian synagogues women are full participants, and in some progressive communities women are introducing new rituals and changing old ones. In *chavurot*,[79] women-only communities, and organizations such as the Alliance for Jewish Renewal, women are to be found in key leadership roles. However, in the synagogue (even egalitarian synagogues) women are more reticent. One recent study has examined some of the psychological factors that underlie this.[80] The author, Nora Gold, interviewed thirty actively involved women members of an egalitarian synagogue in Toronto. During the interviews the women were asked to describe how they saw their role in the synagogue, and to participate in a word-association task in which the stimulus words were, for example, "a Jewish woman," "a woman wearing a *tallit* (prayer shawl), and "a women leading services." Finally they were asked to put into their own words why they thought women did not take on prayer leadership roles in the synagogue, when they were so

---

78. Shulman (1996) p. 8.
79. Small, usually egalitarian, informal communities.
80. Gold (1995).

active in other aspects of leadership (e.g., committee and welfare work).

The results of the study were revealing about the psychological barriers that women experience when they consider undertaking prayer leadership. A number of the women had difficulty imagining themselves in this role simply because they had never, or rarely, seen other women do it. They had no role models. Others experienced psychological reticence. Even though intellectually they thought they should be more active in this way, emotionally they experienced within themselves a taboo against doing so, which they found hard to overcome. Surprisingly, the more Jewish education the women had experienced, especially during childhood, the harder it was. One woman commented:

> In terms of religious leadership, I've had it hammered into me that this is not allowed, it's not for me. I think that's true for many women, especially for those of us who have had the "advantage" of a strong Jewish educational background. Basically, the stronger your traditional network, the harder this is going to be.

Nora Gold concludes from her research that the intellectual acceptance of feminism and egalitarianism within Judaism is necessary but insufficient to empower women in the synagogue. Psychological change is also required. Women need encouragement to actively challenge the stereotypes and their internalized role models of prayer leaders. In addition, women need to support each other in taking the risk of actually putting themselves into prayer leadership roles. "In brief," she concluded, "the process of empowering ourselves involves a reversal of the traditional injunction, 'na'aseh v'nishma' (do and then hear) from Exodus 24:7. We must first hear ourselves and each other and then we must do (nishma v'na'aseh)."

3

The Psychological Framework

P sychology sets out to answer questions. Why do we do such and such? What is the nature of experience? What can we say about consciousness? How do we learn? Do people behave differently in groups compared to when they are alone? Those psychologists who have concerned themselves with religion have had their own set of questions. What is the nature of the religious experience? What do people believe and why do they believe it? Why does religion have such a hold over us? Are there certain types of people who are more likely to be religious than others? What do people feel when they pray? Asking questions and holding a religious belief do not always seem to fit well together. People sometimes speak of "blind faith," as if somehow being unable to see enhances our belief. Or perhaps we give up our intellectual faculties when we walk into a synagogue, church, temple, or mosque.

The questions one asks often influence the types of answers one receives. For example, it makes a difference if we ask questions about our own experience or about someone else's. It is more than a simple matter of bias. When we ask questions about ourselves we are interested in self-knowledge, and then psychology becomes a tool for personal growth and development. A. J. Heschel fully developed this approach in the context of religious philosophy. He distinguished between the attitude of the *conceptual* thinker, which is one of detachment, and that of the *situational* thinker, which is one of concern. Situational thinkers realize that they are involved in a situation that needs explaining.[1] This is also the approach to psychology adopted in this chapter.

We have already referred to research pointing to the discrepancy between religious belief and actual practice.[2] What then accounts for the maintenance of practices when participants do not actually believe in the religious precepts that underlie them? The researchers themselves suggested a psychological explanation. Their study found that most of the Jewish women who completed the questionnaires felt themselves to be strongly identified with Judaism and with the Jewish people. The researchers surmised that the women continued with the customs, and indeed chose to participate in particular customs (such as the Pesach Seder), because doing so helped them affirm their sense of ethnic identification. It helped them feel that they belong.

This is not so strange, especially in today's society when many people bemoan the breakdown of community and the alienation induced by "mass-produced" culture. I have heard many nonreligious Jews explain their adherence to customs in terms that reflect this sense of community and ethnicity. "It is important to celebrate Jewish history," "the customs keep the family together," and "it's something I share with my friends." I have also heard people give similar explanations of why they pay their synagogue fees and, in so doing, contribute toward the salary of the rabbi (who will likely hold views and opinions on religious matters completely contrary to their own). "Someone has to be religious" and "so that there is a *minyan* available when someone needs it."[3] It would be unfair if we were to say that people who hold such attitudes are hypocritical; there are no double standards here. Their behavior reflects and expresses faith, not faith in God perhaps but in the "faith of their ancestors." Each custom followed, each precept fulfilled, is an act of fidelity. It is an ex-

---

1. Heschel (1955) p. 5.
2. *See* Introduction.
3. In order to say the memorial prayer for the dead (*see* Chapter 5).

pression of belonging, a way of connecting more deeply with the Jewish community.[4]

In this book we set out to find an additional kind of explanation and ask another set of questions. It seems likely that the traditions contain psychological truths that have value in themselves. Our purpose is to examine some of these traditions, unearth their hidden meanings, and express these meanings in the psychological language of our times. We will also consider whether the customs promote psychological well-being and provide opportunities for psychological and spiritual growth. In so doing we will need some conceptual tools to help us. Although we will describe the different psychological theories and techniques as we progress, it will be helpful to set out some of the main approaches at this point.

We will begin with the most famous psychologist of all.

SIGMUND FREUD[5]

> Religious ideas are teachings and assertions about facts and conditions of external (or internal) reality which tell one something one has not discovered for oneself and which lay claim to one's belief. Since they give us information about what is most im-

---

4. There is also a theological justification. From the Orthodox viewpoint, the emphasis is on ritual observance. The most important thing is to fulfill the religious obligations set out by the tradition (particularly those laid out in the *Shulchan Aruch*), for belief is secondary. There is also a further point that can be derived from Franz Rosenzweig's perspective (*see* Chapter 2): God is revealed in community and, therefore, adherence to the community is adherence to God.

5. It is not possible in this work to outline all of Freud's contribution to the psychology of religion and the precepts on which his approach is based. Freud's ideas are well known and descriptions of his theories are easily available. For those who are not already familiar with Freud it is worth pointing out that reading Freud himself, rather than relying on secondary sources, is often well worth the effort. Much of his writing is accessible to the nonspecialist, and Freud conveys the subtlety and nuance of his ideas far better than some of his summarizers.

There has been much debate about the extent to which Freud was influenced by his Jewish background. Freud never hid his origins and, indeed, referred to them occasionally in his writings (for example, in *Moses and Monotheism*). In general, however, he understood religion as something to be overcome and transcended. For a detailed discussion *see* Bakan (1958) and Klein (1981).

portant and interesting to us in life, they are particularly highly prized. Anyone who knows nothing of them is ignorant; and anyone who has added them to his knowledge may consider himself much richer.[6]

Sigmund Freud (1856–1939) was most interested in the psychology of personality and psychopathology. Toward the end of his life, however, he began to write about religion.[7] Freud had by this time more or less completed his psychoanalytic studies of the individual, and he now turned his attention to issues affecting society as a whole.

The popular view of Freud's attitude toward religion is that he was predominantly negative. This was not entirely the case, however, as the quotation at the beginning of this section makes clear. Nevertheless, Freud did believe that religious ideas are illusions and that it is possible, and for some it is desirable, to live without such illusions.

Freud's starting point was his perspective on civilization and culture. He held strongly the view that without civilization society would be chaotic, anarchic, and intolerable. This was because the instincts and passions of individuals, which he had uncovered by means of his psychoanalytic technique, would be unchecked in the majority of people. Without the restraining forces of culture, the frustration of their desires would be too much for people to bear, and they would overthrow those who held power and privilege, in order to gain relief from their frustration and satisfy their needs. He wrote that ". . . civilization has to be defended against the individual, and its regulations, institutions and commands are directed to that task."[8] Religious ideas are an important part of civilization.

Freud considered the role of religious ideas to be far greater than just a force for social and economic control. He pointed out that the

---

6. Freud (1985) p. 206.

7. Freud wrote three major works on religion: "Totem and Taboo" (1913), "The Future of an Illusion" (1927), and *Moses and Monotheism* (1938). The present description is derived mainly from the 1927 work as it contains most of his seminal ideas on the topic, some of which were developed at greater length in his other works.

8. Freud (1985) p. 184.

natural world holds many dangers, and that ordinarily the individual has no means of controlling the influence of nature. There is no sure defense against an earthquake, storm, sudden unexplained illness, or death, and because of this it would be natural for all of us to be in a state of perpetual anxiety. We are not continually anxious, however, because of the psychological defenses that we construct. The first step in the construction of these defenses was, for Freud:

> ". . . the humanization of nature. Impersonal forces and destinies cannot be approached; they remain eternally remote. But if the elements have passions that rage as they do in our own souls, if death itself is not something spontaneous but the violent act of an evil Will, if everywhere in nature there are Beings around us of a kind that we know in our society, then we can breathe freely, can feel at home in the uncanny and can deal by psychical means with our senseless anxiety.[9]

The next step, according to Freud, was to deal with the fear in exactly the same way as we dealt with a similar situation experienced in infancy. Then we were helpless in relation to our parents (especially the Father), yet we were also sure of their protection. Now we turn the forces of nature not into persons, but into gods who have the character of a father,[10] who have the power to protect us, reconcile us to fate, and compensate us for the "sufferings and privations" that civilized life has imposed.

The beliefs and doctrines that constitute a religious faith have a particular psychological power. Freud calls these beliefs "illusions," by which he meant that they are "derived from human wishes" and are "insusceptible of proof."[11] Sensible and rational people should eradicate such beliefs and face reality. However, Freud observed that this is not always the case and people bring all sorts of defenses for their religious opinions. He writes disparagingly of them:

---

9. Ibid p. 196.
10. Freud discussed these ideas at great length in "Totem and Taboo" (1985).
11. Ibid p. 213.

In other matters no sensible person will behave so irresponsibly or rest content with such feeble grounds for his opinions. . . . It is only in the highest and most sacred things that he allows himself to do so. In reality these are only attempts at pretending to oneself or to other people that one is still firmly attached to religion, when one has long since cut oneself loose from it. Where questions of religion are concerned, people are guilty of every possible sort of dishonesty and intellectual misdemeanor.[12]

Freud's conclusion is that for those with the capability and opportunity of completing a personal psychoanalysis, religious ideas are of no value and should be dispensed with. If some religious ideas happen to have, encoded within them, a truth value that is of benefit to society, then those ideas should be separated from their religious context and made plain. To continue to maintain a religious outlook, in his view, was regressive. In fact he considered it neurotic. During childhood ". . . so many instinctual demands which will later be unserviceable cannot be suppressed" by rational means, so must be actively repressed.[13] Most of these infantile neuroses are overcome spontaneously during the course of growing up. So too with religion. Those individuals, however, who hang on to religious beliefs may not actually show the symptoms of a neurosis as they are protected from doing so. ". . . devout believers are safeguarded in a high degree against the risk of certain neurotic illnesses; their acceptance of the universal neurosis spares them the task of constructing a personal one.[14]

It is well known that Freud's argument has not been without its critics on many grounds.[15] Freud himself spoke about the risks in-

---

12. Ibid p. 214.
13. Ibid p. 226.
14. Ibid p. 227.
15. Freud has always had his admirers and his critics. At first he was criticized simply because what he said, particularly about infantile sexuality, was unpopular. It did not sit comfortably with either the religious or secular European middle class mores of the day. Later he was criticized for generalizing too widely from his limited sample of Viennese patients. He has been taken to task by philosophers for the unscientific and tautological nature of his conclusions and by empirical psychologists for failing to provide good scientific evidence in support of

volved in making public some of his more controversial views about religion. In *Moses and Monotheism* he explained that while living in Austria he feared that if his essays on the subject were to be published the reaction of the Catholic Church might be so antagonistic as to seriously threaten the practice of psychoanalysis. He only felt safe to publish his essays after he had escaped to England to avoid the persecution of the Nazis, who had burned his books.[16] The main point to be made here, however, is about a limitation of Freud's interests and concerns. It seems that Freud was addressing himself primarily to the doctrines and the beliefs of established religions and, unlike other writers such as William James (see next section), did not attach any significance to personal religious experience. "If one man has gained an unshakable conviction of the true reality of religious doctrines from a state of ecstasy which has deeply moved him, of what significance is that to others?"[17]

Personal religious experience may not have had much significance for Freud, but it did for many of the other psychologists and philosophers who studied and wrote about religion.

WILLIAM JAMES

Without doubt the founder of the "psychology of religion" as a field of study in its own right was William James (1842–1910).[18] His book *The Varieties of Religious Experience* has become a classic of the field. William James described, sometimes in considerable detail, the religious experiences of people in a wide range of cultures. He adopted

---

key concepts such as the Oedipus complex and for the lack of proven efficacy of psychoanalysis as a form of psychotherapy. Recently he has been castigated for his apparent turnaround on the complex issue of the "seduction theory." His supporters, however, have established themselves as successful practitioners, and he is no doubt the "Father" or "Grandfather" of many forms of psychotherapy and psychological theory.

16. *See* Freud (1939) pp. 68, 132.

17. Freud (1985) p. 210.

18. William James was a Bostonian and the brother of the novelist Henry James. He gave the Gifford lectures, on which his book was based, in Edinburgh in 1901–1902.

a systematic approach to understanding religious experience and attempted to deal with all the pertinent questions related to it. He discussed whether those who had religious experiences were deluded or highly sensitive and whether they really had access to unseen worlds, as the doctrines claimed. He considered the power of religion to heal the sick, the nature of conversion experiences, and what happened during prayer. William James also described and analyzed the concept of sainthood and the nature of the experiences enjoyed by those who have been called saints. He broke new ground, for his day, when he validated the fact that personal religious or mystical experiences are not confined to members of religious institutions such as churches. In fact, James took care to distinguish between institutional religion, which he largely disdained, and personal religion, which he valued highly.

Although James adhered to his commitment to a scientific approach, his book is also a work of art. His prose is captivating and his perceptions enlightening. *The Varieties of Religious Experience* is also a committed book in the sense that James was an advocate of the active pursuit of spiritual experiences by individuals. Although he was interested primarily in studying religion, it was the practice of religion that counted. It was not the abstract philosophizing of the universalist theologians and the mystics that was significant, but the everyday involvement of men and women in the ordinary activities of a religious life.

We will briefly take one example, that of prayer, to illustrate his approach. William James collected many accounts of prayer from a number of different cultures, but his own background and training were in the Christian tradition and he was never totally able to shake himself free from this. Nevertheless, James approached prayer in its generic sense. He was careful to state that he did not consider prayer to be only petitional, but something central and essential to the religious experience itself. It was not the supernatural element of prayer that interested him, but the experience of the one who prayed.[19]

---

19. Of course, not everyone who prays experiences the effects that James describes. At several points throughout his book James takes care to point out that his accounts are biased toward the unusual and the ecstatic rather than the typical and the mundane. It was these extraordinary characteristics that made these experiences worth reporting.

"Religion is nothing if it is not the vital act by which the entire mind seeks to save itself by clinging to the principle from which it draws its life. This act is prayer, by which term I understand no vain exercise of words, no mere repetition of certain sacred formulae, but the very movement itself of the soul, putting itself in a personal relation of contact with the mysterious power of which it feels the presence. . . ." [20]

James considered that the effect of prayer is to change the experience of the one who prays. The act of engaging with the "divinity of the world's authorship," the supreme mystery, charges the world with meaning. "Fear and egotism fall away" and it leaves the one who prays enriched with a deep sense of equanimity. "The outward face of nature need not alter, but the expressions of meaning in it alter." "It is as if all doors were opened and all paths freshly smoothed." [21]

At the end of the work James allowed himself to move away from description and to draw some conclusions about the nature of the religious experience itself. He was clear that during such experiences the individual engages in contact with something that is more than the everyday objective world and that this "more" can have transformative effects. James considered the "more" on two levels. At the first level he suggested it is an aspect of the "subconscious self." [22] This part of the self has many aspects including, but not exclusively, religious elements. These elements are subliminal perceptions, incomplete memories, and other parts of the "transmarginal" self. Invasions from these regions play an important part in the religious life. "Let me propose, as an hypothesis, that whatever it may be on its *farther* side,

---

20. James (1960) p. 444.
21. James (1960) p. 453.
22. The "subconscious self" and the "transmarginal self" that James refers to were concepts that had emerged from the then relatively new fields of cognitive psychology and psychophysics. These categories may seem obvious to the modern reader, who has the benefit of the work of Freud and modern cognitive science, but at the time they were innovations. These ideas had developed out of the philosophical writings of Kant and were a challenge to both the religious way of thinking and the scientific doctrine derived from Newtonian mechanics and nineteenth-century science. In a similar way the later thinking of Rabbi Salanter (*see* Chapter 2) was influenced by some of the same factors.

the "more" with which in religious experience we feel ourselves connected is on its *hither* side the subconscious continuation of our conscious life" (italics original).[23]

Moreover, these invasions from the individual's subconscious take on an objective appearance and suggest to the subject that their source is an external, higher power. For James, however, it is actually union with our own higher selves that we are experiencing at such moments.

The second level of the "more" is the "remoter side" of the "transmarginal consciousness." Here we encounter theologies and religious doctrines about the spiritual worlds which are the products of the mystical experiences of others. James does not wish to ally himself with any particular set of religious beliefs, but he makes clear that the *"conscious person is continuous with a wider self through which saving experiences come"* (italics original).[24] This "wider self" is a dimension of experience that we cannot normally understand and is the origin of our ideals. When we connect with this wider aspect of our existence we reap the benefits—we are transformed and regenerated. Although there is no way of directly grasping the nature of this reality, we can know it by its effects, which are in themselves real enough.

These two aspects of our transmarginal selves—the *hither* and the *farther*—give rise to religious experiences and changes in our being and behavior. "The unseen region in question is not merely ideal, for it produces effects in this world. When we commune with it, work is actually done on our finite personality, for we are turned into new men, and consequences in the way of conduct follow in the natural world upon our regenerative change." [25]

CARL GUSTAV JUNG[26]

Jung (1875–1961) was one of Freud's closest and most enthusiastic followers, but his eventual split with Freud is well known, and the

---

23. James (1960) p. 487.
24. James (1960) p. 490.
25. James (1960) pp. 490–91.
26. As with Freud, only a limited account of Jung's approach, his "analytical psychology," will be attempted here. I will also not address his alleged anti-Semitism

argument between them was very bitter. Jung considered Freud's view of spirituality inadequate, seeing it as far more than repressed sexuality. Conversely, Freud could not accept Jung's notion of the collective unconscious and dismissed outright his interest in the paranormal and in Eastern religion.

The collective unconscious was Jung's greatest innovation in psychology. He described it as composed of images (thought forms, impressions, and images) that exist as a kind of memory drawn from the common experiences of countless generations. These images are held in potential by us all. They emerge in the personal unconscious in the form of symbols that we can learn to decipher. It is only in this manner that the material of the collective unconscious can become known and manifested in conscious life. The number of images and thought forms in the collective unconscious is virtually limitless, but some of them, because they are associated with powerful emotions, are of greater importance than others and emerge more frequently in the personal unconscious. Jung referred to these images as archetypes and explained that they are "forms without content, representing merely the possibility of a certain type of perception and action." [27]

Symbols are the most outward expression of archetypes. They have layers of meaning and can be contemplated repeatedly without exhausting their depths. Jung devoted himself to collecting and analyzing mandalas and meditated at length on the meaning of the symbols in alchemy. It is no surprise that the most common symbols are religious, because religious ceremonies are associated with occasions such as births, funerals, weddings, and harvests, which are characterized by a considerable degree of emotion.

Myths are also expressions of the collective unconscious. A culture's myths convey in symbolic form the important values of its members. Myths have a universal quality and are found in similar

---

but will confine myself to outlining his views on religion. I will identify some of the key concepts that will be useful when later we examine some Jewish customs and traditions.

27. Jung (1935) p. 48.

forms in all human communities. All religions have a rich store of myth. The central figures in these mythic stories are archetypal. Although the external aspects of the symbols may vary between cultures (having been influenced by conscious forces), Jung's analysis of them often revealed similarities in their unconscious content.

Signs, symbols, and myths are important concepts in the psychology of religion and need further discussion. Rabbi Zalman Schachter has described the differences between them as follows:[28] A *sign* is static and conveys limited and specific information. For example, a schematic representation of a man or woman on a door is sufficient to tell us whether a public bathroom is intended for men or women. Another example is a traffic sign that tells us whether to go or stop. A *symbol* is more complex and conveys information at a number of different levels simultaneously; it can be both a sign and something deeper. The Star of David or, in Hebrew, *Magen David*, is a good example. It is instantly recognizable as the design on the Israeli national flag and, as such, is a sign that the country is Jewish. Many Jewish organizations have adopted the symbol in order to convey the same message. However, for the alchemists, the two interpenetrating triangles represented the marriage of heaven and earth (the upper triangle heaven and the lower triangle earth) and referred to it as "the kiss." The Cross of Christianity also has multiple meanings. It symbolizes the Christian religion and the ideas of suffering, martyrdom, love, and much else. It has also been used to refer to the four directions and as the Staff of Life. Mandalas are symbols that are the focus of meditation. Symbols are rarely deliberately or consciously designed or created, but emerge out of a deeply rooted tradition and culture—the collective unconscious. They slowly acquire layers of meaning, which are overdetermined, and a rich repository of wisdom for contemplation.

The idea of *myth* has nothing to do with whether a narrative is factual. Often the "facts" are unknown or bear only a passing resemblance to actual historical events. For the person fully engaged with the myth, the facts are irrelevant. What is important about a myth is

---

28. Lecture at the Elat Chayyim Retreat Center, New York, 1993.

that it is *psychologically* true. A child once explained a myth as "a story that is true on the inside." [29] Myths have universal significance and are timeless. The Greek myths still tell us a great deal about human nature as do the Hebrew Bible stories. This is why Freud chose the story of Oedipus to describe the relationship between a boy and his parents. Zalman Schachter described a myth as "a symbol in motion." The meaning of a myth cannot be exhausted. [30]

Marc Ellis, a radical Jewish theologian, has pointed out that three of the greatest world religions, Judaism, Christianity, and Islam, all share a common theme in the mythic events that founded them. All tell of a time in which the people made journeys, "walking and talking," telling each other stories of how they came into being and relating to each other the founding events of their group. These historical myths (the Exodus, the wanderings of Jesus in the Galilee, and the great march of the prophet Mohammed) have become the definitive events of each religion.

For Jung, the importance of symbol and myth is that they allow us to keep in contact with our unconscious selves. When we lose contact with our culture's myths, we lose something of our creativity and vitality. It is through the creation of mythologies that consciousness can be raised.

> Myth is the natural and indispensable intermediate stage between unconscious and conscious cognition. True the unconscious knows more than consciousness does; but it is knowledge of a special sort, knowledge in eternity, usually without reference to the here and now, not couched in the language of the intellect. Only when we let its statements amplify themselves . . . does it come within the range of our understanding; only then does a new aspect become perceptible to us. [31]

The study of archetypes, symbols, and myths led Jung to consider deeply the role of religion in an individual's life. It was appar-

---

29. *See* Johnson (1983) p. 2.
30. This is in many ways similar to the way in which the hasidic *rebbes* interpreted the biblical stories (*see* Chapter 2) and *midrash* (*see* Chapter 1).
31. Jung (1983) p. 343.

ent to him that we involve ourselves in religion (with its rich heritage of symbol and myth) because this enables us to attune ourselves, in a dynamic way, to the natural world and natural forces. Through religion we are better able to contact the archetypes within us and, therefore, be psychologically healthy. Unlike Freud, Jung did not consider religious commitment always to be a regressive step (although sometimes it could be). In some circumstances Jung advocated that his patients return to their religion, whatever that happened to be. One of his most famous cases in this regard involved a young Jewish woman who had "lost her faith."[32] Jung detected that her grandfather had been a hasidic leader, a *tzaddik*, although her own parents were irreligious. He told her, "Now I am going to tell you something that you may not be able to accept. Your grandfather was a *tzaddik*. Your father became an apostate to the Jewish faith. He betrayed the secret and turned his back on God. And you have your neurosis because the fear of God has got into you." Jung saw her on only one further occasion and after that, we are told, her neurosis was cured.

PSYCHOTHERAPY AND SPIRITUALITY

Jung's work has been one of the springboards for today's explosion of interest in the relationship between psychotherapy and spirituality. Another influence on this trend was also anticipated by Jung, namely the introduction of Eastern spiritual teachings and practices (such as meditation, Yoga, Akido, tai chi) into the West. This cross-fertilization has been so influential that there has sometimes been an almost total identification between the methods promoting psychological growth and those fostering spiritual development. While psychoanalysis has bucked this trend and has tended to remain within its traditional medical and scientific territory, other schools of psychotherapy have either explicitly or implicitly incorporated a spiritual perspective into their approach. Some psychotherapists see spiritual exploration and growth as the ultimate goal of therapy and as the culmination of

---

32. *See* Jung (1983) p. 161.

a process of change. Among these schools are, to a greater or lesser extent, person-centered therapy, psychosynthesis, Gestalt, rebirthing, primal therapy, some forms of body psychotherapy and, of course, transpersonal psychology. Similarly, some physical/medical problems that were once purely the domain of the physician are now also treated by means of nonphysical and spiritual techniques such as healing, past-life regression, crystal healing, and homeopathy. During the last thirty years or so we have witnessed the welcome attempt to develop holistic approaches to the treatment of both physical and psychological problems.

> How is one to distinguish the silent Sage from the silent fool?
> The Sage doesn't mind being silent.
> —Rabbi Israel of Rizhin[33]

There is, however, a difficulty. Are psychological development and spiritual development the same thing or is something important lost when we fail to make a distinction between them? Two of the best known advocates of meditation in the West are also psychologists. Ram Dass (also known as Richard Alpert) was a lecturer in psychology at Stanford and Harvard universities and became a teacher of Hindu thought. Jack Kornfield has a doctorate in psychology, was ordained as a Buddhist monk, and teaches Vipassana (insight) meditation. Both of these individuals participated in a panel discussion about the relative merits of meditation and psychotherapy for emotional change and development.[34] The moderator of the discussion suggested that some people may spend time in meditation as a way of avoiding the "knots" of their personality. Jack Kornfield accepted that there is always a risk of this, but that a good meditation teacher would guide a student away from this trap. He also strongly expressed his view that while psychological techniques could be very useful, they were limited as "they do not help one develop the penetrating insight that helps one cut through the deeper layers of illusion. . . ." Ram Dass went on to say that meditation and psychology had different aims.

---

33. Wiesel (1972) p. 117.
34. *See* Chapter 3 in Welwood (1983) p. 36.

Meditation could help one dissolve the ego, whereas psychological techniques were developed to strengthen the ego and to help it become more adaptive to its situation. The danger in the West, he thought, was that Westerners take from the East only those techniques that build up the ego and not the rest of the package.

The psychotherapeutic process and the spiritual quest seem to share many characteristics. The British group analyst and family therapist Robin Skynner has found several.[35] In both psychotherapy and spiritual tradition there is the idea that our perception is clouded, that we are fragmented and need to become whole, that integrity can be achieved via self-knowledge, and that gaining this self-awareness can be initially painful, but eventually leads to healing and growth. That which was previously unconscious and unknown reaches awareness either through meditation and prayer or through the interpretation and feedback from a therapist. Similarly, both approaches believe that we possess hidden resources that only become available when we have achieved this greater self-knowledge and that much of our suffering and pain is a product of our blindness and ignorance. Finally, both psychotherapy and spiritual tradition require regular contact with a teacher, therapist, or guide who has made the journey, or some of the journey, his or her self and can help us to become more objective and to free ourselves from delusion.

The similarities, however, are not the whole story. Robin Skynner suggests that there are important differences and that the two approaches are really at "right angles" to each other, rather than being identical paths. Sacred traditions proceed from the idea of hierarchy within the universe. The human is not at the center of creation; rather, we have a crucial role to play in a drama that is bigger than the life of any single one of us. We all have choices to make in the way we lead our lives, which may align us either with the real world and a "higher" purpose or with the world of illusion and personal appetites and preferences. Spiritual tradition assumes that we are all capable of awakening ourselves to this other level of reality and in so doing we may become disillusioned with the lives that we have previously led.

---

35. *See* Welwood (1983) Chapter 3.

As Ram Dass pointed out, spirituality is concerned to weaken the hold the ego has over us, whereas psychotherapy seeks to strengthen it. There is, however, an alternative to this simple dichotomy. The development of a strong healthy ego that is a servant of the higher self, rather than its master, is a necessary part of spiritual development.[36]

Robin Skynner explains that the source of spiritual tradition and authority is entirely different from that of ordinary psychology. Spiritual tradition is revealed knowledge, a manifestation of the spiritual in and through the lives of individuals. Such individuals embody the teachings by the way in which they live their lives and maintain an enduring authority over their followers. Clients in therapy, however, can reasonably expect to "dissipate the transference," meaning that as a result of successful therapy they no longer see their therapist as an inevitable source of authority over them.[37]

So what can we conclude? Psychotherapy and spirituality each need to find their own place. Whilst it is true that, as William James and others have noted, an encounter with another, nonordinary level of reality may have a profound effect on one's life and well-being, this cannot be relied upon. It might as easily divert us from the real concerns of living. The place of psychotherapy is to help us ground ourselves in reality, establish relationships, and perform our everyday responsibilities. Without such capacities we cannot expect to fully develop our spiritual selves, but with them, there is much to explore. "Given this ground the sacred traditions have some possibility of guiding us back to the source of our lives."[38]

---

36. This is a point made both by transpersonal theorists such as Ken Wilber (*see* below) and by teachers of spiritual traditions such as Kabbalah (e.g., Zev ben Shimon Halevi, discussed below).

37. This issue is far more complex than it appears. Some spiritual traditions have never invested individuals with any form of divine authority. In particular, the Quakers maintain that the "still small voice" can be heard by anyone and that this voice can be best heard in community. The innovation of the Baal Shem-Tov was that anyone, not just the learned, could hear the *bat kol* (voice of God), despite the enormous authority of the *rebbes*. Conversely, the leaders of some religious cults have made great use of the authority vested in them as a result of "ordinary" psychological processes, such as transference and projection, in order to maintain their positions of power.

38. Skynner (1983) p. 32.

The question to be addressed to religion and to religious practices is, how well do they help us to accomplish each of these tasks? Within Judaism a great deal is taught about how to conduct one's ordinary life. The teachings about the inner life and spiritual practice, however, are less well known, and we will need to consider these before addressing the traditions in detail. Before doing so there is one further field of psychology that we need to examine briefly.

TRANSPERSONAL PSYCHOLOGY

Transpersonal psychology is the general name given within psychology to studies of "higher consciousness." Until recently it has been a relatively neglected field of research, but has generated a lot more activity of late. We will not review this research here, but will outline some of the main theoretical ideas to provide us with a context for our later studies. Two names stand out for our attention: the humanistic-existentialist psychotherapist Abraham Maslow and the psychologist-philosopher-theologian Ken Wilber.

Abraham Maslow set himself the task of reversing the direction of academic and empirical psychology. He concerned himself, not with neurosis and misery, but with that which is noblest and highest in human nature. He was interested in human potential and how to help people actualize this in themselves. As such his approach is closer to those of spiritual teachers than any of the psychologists that we have considered thus far. Maslow assumed that we all possess a healthy desire to grow closer to the lines of our inner nature and that when this desire is inhibited, blocked, or distorted we become psychologically unhealthy.

Maslow's most famous contribution was his theory of motivation, which he expressed as a hierarchy of needs.[39] When basic needs have been satisfied, higher needs emerge. At the base of the hierarchy are *physiological needs* that our bodies demand we satisfy. These are followed by *safety needs*, such as for security, stability, protection, and so forth. When these have been met, we become aware or our

---

39. Maslow (1970, 1st edition 1954).

need to belong, which we pursue by joining groups, establishing community and homes and, as part of this, experiencing loving relationships with others (not necessarily, but including, sexual relationships). These social needs are followed by *esteem needs*, which are often diverse. They may include the development of strength, skill, mastery, and confidence, but also may include prestige, respect, and status bestowed upon us by people we value. It is from the satisfaction of these esteem needs that we develop feelings of self-confidence and self-worth.

At the top of the hierarchy is *self-actualization*, which emerges only when the other four categories of need have been met. At this stage "meta-needs" become apparent. These are needs that are facets of our inner (spiritual) nature and may be expressed as creativity, a sense of justice, truth, or beauty. One important part of Maslow's work has been to conduct psychological research with those people he termed self-actualizers.[40] Many of these people described to him mystical experiences similar to those recorded by William James. Maslow referred to these as "peak experiences." Like James before him, Maslow made it his task to record the nature of these experiences and to describe the qualities shared by those people who had them.[41] He found that during these experiences the nature of cognition changed and that these experiences closely resembled the moments of mystical union described consistently by spiritual seekers and meditators. Similarly, the personal qualities of self-actualizers, such as openness, spontaneity, and fearlessness, have much in common with the qualities often attributed to saints, rebbes, gurus, and other charismatic leaders.

The grand theorist of transpersonal psychology is Ken Wilber. Like Maslow, Wilber provides us with an overview of human consciousness and shows how the spiritual and the psychological are interconnected with each other. Rather than setting forth another hierarchical model, however, Wilber describes how consciousness evolves in a magnificent cycle. Each individual, and all of us collectively, move

---

40. Including Eleanor Roosevelt and Albert Einstein as well as ordinary people who were unknown to the public.
41. Maslow (1968).

first of all in an outward arc from subconsciousness to self-consciousness and then begin to traverse the inward arc to superconsciousness. The development of the individual mirrors the spiritual development of humanity as a whole.[42]

Our individual journeys start in infancy or even at conception. Sub-consciousness is the first stage, and at this stage there is no separation of the self from the environment, as there is almost no self to be aware of its situation. At this level we are ruled by our instincts, and our experience is that of timeless, oceanic oneness with our environment. As we progress along the outward arc and learn to control our bodies, develop language, and develop ego, we become fully self-conscious. At this point we may begin the inward arc, the return to nonduality and integration. This inward arc is the journey undertaken by mystics and spiritual seekers and is the path along which Wilber sees humanity slowly evolving.[43]

Classical psychology has been mostly concerned with the early part of the cycle of consciousness and has detailed the processes of the pre-egoic stage very well. Freud and others either denied or ignored the second half of the cycle. Ken Wilber, however, has taken us further and has analyzed the mystical literature of the sacred traditions, where the meditators and mystics have described their journeys and the stages through which they have passed. In this way Wilber has been able to describe the psychological processes involved in the inward arc, the development of superconsciousness.[44]

Wilber shows how the psychologically normal adult, with a functioning persona and ego, is not the necessary endpoint of our evolution or the "highest" developmental stage we can achieve. However, it may represent the level at which most of us currently function. In every age there are those individuals who have developed further and have experiences that break down of the illusion of the separation of body and mind and indeed the illusion of our separateness from each other and from existence as a whole. This requires the "death" of the ego,

---

42. *See* Wilber (1981).
43. *See* Wilber (1981).
44. *See* Wilber (1977).

meaning the disidentification of the ego with its achievements. Wilber thinks of such individuals as the "growing tips of consciousness" and says that they provide the inspiration and guidance for the rest of us.

The evolution of consciousness occurs in stages, and these stages form a kind of ladder on which we climb.[45] As we progress up the ladder we do not jettison the old stages, but they remain within us and are the platform on which we stand. In fact it is the transformation of these previous stages that provides the structures on which later development is based. The lower stages of consciousness contain in potential, enfolded within them, the higher structures themselves. In many ways the structures, therefore, resemble each other.

This brings us back to the difficulty that we identified earlier. How do we distinguish between true spiritual development and infantile regression? Wilber assists by reminding us of the important distinction between "pre" states and "trans" states. In particular he shows that the infantile state of bliss, in which the baby is in the womb and fused with his or her mother, is not the same as a state of transcendence following the awakening of consciousness, even though both may experience calmness, peace, oneness, and so forth. The process of development through the stages of consciousness, and through each stage, has a distinctive and necessary form. First there is *fusion*, for example of mind and body in early infancy, from which there is a later *differentiation* in which the self rises above the confinement of simple sensations, perceptions, and impulses.

There will be a problem, however, if instead of the healthy differentiation between mind and body there is *dissociation* and the body/mind connection becomes fragmented. "Successful development means a series of clean differentiations with little or no dissociations . . . dissociation simply means the exile of a structure to the submergent-unconscious; not its transcendence, but its repression." [46] This process is repeated at all levels of the evolution of consciousness.

---

45. The notion of a spiritual ladder is also popular in Kabbalah and in hasidic thought. It is sometimes known as Jacob's ladder (after Jacob's famous dream in Genesis 28:12).

46. Wilber (1980) p. 131.

There is then an enormous difference between the inner peace of a meditator and that of a baby feeding at the breast. The meditator may, of course, choose to remain meditating because the transcendent state is preferable to the challenges of everyday life. Such regression is possible at any level of development.

THE INHERENT PSYCHOLOGY WITHIN JEWISH TRADITION

We saw in Chapters 1 and 2 how Jewish tradition has changed and evolved over time and how in the course of its long development it has incorporated many psychological insights and perspectives. In the final part of this chapter we will look at some psychological ideas that have been present from the earliest periods of Jewish history. These are the distinctive approach to biblical exegesis known as *PaRDeS* and the Kabbalah. We will finish by briefly considering some Jewish approaches and concerns relating to psychotherapy.

PaRDeS

The Hebrew word *PaRDeS* is usually translated as "orchard", but in rabbinic literature it also carries the connotation of the "heavenly orchard," the Garden of Eden, and Paradise.[47] *PaRDeS* is also an acronym of four other Hebrew words: *P'shat*, *Remez*, *Drash*, and *Sod*, and these four refer to a traditional and profoundly psychological approach to exegesis. The implication is that when one has achieved a level of understanding of a verse at all four levels of interpretation, then one knows and experiences something of the "orchard."[48]

The first level, *P'shat*, refers to the simple, straightforward and literal meaning of a text. It is an approach whereby one uses logic

---

47. This is based on the account in the Talmud of the four sages who "entered the orchard." Their travels are understood as a spiritual ascent accomplished by means of meditation (*see* Kaplan [1982]).

48. *See* a discussion of its similarity to psychotherapy by Rotenberg (1994).

and the analysis of grammar, syntax, and variant word meanings to arrive at the most parsimonious interpretation of a text.[49]

Remez means a "hint" or an "allusion." Here meaning is not explicit but is encoded in symbolism. Interpretations are often based on numerological manipulations of the Hebrew letters.[50] The assumption underlying this type of interpretive activity is that, because the text is holy, the meanings discovered in this way were always present within the text in potential and awaited the revelation achieved by this kind of interpretive manipulation.

Drash is "to enquire" and is closely related to *midrash*. This level of interpretation or commentary is usually allegorical and commonly understood to be interpretation in the sense of "giving one's interpretation." It is the stuff of rabbinic sermons and homily.

Sod means "secret." It is the deepest level, the most hidden, available only to the initiated.

Traditionally understood, these four levels of interpretation are hierarchical. As with Wilber's stages of consciousness, each stands on the other and incorporates the levels below. Rabbi Zalman Schachter has suggested that each one relates to a different approach to psychol-

---

49. This is the approach favored by the most famous biblical commentator, *Rashi* (Rabbi Solomon ben Isaac).

50. There are essentially two approaches. The most well known is Gemmatria. Each letter is assigned a number value based on its position in the Hebrew alphabet. The numbers are totaled for each word, and words with the same number values are considered to be semantically, and perhaps spiritually, related. For example, *Elohim* is one of the names used in the Bible for God, particularly in the account of creation contained in the first chapter of Genesis. It has the same number value as *Tevah*, which means "nature." Hence, a relationship between this particular holy name of God (the creator God) and Nature is perceived. The second type of analysis is Notarikon. This is the approach whereby each letter of a word is used as the first letter of another word, and a sentence is constructed based on these words. An example is the first word of the ten commandments, *Anochi*, which means "I." This has been expanded to a sentence translated as "I myself came and gave them."

Another approach to *Remez* is the interpretation of the Zohar (*The Book of Splendor*—a key kabbalistic text). For example, Rabbi Levi-Yitzchak of Berditchev frequently refers to Zoharic passages as *Remez* in his book *Kedushas Levi* (a mystical commentary on the Torah portion).

ogy. "I discovered that psychology too had its own *PaRDeS* of *P'shat* = behaviorism, *Remez* = psychoanalysis and Gestalt, *Drash* = humanistic and cognitive psychology, and the *Sod* = transpersonal psychology." [51] As we go on to discuss the different areas of Jewish tradition, we will find that we need to draw on different levels of interpretation to achieve a holistic view.

Kabbalah

Kabbalah means "received" and refers to much of the corpus of Jewish mysticism developed over thousands of years. As with the Written and Oral Torah, the Kabbalah is considered to be of divine and ancient origin. Legend tells us that kabbalistic knowledge was first possessed by the earliest biblical character, Enoch,[52] and that one of the most important kabbalistic texts, the *Sefer Yetzirah*, was written by Abraham.

The Kabbalah is commonly divided into three sections: the magical tradition, the meditative traditions and the philosophical tradition. The latter has been by far the most influential on Jewish tradition. It is theoretical and speculates on the nature of the divine world and its connection with our physical world. It is the framework within which the other two traditions sit, and both are guided by it.

Jewish mysticism, like all mysticism, is a path to knowing God and, as such, is concerned with self-perfection. It is full of psychological insights and models, but they are expressed in a theological and supernatural language.[53] Traditionally Kabbalah has been a secret tradition and a closed book to most people. Today we are fortunate

---

51. Schachter-Shalomi (1991) p. xv.
52. Based on the verse in Genesis (5:24) that "Enoch walked with God" and, according to midrashic interpretation, that he did not suffer a normal death but was "taken by God."
53. I do not mean to say that mysticism is *only* psychological, although in the light of the discussion above we do well to recognize the important influence psychology plays. Kabbalah is obviously concerned with the supernatural and the transpersonal and speaks of forces beyond ordinary human awareness and capacities.

that many teachers of Kabbalah have translated kabbalistic texts and have presented Kabbalah in a modern, often, psychological language.[54]

Attempting to describe some of the ideas of Kabbalah in only a few brief paragraphs carries the obvious danger of oversimplification. However, this is not a book about Kabbalah, and I trust that some of the concepts become clearer as they are expanded upon in other chapters.

Among those who have expounded the psychological aspects of the kabbalistic system has been Z'ev ben Shimon Halevi. In a series of books he has described in detail the inner workings of the kabbalistic "Tree of Life."[55] The "Tree of Life" portrays the interrelationships of the revealed attributes of God (known as the *sephirot*). Halevi shows how the "Tree" also represents all the levels of an individual: the body, the soul, the spirit, and the divine. He describes how the sephirotic Tree can be utilized by the serious seeker as a map of the psyche and as a tool for identifying areas within oneself that need exploring or balancing in order to become whole and closer to God. Halevi chooses to emphasize particularly the role of the mind because it ". . . has access to (the) body, contains the soul, is penetrated by spirit and touched by the Divine."[56] He also relates the different approaches to psychology to different levels of the "Tree."

Kabbalah teaches that the physical world of our ordinary senses is only one level of reality. The Kabbalah speaks of four spiritual worlds that are expressed in the four Hebrew letters of the Divine Name known as the Tetragrammaton.[57] Both Z'ev ben Shimon Halevi and Zalman Schachter have taught how we might understand these worlds in psychological terms. *Olam HaAssiyah* is the physical world or the world of action. This is the realm of the body and of activity and behavior. It is the densest and most corporeal of all the worlds and is

---

54. The interested reader could consult, for example, Green (1992), Halevi (1986), Hoffman (1981), and Steinsaltz (1980).

55. Primarily following the system of Moshe Cordovero who was later superseded in popularity and influence by Rabbi Isaac Luria (The Ari).

56. Ibid (1986) p. x.

57. *Yud*, *Hey*, *Vav*, and *Hey*.

the object of creation. *Olam HaYetzirah* is the world of "Formation." It is within this level that we have feelings and dreams and experience ourselves in relationship with other beings. *Olam HaBriyah* is the world of "Creation." It is the realm of intellect, mentation, and pure thought forms. It is comparable to Plato's notion of the world of "Ideals." *Olam HaAtzilut* is the world of "Emanation," the purest and most refined level of being, most closely connected with the Divine Being.

As with *PaRDeS* we can find a degree of correspondence between Kabbalah and the different approaches within psychology. *Olam HaAssiyah* is the world of the behaviorist, whereas *Olam HaYetzirah* is the concern of the Freudians and of psychodynamics. Jung and many transpersonal psychologists are most at home in *Olam HaBriyah*.

THE PSYCHOHALACHIC PROCESS

An entirely different approach to the relationship between Judaism and psychology has been the concern about whether there is a basis within Jewish law for the practice of psychotherapy. Are these two traditions compatible or is there a clash of values? An Orthodox response might be as follows. To the extent that psychology supports and encourages behavior consistent with *halacha*, then it can be supported; otherwise it should be rejected.[58] In particular, psychoanalysis is problematic because of the open way in which sexual behavior and fantasy are discussed, and also because God is construed (particularly by Freud) as a projection rather than as a reality.

We can see straight away that this approach to the question assumes the primacy of *halacha* as a core set of values. However, even for religious and observant psychotherapists a more sophisticated approach is called for.[59] This has been provided by a group of observant psychodynamically trained psychotherapists working in Israel and

---

58. *See* Amsel (1969).

59. *See*, for example, Spero's (1990) article on how a religious client's experience of God can be addressed in psychoanalytic psychotherapy.

North America.[60] The concept of psychohalacha is an extension of the approach of Rav Soloveitchik (considered in Chapter 1). The principle that one's day-to-day life should be governed by halachic considerations is extended to include a sensitivity to psychological concerns.[61] Initially this is the talmudic concept of *Lifnim Mishurat Hadin*,[62] which is "going beyond the letter of the law." There are also the application of biblical precepts such as "rebuking one's neighbor" and "not putting a stumbling block in front of the blind" and the rabbinic discussion of these ideas.[63] For these rabbis and therapists, the *halacha* provides a living framework for their psychotherapeutic work.

The religious leader as therapist and spiritual counselor is, of course, a traditional role. Rabbi Zalman Schachter has made an in-depth study of the special case of the encounter between a hasidic *rebbe* and his followers.[64] These occasions, known as *yihudim*, have a special place in the life of a *hasid* because they provide an opportunity to receive personal guidance and instruction based on the *rebbe's* perception of their current spiritual status and needs. Rabbi Schachter shows how both the *hasid* and the *rebbe* undertake careful preparation for these meetings. He also reveals the similarities and dissimilarities between these encounters and psychological therapy. In the *yihud* both participants share the same set of beliefs about cosmology and the inherent authority of the *rebbe*. Because of this the *hasid* is open to profound and significant changes that might not be so easily affected by an ordinary psychotherapist.

Rabbi Schachter also extends the boundaries of the concept of psychohalacha. Contained within each of the *mitzvot* is a profound teaching that provides an opportunity for further spiritual growth. Often it is only the outward content of the *mitzvah* that is available to us. The spiritual teachings are encoded in mystical language that

---

60. Reuben Bulka, Moshe Spero, Levi Meier, and others. Much of their thinking has been published in the Journal Of Judaism and Psychology, which is largely devoted to this type of exploration.

61. *See* Meier (1988).

62. Baba Mezia 30b.

63. *See* Meier (1988) p. 69.

64. Schachter-Shalomi (1991).

we may not understand. Rabbi Zalman urges us to pay more attention to the inner teachings, as these were the meanings originally intended. One of his examples will give us a clearer idea of what he has in mind. The Talmud asks the following question. How long is one required to wear the *tephillin*[65] during morning prayers? The Talmud responds: the length of time required to walk four cubits. Rabbi Schachter explains that walking four cubits refers to the four worlds of Kabbalah and that the Talmud is teaching that prayers must not be performed in a mechanical fashion and that their purpose is to help us switch our attention to deeper levels of reality.

Psychohalacha is an approach that is about the attunement of consciousness. It reminds us of William James's observation that the practice of religion has transformative possibilities and that it needs to be evaluated on these grounds. We have also seen in this chapter that through the encounter with symbols we make contact with the level of reality that Jung referred to as archetypes of the collective unconscious. Finally, psychohalacha directs us toward a growthful, not regressive, religious and spiritual life. It is with this framework that we can now turn our attention to the richness and details of Jewish traditions.

---

65. Phylacteries.

II

4

The Ceremony of *Havdalah*

May the One who blessed our ancestors . . . bless all this holy congregation, together with all other holy congregations, them, their families and all that belong to them; those who establish synagogues for prayer, and those who enter therein to pray; those who give lamps for lighting, and wine for *Kiddush* and *Havdalah*, bread to the wayfarers, and charity to the poor. . . .[1]

Within most religious traditions there are a variety of ceremonies and rituals. This is true, also, of Judaism. From a halachic perspective the main question to be asked of a Jewish ceremony is about its correct performance. Does it conform to the detail laid down in the codes? There may be varying versions of a ceremony, depending on the customs of different communities, but in essence there is usually a consensus of rabbinic opinion detailing the correct performance of the rite. The student of Jewish mysticism will ask additional questions: What is the meta-structure of the ceremony? What spiritual energies are invoked, how is the ceremony connected with the Divine Will, and what is the spiritual purpose of the ceremony?

---

1. Abridged from the prayer for the congregation, *Shabbat* morning service.

From a psychological perspective an entirely new question emerges—a question about meaning. The outstanding finding of the Women in the Community review[2] was that although many rituals are regularly observed, they are observed in the absence of religious belief and that the selection of rituals has become a matter of individual choice and preference, rather than of theological doctrine or guidance." . . . the importance given in general life to consumer choice and personal growth has contributed to a selective Judaism; a philosophy in which individuals feel it is permissible to choose which practices they maintain and which they neglect." What, then, are the psychological factors at work in the maintenance of these rituals?

In this chapter we will examine, in some detail, the *Havdalah* ceremony, which takes place at the end of *Shabbat* and some festivals. It is a custom that is not observed as widely as, for example, lighting candles on Friday night or the Seder service at Passover; nevertheless, it seems to be making a comeback and is growing in popularity. Our main reason for choosing *Havdalah*, however, is that it is an unusually elaborate and complete ceremony. Contained within it are customs and symbols that signal important psychological concepts that will help us understand other Jewish customs.

THE PSYCHOLOGY OF CEREMONY AND RITUAL[3]

From a psychological perspective the performance of a religious ceremony has two primary functions: first, the expression and moderation of emotions, and second, the transmission of information that is important to a particular religious culture. In other words, they have both an emotive component and an educational one. In order to facilitate this, ceremonies and rituals have certain key characteristics. These include repetition, the use of symbols, a recognizable and de-

---

2. *See* Introduction.

3. For our present purpose we will use ceremony and ritual more or less interchangeably. It may be argued, however, that ceremony is more properly a religious enactment defined by a particular liturgy, with the primary function of preserving a religious culture, whereas a ritual implies a quality of transformation and change.

fined structure, and flexibility enabling adaptation to new circumstances. We will briefly consider each of these in turn.

Some ceremonies are performed daily or weekly. These are well known to any regular attendee of a church, synagogue, temple, or mosque. The regular cycle of services usually includes elements of ritual that are so familiar to the participants that they are able to perform them automatically, without necessarily paying a great deal of attention to what they are doing.[4] Other ceremonies are less frequent, such as those that occur on festival days and those that mark important events in the life cycle, such as births, marriages, and deaths. Nevertheless, these ceremonies also become familiar over time. So an adult who has lived and matured within a particular religious community will know the main elements of each ceremony and will have developed some understanding of their significance and meaning. In this way, by means of repetition, the rituals and ceremonies are incorporated into the consciousness of the group and the individual.

It is no coincidence that a great deal of the significance of a ceremony is expressed symbolically. We saw in Chapter 3 how symbols are containers for depths of meaning. Another important aspect of symbols is their essential ambiguity. This idea is explored by the Jungian analyst Bani Shorter:

> . . . Jung defined symbols as "intuitive ideas that cannot yet be formulated in any better way." Symbolic communication acts as a kind of sign language which is resorted to at the borders of comprehension, not selected to please an audience but made use of as the only appropriate instrument available at the time, and it works both ways. For just as a worshipper can only approach the unknowable awakener of being by way of symbolic utterance, the presence of that mysterious other is apprehensible only by way of a statement open to many interpretations.[5]

---

4. Of course, all traditions consider that rituals should preferably be performed with conscious awareness and attention. Nevertheless, a great deal of religious adherence is automatic and overlearned, although automatic performance may still have a pyschological influence on the performer.

5. Shorter (1996) p. 24.

Symbols, then, are conduits enabling the flow between the individual (and personal levels of awareness) and that which is beyond the individual—the transpersonal.

Ceremonies and rituals are also dynamic. Their distinctive feature is that a state of affairs pertaining at the beginning is transformed, by performance of the ritual, to something new at its completion. The structure of the ceremony, therefore, follows a pattern, and in a well-developed ritual this pattern is not arbitrary but drawn out of the religious tradition itself. In attempting to apprehend the divine, a religious culture perceives a pattern that seems to be inherent in the cosmos, a pattern larger than itself, and it seeks to express this pattern in its ceremonial forms.

One such basic pattern is the circle, wheel, or spiral, possibly following the movement of the sun from the east through the south to the west (in the northern hemisphere). These might be the "rounds" in the Native American Sweat Lodge or, to give an example from within Judaism, the waving of the *lulav* during the festival of Sukkot. Structuring a ceremony after a pattern found in nature is, perhaps, an attempt at attunement to forces larger than oneself, and the creation of an opportunity for the interpenetration of worlds—the spiritual with the psychological. Another pattern is found in the regular symbolic enactment of a cultural myth. Judaism is full of examples: the lighting of candles at Chanukah as a commemoration of the lamp burning in the Temple, theatricals at Purim enacting the story of the book of Esther and, of course, the Seder service at the Passover meal, during which the most crucial story, that of the birth of the Jewish people, is retold annually in ceremonial form.

A pattern found again and again in ceremony is that of the journey of ascent and descent. There are many examples. When receiving the Host during a High Catholic Mass, the participant moves slowly toward the priest and then away from him, with the central act itself surrounded by magisterial music and procession. Reading from the Torah in a synagogue service follows a similar pattern. First the Torah is ceremonially removed from the Ark, then it is processed around the synagogue before being placed on the desk from which it will be read. After the reading it is held aloft for the congregation to see and is once again paraded around the synagogue before being returned to the Ark. It is the highlight of the service.

This journey of ascent and descent often represents a path of initiation, a journey with a number of stages. The beginning of the ritual frequently includes an element of purification and buildup of energy, the central section contains the moment of the most intimate connection with the source, and the final section facilitates integration and return to the ordinary, nonceremonial reality. This pattern too is modeled on a perception of the universal, and it finds a variety of expression: birth and rebirth, the cycle of the orgasm, the mythic journey.

By engaging with one of these "universal" patterns, through ritual, we seek an encounter with the sacred. For it is through such an encounter, enabling us to identify the cosmic pattern within ourselves, that ritual has potential for transformation. This idea is expressed powerfully by Bani Shorter:

> "Taking in" the sacred is nothing more than seeing it as the pattern fundamental to all other patterns in ourselves, inescapable and essential. It is an acknowledgment that, being human, we are in possession of a godforce as vulnerable, laudable, dangerous, wise as any other of the most basic archetypal forces which we carry within but with a difference—that its strength outweighs all others, interferes with and permeates all other of our stories, is the subplot of all we do. It is not "the unconscious" but that which calls attention to all that can be made conscious within us.[6]

We saw earlier how Jewish liturgical rites, *halacha*, and customs have evolved over time as an adaptation to changing circumstances and requirements.[7] This is a particularly obvious feature of Jewish ceremonies as well. Ceremonies change to better fulfill the needs of a community, and new rituals evolve. A few brief examples will suffice. Ezra introduced the custom of publicly reading from the Torah in the vernacular in biblical times. There have been significant changes

---

6. Ibid p. 26.
7. *See* Chapter 1.

to the marriage ceremony in response to political and historical considerations.[8] Some families light more than two candles on Friday nights, perhaps one for each child. Coming of age ceremonies for teenagers were originally restricted to Bar Mitzvah celebrations for boys at the age of 13. Nowadays 12-year-old girls have Aishet Chayil ceremonies in Orthodox synagogues or Bat Mitzvahs in progressive ones. Finally, the inclusion of space and time for extra poetry and music, within a preset ceremony, allows for the possibility of personal and emotional expression—the psychohalachic element.

We will now turn to our example of Jewish ceremony, *Havdalah*.

HAVDALAH

Havdalah is one of the most colorful and complete ceremonies in Jewish life. It marks the end of Shabbat and the end of many festivals. It takes place when the sun has just set, the mood is ideally quiet and contemplative, and we feel at our most removed from ordinary, daily life. The word *Havdalah* can be translated as meaning "separation," and its function is to mark the transition from the sacred and holy time of Shabbat or a festival, to the ordinary mundane time of the rest of the week. The ritual itself has a number of distinct elements. It is both a piece of liturgy and a ceremony. In its present, modern form, *Havdalah* begins with the recitation of biblical verses taken from the Book of Psalms and the Book of Esther (see below for text[9]). A blessing is made first over a cup of wine, then over spices, and then over the fire emanating from a plaited candle. The spice box, containing a blend of aromatic spices, is passed around all those present who, after reciting the appropriate blessing, inhale deeply in order to experience the reviving effects of the scents. The candle is raised aloft so that the light can be clearly seen and reflected on the faces of all the participants.

The actual moment of transition between holy time and mundane time is marked by the recitation of the *Havdalah* blessing. As

---

8. *See* Chapter 6.
9. This is the conclusion of Shabbat version of *Havdalah*. The text quoted here is from Singer (1962).

this blessing is concluded, the candle is suddenly and dramatically doused by plunging it into the glass of wine or, in some communities, a glass of spirits, such as vodka, which is then set aflame and burns for a few moments illuminating the darkness. As this happens, the room is thrown into light by either lighting more candles or, in modern households, flicking the switch of the electric lights. The ceremony is concluded by songs, poems, and the traditional greeting in Yiddish "Gute Woch," or in Hebrew "*Shavuah Tov*," or in English "Have a good week."

The *Havdalah* Service

Behold God is my salvation; I will trust, and will not be afraid: for Jah the Lord is my strength and song, and he is become my salvation. Therefore with joy shall ye draw water out of the wells of salvation. Salvation belongeth unto the Lord: thy blessing be upon thy people. (Selah.) The Lord of hosts is with us; the God of Jacob is our refuge. (Selah.) The Jews had light and joy and gladness and honor. So be it with us. I will lift up the cup of salvation, and call upon the name of the Lord.

* Blessed art thou, O Lord our God, King of the Universe, who createst the fruit of the vine.

* Blessed art thou, O Lord our God, King of the Universe, who createst diverse kinds of spices.

* Blessed art thou, O Lord our God, King of the Universe, who createst the light of the fire.

* Blessed art thou, O Lord our God, King of the Universe, who makest a distinction between holy and profane, between light and darkness, between Israel and the other nations, between the seventh day and the six working days. Blessed art thou, O Lord, who makest a distinction between holy and profane.

The *Havdalah* ritual and liturgy have been studied and analyzed by Professor Larry Hoffman.[10] He points out that although the

---

10. Hoffman (1987).

Havdalah ceremony has its origins in Mishnaic times, a ceremony of some kind was known even earlier, probably around the time of the Second Temple. The present ceremony derives from eleventh-century France, although there are many different versions of the rite. According to Hoffman, the *Havdalah* ceremony contains, sometimes symbolically encoded, a subtext delineating fundamental *categories* of Jewish thought, perception, and consciousness. In this chapter we will briefly examine the history of the ritual, the psychological categories that it establishes, and certain mythological themes contained within it that surface in other Jewish ceremonies as well. In so doing we will glimpse some of the psychological meanings contained within the ritual, meanings that may account for its survival and vitality.

The Continuing Development of the Havdalah Ceremony[11]

The modern text of the *Havdalah* ceremony varies slightly according to the point in the cycle of the week and festivals that it occurs. For example, there are different versions for the end of Shabbat, the end of a festival, and between Shabbat and a festival (when a festival begins on Saturday night). This means that when the next day is a week day, the liturgy differentiates between holy time and ordinary time, but when the next day is a holiday, the liturgy differentiates between different levels of holiness, and the final part of the *Havdalah* blessing reads, "You have distinguished between the holiness of the Sabbath and the holiness of a holy day." The earliest versions of the *Havdalah* blessings were probably recited in the Temple and are associated with the time of Ezra and the *Anshe Knesset Ha G'Dolah* (the men of the Great Assembly). They therefore constitute a putative historical link to the Oral Law and Sinai Revelation.

The Talmud records different versions of the *Havdalah* text, and attempting to reconstruct what might have been the original ceremony is a little like a psychotherapist trying to reconstruct a client's dream from those fragments that can be remembered. The liturgy of the current rite emphasizes the distinctions between holy and secular, light

---

11. *See* Hoffman (1987) for a full account of the development of the rite.

and dark, and the Jewish people and the other nations. However, in the Talmud, we find in the text other distinctions that contemporary versions leave out. These are: clean and unclean, sea from dry land, upper waters from lower waters, Levites from Israelites, and priests from Levites and Israelites.[12] These distinctions have been dropped from the original *Havdalah* ceremony, and we can only assume that they are no longer included because these categories are no longer pertinent to Jewish experience.

It is interesting that in modern times there has been a resurgence of interest in the *Havdalah* ritual, especially in Zionist youth groups, *chavurot*, and various minority groups that have been marginalized within Jewish tradition. So now, modern versions of the *Havdalah* ceremony emphasize distinctions that these groups feel are important. Examples are Zionist groups emphasizing the importance of national identities, gay and lesbian communities celebrating difference and diversity, and antiracist groups emphasizing the values of internationalism and antiracism.

The liturgy that surrounds the central ceremonial acts of *Havdalah* has also undergone various changes. For example, in the ninth century, Rav Amram contributed a lengthy poem that has now been omitted from most prayer books, although it was fully recorded in the authoritative code the Tur.[13] A glance at modern prayer books today will show the differences that exist between Ashkenazi and Sephardic versions, and even within the Ashkenazi texts there are differences. For example, the Singer's prayer book, which is the normative text for the Orthodox Anglo-Jewish community, has only a brief number of songs following the *Havdalah* ceremony; however, another traditional Orthodox prayer book, the Art Scroll *siddur*, has a much longer set of songs and poems.

The development and evolution of the *Havdalah* ritual may have reflected changes in the historical situation of the Jewish people. It probably gained prominence as a home-based ritual only in modern times and previously took place in the synagogue. If, as seems likely,

---

12. *Pesachim* 103b–104a.
13. Code preceding the *Shulchan Aruch* in the fourteenth century.

Havdalah originally occurred within the precincts of the temple, then it would have become particularly popular around the time of the great dispersion. It served to emphasize and reinforce categories important to Jewish life at a time when these categories were most under threat because of the breakup of the Jewish communities. Similarly, the inclusion or exclusion of different elements of the ritual was probably determined by the prevailing concerns of the time. For example, the highly respected codifier Moshe Isserles proffered the opinion that the biblical verses preceding the ritual were not compulsory (i.e., not required according to the *halacha*) but were included only for "good luck."[14]

Psychological Interpretation of the Ceremonial Symbols

Each symbol has multiple interpretations. Some of these are homiletic; others are mystical.

Wine

The blessing over the wine at *Havdalah* echoes the blessing of the wine drunk during *Kiddush* the previous evening. On Friday night the wine is drunk in fulfillment of the biblical commandment to sanctify the Shabbat and to make it holy. In Judaism the consumption of wine is the literal manner in which something is made holy. Wine raises the spiritual status of an act. At *Kiddush* on Shabbat evening the wine also acts as a marker, separating the days of the week from Shabbat. So too is wine a marker at *Havdalah*, only this time in the opposite direction: from Shabbat to the week.

The symbolism of wine has been extended by those mystics who make use of *gematriah*.[15] They have calculated that the numerical value of the letters that make up the Hebrew word for wine is seventy.[16]

---

14. Moshe Isserles was the author of the authoritative gloss on the *Shulchan Aruch* that set out the Ashkenazi *minhagim*.

15. A method of numerology based on the Hebrew letters (*see* Chapter 3).

16. *See* Adin Steinsaltz (1980) for a fuller discussion of the significance of wine at *Kiddush* (especially pp. 178–180).

Seventy is a highly significant number in Kabbalah. It represents the ten *sephirot*[17] multiplied by the seven days of the week. In other words, it symbolizes fulfillment because each of the *sephirot* has become manifest in each day of the week. On Friday night it is the completion of the week that is celebrated, whereas at *Havdalah* it is the completion and unification of the Shabbat that are sanctified. Drinking wine, therefore, is a symbolic taking in of the holiness of Shabbat.

Spices

The primary importance of the spices is their smell. The Hebrew word for fragrance is *rayach*, which is closely related to, and has the same Hebrew root as, the word for spirit, which is *Ruach*. This suggests the symbolic significance of the sniffing of aromatic spices during the ritual. We might speculate that the spices are in some way associated with the *Rayach Nichoach* ("a pleasing fragrance") referred to frequently in the biblical description of the sacrificial rites that occurred originally in the *Mishkan*.[18] However, the Jewish folk traditions have given us a rich and elaborate mythology about the *Havdalah* spices that is closely linked to the spiritual significance of Shabbat and the festivals.

The folk tradition teaches us that during Shabbat we are each given a *neshama y'tairah* (an extra soul). We receive this soul at the beginning of Shabbat, and this is a symbolic way of stating that the Sabbath is intended as a time of deep rest, contemplation, and renewal. At the end of the holy time, at *Havdalah*, this extra soul is taken from us and, because of this, we feel depleted. The purpose of smelling the spices is to refresh us; otherwise, we may feel weak and faint at this sensitive time. An alternative version of the folk tradition suggests that the *neshama y'tairah* is reluctant to leave at the end of Shabbat and has to be drawn out of us by the lure of the spices. The reluctance is also within us, as another explanation of the spices implies. Just as the smell of the spices lingers in the atmosphere, so too, we hope,

---

17. *See* Chapter 3.
18. Portable sanctuary desert constructed by Moses.

will the spirit of Shabbat remain with us during the forthcoming week. We are reluctant to let go.

There is yet another explanation of the spice sniffing that draws on a separate mythological narrative. According to the traditions surrounding death and bereavement, some souls are tested or punished during the year following the death of the body. During Shabbat, however, the entire universe is at rest (including the world to come); therefore, these souls are also at rest and no longer in torment.[19] *Havdalah* marks the end of this period of respite. It is the time when the fires of Gehinom are rekindled.[20] Inevitably we will feel sad at this moment because of our awareness that departed loved ones may be suffering, so the spices come to cheer us and revive us.

Fire

The most obvious significance of lighting a candle at this time is that it is an action of "work," that is, something that has been prohibited during the preceding festival or Sabbath. Lighting a fire, therefore, symbolically indicates that we are no longer in a festival or Sabbath time, and that ordinary life has resumed.

In symbolic terms, fire is the agent of transformation. It converts the material into the nonmaterial, and as such it is an expression of the assumed mystical task of the Jewish people: transforming the material into the spiritual by conscious activity. This, of course, has practical implications. During the ordinary days of the week we are busy, doing our best to perfect the world and to hurry forward the future Messianic age. During Shabbat and festivals we rest from this task and, instead, experience a foretaste of the messianic era, which becomes available to us during the holy day through its inherent spirituality. This idea is expressed mythologically in various Jewish traditions. There is a *midrash* that Adam, in the

---

19. See Chapter 5.

20. Traditional and poetic reference to Hell, although the concept of Hell is rather different in Judaism than in the traditional Christian images, such as that of Dante.

Garden of Eden, was afraid of the dark. Adam was created toward the end of the sixth day and when Shabbat arrived, it was his first experience of darkness and, therefore, unknown to him. At the end of Shabbat God gave Adam two stones to rub together to make fire, and this brought his illumination and ability to begin transforming the world. It is interesting to notice the difference between this *midrash* and the Greek myth of Prometheus. Prometheus had to steal fire from the gods, whereas in the Jewish version, God *gave* Adam a gift of fire. Another version of the *midrash* states that Adam feared the return of the snake, who might lead him astray, and a pillar of fire was sent to protect him.

The symbolism of the plaited or twisted candle is also highly significant in the *Havdalah* ritual. The lighting of the *Havdalah* candle as Shabbat comes to a close is reminiscent of the lighting of the two individual candles in the home as part of the ceremony that inaugurates the Sabbath on Friday night. At the beginning of Shabbat the candles are separate, representing disunity, schism and, to some extent, fragmentation. The enjoyment of Sabbath rest, prayer, contemplation, and inward reflection brings about a healing of this separateness, a unification that is symbolized by the plaited candle of *Havdalah*. The very full and bright flame of the plaited candle symbolizes the brightness of the soul that has celebrated the Sabbath and renewed itself. In the language of the Kabbalah, the right-hand Friday night candle represents *Chesed*, which is love and expansiveness, whereas the left-hand candle represents *Gevurah*, signifying the qualities of strength, judgment, and receptivity. At the end of the Sabbath these two qualities are symbolically interwoven to form a unified "tree of life"—the quality of *Tiferet*, expressing the attributes of beauty, balance, and harmony.

Taken as a whole the *Havdalah* ritual incorporates all four elements known to the ancient world. There is fire in the form of the flame of the *Havdalah* candle, water in the wine, earth in the spices, and air in the aromatic fragrance and in the sound of singing and prayer. Once again we see a symbol of unification and completion.

Elijah

The prophet Malachi prophesied that the coming and return of Elijah would herald the coming of the time of the Messiah.[21] It is for this reason that a song calling upon and welcoming Elijah into the community is sung joyously and vigorously after the recitation of the *Havdalah* blessing and the dousing of the candle. The mythology surrounding the Elijah figure is highly developed in Jewish thought. We will consider him from two perspectives: first, in terms of why we should welcome him, particularly at the end of the Sabbath, and second, in terms of his mythological significance within Judaism.

The Jewish tradition understands the primary task and purpose of the Jewish people to be working toward bringing forward the time of the messianic era.[22] For six days each week we work in the world doing our best, according to our varying talents and abilities, to bring the time of the Messiah a little closer. The Sabbath, however, is considered to be a foretaste of the world to come, and consequently it is our duty to rest on the Sabbath and enjoy the experience. As, according to the traditional view, Elijah will herald the messianic era, the first possible instance that he could arrive would be immediately after Shabbat, that is, after *Havdalah*. The tradition expresses this perspective in a number of imaginative and colorful ways. Elijah is unable to travel during Shabbat (so as not to break the commandment of avoiding traveling on Shabbat); therefore, he will travel as quickly as possible after Shabbat has been concluded.[23] In addition, he would not arrive on a Friday because of his consideration of housewives— in other words, because housewives (or whoever takes this role) have

---

21. *Malachi* 4:5.

22. There are alternative opinions within Jewish tradition concerning the nature of the messianic era. Maimonides, in his Mishnah Torah, argued that biblical references to a messianic age refer to political changes only, whereas Nachmanides and, later, the Hasidim held a more mystical perspective. In the modern world there are those who wait for the imminent arrival of the person of the Messiah and others who occupy themselves with practical steps of charity and social action as a means of realizing the messianic dream.

23. *Kitzur Shulchan Aruch* Chapter 96, Section 12 (Ganzfield [1961] p. 147).

been busy preparing beautiful foods for the Shabbat and cleaning the house. He would not want to arrive on Friday afternoon, as this would mean that the messianic age would have begun and their preparations would then have been for nothing.

The messianic qualities of Elijah are also expressed in a midrashic form. One *midrash* describes Elijah as sitting in the Garden of Eden underneath the Tree of Life.[24] While sitting, he is counting the merit of all those who keep Shabbat. This *midrash* draws on another Jewish tradition that the messianic era will begin when every living Jew has kept perfectly, and in all its details, two consecutive Sabbaths. Only when this has occurred will the Messiah come. It is interesting to compare this tradition with the parallel insight from Buddhism. According to the Buddhist doctrine, the Buddha sat under the bodhi tree meditating. It was through this meditation that he became enlightened, but the Buddha refused to go into Nirvana until everyone else was enlightened and could enter Nirvana with him.

The figure of Elijah has tremendous psychological significance in Jewish tradition. According to the depth psychologist Aharon Wiener, he is an archetypal/mythical hero no different, psychologically speaking, from other mythological heroes such as Zeus, Hermes, Buddha, Jesus, or Mohammed.[25] The biblical accounts of Elijah's life show him as a character who undertakes a personal spiritual journey and, in so doing, becomes transformed from a mortal to an immortal being who eventually ascends to Heaven in a fiery chariot. The biblical account describes Elijah as working miracles and battling with evil forces. He appears to be both human and angelic and to exist in both this world and the spiritual world. Elijah occupies an important place in the Jewish imagination. In countless folk tales he turns up unexpectedly and rescues people, appearing in disguised form and only later revealing his identity.[26] In the folk traditions it seems that he has had encounters with almost every major Jewish leader since bib-

---

24. Ibid.
25. Wiener (1978).
26. Very much like the figure of Merlin in the Arthurian legends and Celtic tradition.

lical times. It is no wonder that the figure of Elijah is associated with a number of Jewish festivals and ceremonies including *Havdalah*, the Pesach Seder, and *Bris milah* (ritual circumcision). What these occasions all share, in one form or another, is a sense of danger and risk, transition, and heavenly intervention.

What, then, is the risk associated with the *Havdalah* ceremony? In order to understand this, we need to consider an idea from anthropology, that of liminal time. This concept can help us to understand aspects of the *Havdalah* liturgy that are no longer extant in their contemporary versions, or that continue only in reduced and distorted forms.

Crossing the Threshold (Liminality)

Observers of premodern cultures have pointed out that religious ceremonies are often associated with times at which there is a perceived crossing from one category of being to another. The most obvious of these are birth, death, and weddings. They also occur just as the sun is rising or when the sun is setting. For example, the Jewish daily prayers are traditionally recited at dawn (*shacharit*), and at a time just before sunset (*mincha*). Such times are considered to be times of great danger, because they occupy a kind of no-man's land where normal rules and categories may no longer apply. Similarly the return of the moon is marked each month by the minor festival of Rosh Chodesh. We can consider the *Havdalah* ceremony in this light. *Havdalah* is the ceremony that shepherds us from the feeling of safety and security engendered by Shabbat or a festival, to the harsher reality of ordinary time. The tradition expresses this in terms of our living in the presence of the *shechinah*, which leaves as the festival or Shabbat ends, or the departing *neshama y'tairah* and our feeling of depletion.

With these ideas in mind, let us look at the poem attributed to Rav Amram referred to earlier. This text makes explicit reference to certain cosmological entities that were presumably familiar to the medieval Jewish mind. In some ways the poem resembles a spell in which angels of protection are conjured (just as angels are invoked at the beginning of Shabbat during the *shalom aleichem* prayer). An angel called Putah[27] is called upon to remove foolish hearts and cast them upon the high mountains. This is accomplished by means of the power of certain holy names. The text then goes on to mention various biblical examples of heroes who were granted success in life (as if their power could be added to our own by virtue of their merit). The text includes all, or in some versions only a part, of Psalm 12, which asserts that help comes from God. The second part of the prayer asks for a good week in which the evil designs of others will be thwarted, and some versions include a section asking God, three times, to grant good luck (*simman tov*).[28]

It may seem that this latter text, which is undoubtedly medieval in origin, only reflects superstitions commonly associated with that period and has no relevance today. Nevertheless, remnants of this ritual can be found in the modern version. For example, we have already referred to the Ashkenazi tradition of wishing people a *gute woch* at the conclusion of the *Havdalah* ceremony. However, there are other contemporary customs that also seem to have a superstitious quality to them. One is the custom of watching the reflected light of the *Havdalah* candle on one's fingernails during the blessing over fire. In so doing, the participants are attempting to accomplish two things. The first is relatively well known; by seeing the reflection of the candlelight in the fingernails one symbolically distinguishes between dark and light. It is thus a symbolic enactment of the words of the blessing and easily accepted by the modern mind. The second, however, is much more reminiscent of the medieval period and resonates with Rav Amram's poem. Darkness is associated with evil, and the light of the candle represents the power of good. This light is perceived as being driven out by evil or dangerous powers that may be present during this liminal period. A further practice, which may seem bizarre to the uninitiated observer, is to dip one's little fingers into the mixture of candle wax and wine that remains at the conclusion of the

---

27. Also referred to as Purah.

28. *Simman tov* can be translated as meaning "a good sign" and probably originally referred to astrological signs, although nowadays it is taken to simply mean a good wish.

ceremony. A little of this mixture is then wiped onto the eyelids and ears and then placed in the pockets. This must surely have been originally a protection ritual, but now has folklore status and is understood to be a wish that one should, for the coming week, only see good things, hear good things, and have a "little something" in the pockets.

What psychological sense can we make of all these things? Elijah, angels, protection rituals, and so forth sound very strange to modern ears. In psychological terms it may be useful to compare the state of liminality that exists around the time of *Havdalah* with other transitional states, other occasions in which we move from a world in which we feel safe and secure to a situation in which we feel more vulnerable. The particular model for this is the transition that a young child makes daily between sleep and wakefulness. The well-respected British psychoanalyst Donald Winnicott named these "transitional states." They occupy a kind of neutral territory between the self-created world and the perceived world.[29] At such times the child may adopt favorite objects, such as a teddy bear, a piece of cloth, or a favorite toy, or may place a thumb or fingers in the mouth. Winnicott named such things "transitional objects." The status of these objects is precarious, fully existing in neither world, but vital to both. "I would describe this precious object by saying that there is a tacit understanding that no one will claim that this real thing is a part of the world, or that it is created by the infant. It is understood that both these things are true: the infant created it and the world supplied it."[30]

There is a certain similarity between Winnicott's description of transitional objects and Bani Shorter's understanding of symbols. The manifold meanings underlying the symbols of Elijah and the angels, the candles, the spices, the wine, and the poetry flicker between worlds. Perhaps the ceremonial of *Havdalah* performs two functions simultaneously. At an emotional level it helps to conduct us safely from our shelter in the divine presence to the everyday reality of the ordinary

---

29. *See*, for example, Winnicott (1989).
30. Ibid pp. 143–144.

world. At a transpersonal level it may provide a porthole between worlds, an opportunity for the perception of something beyond the ordinary.

The *Havdalah* ceremony contains the principal elements of all developed rituals. It educates by restating fundamental categories that constitute Jewish consciousness and awareness. It is a social occasion bringing together families and communities for a celebration, and in so doing builds and enhances a sense of collectivity. The symbols of *Havdalah* re-evoke the powerful feelings and images experienced during the previous Shabbat or festival, and they are transformed from disparate elements into a unity. In so doing, *Havdalah* provides us with a vehicle through which we enter the new week.

5

Bereavement and Mourning

No one ever told me that grief felt so like fear. I am not afraid,
but the sensation is like being afraid. The same fluttering in the
stomach, the same restlessness, the yawning. I keep on
swallowing. . . . At other times it feels like being mildly drunk,
or concussed. There is a sort of invisible blanket between the
world and me. . . .

—C. S. Lewis[1]

A death when it comes is almost always a shock, even when it
has been expected, anticipated, or perhaps even welcomed. How much
more so when it is sudden. In the ordinary way there seems to be
very little we can do to prepare for the reality of a death. Death by its
very nature turns everything upside down, threatens our psychological defense mechanisms, and confronts us with the specter of imper-
manence and vulnerability. In our culture we often react to such a
shock with anxiety and fear—emotions that share psychophysiological features with each other. Sometimes we are also angry or confused,
or experience intense emotional states that we are at a loss to express
adequately in words. These initial feelings in the fullness of time may
give way to intense sadness, loss, and bereavement.

---

1. Lewis (1961) p. 5.

In such a situation do religious traditions help or hinder the adjustment and grieving processes? The Jewish rituals, customs, and practices that surround death and mourning are detailed, complex, and all-encompassing. From the moment someone takes his or her final breath, the tradition provides strict guidelines that govern the behavior of every individual person involved. Is this detail helpful, emotionally containing, and supportive, or does it overly restrict the personal expression of grief? And if it helps, how does it do so?

This chapter examines in some detail the psychological significance of the Jewish customs surrounding death. First, however, we will take a general look at the customs through the lens of two hypothetical case histories.

BUSHEY

The largest Jewish burial ground in Great Britain is situated just outside the small dormitory town of Bushey. Owned and run by the United Synagogue of Orthodox Congregations, it lies just a few miles north of the London suburbs that house much of the Jewish community. To its visitors it is known simply as "Bushey" and, paradoxically, it is frequently a hive of life and communal activity. Most Sundays the large parking lot is filled to the brim. The "grounds," as they are usually called, teem with people attending funerals or stone settings[2] or visiting the graves of departed relatives and friends. Before the high holy days the grounds are even busier as relatives make an annual visit to pay their respects, recite a brief prayer, and leave a pebble on the gravestone to mark their visit. During weekdays Bushey is quieter and the atmosphere somber. Mourners attend simple, hastily arranged funerals of relatives, friends, or work colleagues who died, perhaps, less than twenty-four hours previously. Bushey, along with similar Jewish cemeteries throughout the world, is at the heart of Jewish life.

---

2. Also called an "unveiling." The stone setting is a ceremony, often about a month before the first anniversary of the death, when the gravestone is unveiled and the inscription is read. This may also mark the ending of the prescribed mourning period for close relatives.

At Bushey there are two funeral halls where prayers are said before the actual burial. Sometimes both halls are in use at the same time. The form of service does not vary and is identical in both halls. The Orthodox funeral rite has been fixed for generations. Only the eulogy (*Hesped*)[3] is personalized, and even then the format has been more or less standardized by usage and convention. Imagine a situation in which both halls are full, but the mourners occupying them, despite their common Orthodox affiliations, are located at different points in the religious spectrum. Outwardly they appear similar, but the experience of the individuals involved might be very different. Let us call these families the Silvers and the Rosens.

Mr. Silver had died in hospital after a long illness. Word of his passing was quickly circulated among relatives and friends, and some of the mourners had traveled many miles across the globe to be present at the funeral. Very few members of the family were currently strictly observant, but several generations back an uncle had studied in a yeshiva,[4] and most of the family continued to hold their tradition in high regard. All the men could read Hebrew, even if they couldn't translate what they read, and some of the women had received sufficient religious education to enable them to follow the proceedings. The impact of the service on the mourners was moving and profound. The chanting of the ancient Hebrew in the traditional minor key, the ritual tearing of garments (*K'riah*), the reciting of *Kaddish*,[5] and the performing of other customs touched each of the principal mourners deep within their souls and memories. They felt held in the center of the community who had gathered for the funeral, and the experience provided comfort, meaning, and support.

The experience for the Rosens was quite different. Like his counterpart in the funeral hall next door, Mr. Rosen had also died

---

3. *Hesped* is often equated with the Greek word "eulogy," but it is actually closer in meaning to "reckoning."

4. Advanced religious academy.

5. Memorial prayer.

after a long illness. Similarly, the hall was full of relatives and friends, but the impact on the mourners was far from comforting. The recitation by the rabbi of the ancient Hebrew prose was understood by no one present, and the rituals were experienced by them as arcane and irrelevant. The ceremony reflected little of the personality or life of the deceased, and this mattered enormously to his daughters who were the principal mourners. Because they had no say in the details of the service and prayers, they were angry at their resultant feelings of disempowerment. Particularly painful for them was the Orthodox custom forbidding them from reciting *Kaddish* and replacing them by male cousins who had hardly known the deceased. Even if they had been allowed to participate fully, there was little in the service that could have comforted them or given meaning to their father's death. The entire experience increased their preexisting sense of alienation from Jewish practices.

The impact of the Jewish customs, then, was very different on the two families. But what meanings are there at the core of the traditions? What are the *t'amai mitzvot?*[6] Examined from the perspective of psychology, do the customs make sense? Do the practices contain some deep insights into the process of mourning, the experience of grief, and the place of death in psyche? We will begin our examination by considering what psychology has to say about bereavement and loss. Then we will turn to the Jewish practices and examine them in the light of that psychological knowledge.

IF YOU BELIEVE IN GOD, DOES IT HELP?

It is commonly held that religion provides comfort. That is, those who believe are able to find meaning in a death because they are able to say to themselves that their loved one has "gone to a better place," or that they have died because "their time had come," or "that God had saved them from further suffering." And there is no doubt that

---

6. Literally, "the taste of the *mitzvot*"—the inner meanings of the *mitzvot*.

death improves synagogue and church attendance. Many people turn to religion at times of loss, and in response to this there are myriads of support groups and pastoral counseling services to provide for their needs. The question for the psychologist, however, is whether it is the belief in God or the social support from the church or synagogue community—is it faith or is it friendship—that gets people through.[7]

Bereavement can be, at times, the precipitant of considerable psychological distress and even psychiatric breakdown. The psychological studies on the role of religion in moderating these negative consequences, however, are equivocal.[8] On the one hand there is some limited support for the view that religious belief helps bereaved people overcome their loss. A study conducted in Boston in the early 1970s found that fifty percent of the people they surveyed reported that religion had been a great comfort following a loss. Another study showed that people who attended church regularly were less likely to become depressed after a bereavement than non-church attenders. However, we are unable to tell from such research whether it is belief, such as in God and the afterlife, that is helpful or whether it is the increased availability of social support that institutional religion brings.

More detailed studies have attempted to answer this question about the role of specific religious beliefs. Surveys of the bereaved in Western culture have fairly consistently found that "faith in God," "self-rated religiosity," and "belief in an afterlife" made little difference in how people coped with a loss. In other cultures it may be rather different. Japanese widows, for example, have been shown to cope with an unexpected death better than their counterparts in the United Kingdom. The reasons for this are probably rather complicated. The authors of the study suggest that it may be because their religion, Shintoism, includes belief in ancestor worship and the capacity to maintain contact with the deceased after death. To help with this the

---

7. From a religious perspective this is a false dichotomy. The desire to extend the hand of friendship to the bereaved is understood to be motivated by faith and an enactment of God's will.

8. See Stroebe and Stroebe (1987) for discussion and review of this research.

bereaved prominently display urns containing the ashes of the dead person, along with photographs, in their houses and pray to them regularly. It might be thought that such practices represent a kind of "holding on" and a failure to accept the reality of the death. However, the Japanese belief system is highly sophisticated and able to incorporate the idea that the person is alive in one sense, but dead in another. The bereaved is able to look at the photograph and experience the individual as still alive and then look at the urn and know that the person is dead.

The situation becomes even more complex when the interaction between type of belief and other influential factors is considered. A number of studies were reviewed by Stroebe and Stroebe. For example, in a California study a group of older adults who accepted religious doctrines uncritically experienced greater distress following a bereavement than a similar group who were more discriminating in what they believed. Similarly, those who held religious views emphasizing God as an external agent coped less well than those who understood God as an internal experience. In another study religious faith and belief in an afterlife were found to help the dying person accept death more easily.[9] Those mourners who profess such beliefs are also more likely to describe their relationship with the deceased as having been "very good." Perhaps one important consequence of certain religious beliefs is to improve relationships around the time of death so that the death is then more easily accepted and grieved by all concerned. Or perhaps those with better interpersonal relationships are more likely to hold compatible religious beliefs. At the moment we simply do not know the answer to these types of questions.

In the Jewish world there has been a focus on how mental health practitioners might best provide support to the strictly observant ultra-Orthodox Jews who are having difficulty coping with a bereavement.[10] Grief is often expressed by the ultra-Orthodox through distinctively religious idioms, and therapists must be able to understand these idioms. Furthermore, they must also be prepared to make use

---

9. Cartwright (1991).
10. Bilu and Witzum (1993).

of healing rituals, dream interpretation, and stories that are culturally appropriate for this group.

Simply being religious does not seem to protect strictly observant Jews from psychiatric problems after bereavement; in fact, the converse is sometimes true. Two studies in Israel found a negative correlation between religiosity and outcome.[11] In other words, those who were more religious coped less well than those who were less religious. However, in both of these studies the religious groups were significantly less well educated than the nonreligious groups, and it may be that a high level of education is a moderating factor.

CULTURAL DIFFERENCES

One of the central insights psychology brings to the study of bereavement is that the way feelings are experienced and expressed is not universal. Cultural factors have a large role to play. In order to understand the relevance of particular religious customs it is important to see how they map on to the way a particular culture expresses grief. For example, anthropologists have found that people in most cultures cry after a loss (seventy-three out of seventy-eight cultures studied); however, the Balinese do not cry at funerals, but laugh instead. In Japan smiling is quite common. The existence of such exceptions to what might have been thought of as a universal rule points to the importance of social, cultural, and psychological factors.

Psychologists have proposed a variety of different theories to explain how we process emotions. Early theories were based on the work of William James.[12] James suggested that the experience of an emotion is based on the feedback we get from the biological arousal of the nervous system that occurs in response to certain emotional situations. A more sophisticated view is the "cognition arousal theory."[13] According to this approach, emotional states are determined by both physiological arousal and the meaning that the arousal has for us. For

---

11. Discussed in Stroebe and Stroebe (1987).
12. James (1950).
13. Schachter and Singer (1962).

example, we may experience a sudden increase in heart rate and interpret this as meaning either anxiety or fear. Our interpretation depends on the circumstances that provoked the increase and our interpretation of what the increase in heart rate means. How we interpret these physiological symptoms may depend quite a lot on cultural factors.

It is probably these cultural factors that explain why grief is expressed differently in different societies. Some communities sanction crying at funerals; others do not. Another approach, the "social constructivist" approach, goes so far as to say that because certain emotions are expected in certain situations, individuals control their emotions (presumably unconsciously) to comply with societal expectations. They may attempt to arouse emotions that fit in with what society expects and to suppress feelings that do not fit in. For example, although crying at funerals occurs in many societies, there are big differences in the type and timing of the crying that occurs. Some cultures have ritualized wailing at funerals, while at others restrained and dignified weeping is more common.

From a psychological point of view the outward expression of what we feel in the form of actions or speech has two functions. On the one hand, emotional expression communicates to the people surrounding us what we are feeling so they can respond. On the other hand, it may also help us to regulate the intensity of the emotions we experience. In fact, this is the way we normally think about emotions in Western culture. We cry or shout to "get things off our chest"—a form of emotional catharsis. Psychology, however, suggests that it may also work the other way around. The way we express feelings may influence the way we experience them. One psychological study of crying, for example, found that the experience of crying actually increased physiological arousal (in an unpleasant way) and feelings of sadness. Instead of helping people feel less upset, it made them feel worse.[14]

The way grief is expressed, therefore, may have quite a profound effect on the way people cope with bereavement. A study comparing the reactions of a group of Swazi girls and women with a similar group

---

14. Gross, Fredrickson, and Levenson (1994).

from Scotland bears this out.[15] In traditional Swazi culture there is a clearly defined period of ritual mourning with ritualized crying and grieving, whereas there is nothing similar in the Scottish culture. During this period the Swazi people experienced far more intense feelings of grief than their Scottish counterparts. However, after one year the Scottish group was more likely than the Swazi group to report feelings of guilt (a common bereavement reaction in Western culture). Perhaps this is an example of some customs and traditions facilitating grieving while others do not.

THE PSYCHOLOGY OF BEREAVEMENT

Differences between cultures in the way that grief is experienced and expressed can be profound. Nevertheless, psychologists have identified some common patterns of behavior that most mourners seem to go through.[16] Initially, in the first period after the death of a close person, there is a period of numbness in which the bereaved person is unable to take in and fully experience the loss. This phase is replaced by a feeling of yearning for the dead person. The mourner might dream about him or her frequently and suffer cruel disappointments upon awakening. It is common for the bereaved to imagine having seen the person in the street or on television or to half expect to meet the person upon arriving home. This stage can be followed by a period of disorganization and despair when it finally sinks home that the person has really gone, never to return. It is only after coming to this level of acceptance that the mourner is able to move on and come to terms with what it will mean to live without the loved one in his or her life.

---

15. Lovell, Hemmings, and Hill (1993).

16. *See* Bowlby (1980 pp. 85–96) and Parkes (1991) for full descriptions of the stages and accounts of the research efforts on which these are based. However, it is important not to pay too much attention to the order of these stages. People may go through them at different speeds and in different orders. Sometimes people remain "stuck" in one of the stages and need therapy or counseling to help them move on. Others move through them quickly and then return to earlier stages and go through the cycle again. The stages are best considered as generalizations.

An alternative way of conceptualizing the bereavement process is to see it in terms of the tasks that a person has to achieve in order to fully process a loss. Developed from the original work of Freud, this is an active process of working through grief, rather than passively going through stages.[17] "Grief work" involves accepting the reality of the loss, working through the pain of the grief, adjusting to an environment in which the deceased person is missing and, finally, emotionally withdrawing from the deceased person. While the dead are not forgotten, it is possible for the bereaved person to form new relationships and, to some extent, to "fill the gap."

Before looking at how well or badly the Jewish laws and customs of mourning facilitate the grieving process, we have one more topic to consider briefly. What if the relationship between the mourner and the deceased was poor or even hostile? What if there were resentments between partners, or parent and child, or between friends? How does this affect the process and can religious practices help?

Elizabeth Kubler-Ross[18] has helped us enormously to understand the powerful processes that affect relationships around the time of death. She emphasizes that our unconscious mind cannot distinguish between a wish and a deed. "The child who angrily wishes his mother to drop dead for not having gratified his needs will be greatly traumatized by her actual death—even if this event is not linked closely in time to his destructive wishes."[19] In this way a dead person remains alive and continues to have an influence on the living that prevents the mourning and the letting go that are appropriate after a death.

> A husband and wife may have been fighting for years, but when the partner dies, the survivor will cry and be overwhelmed with regret, fear and anguish, and will fear his own death even more, still believing in the law of talion—an eye for an eye, a tooth for a tooth—"I am responsible for her death, I will have to die a pitiful death in retribution."[20]

---

17. Worden (1991).
18. Kubler-Ross 1969.
19. Ibid p. 3.
20. Ibid p. 3. The rabbinic interpretation of this well-know biblical quotation is rather different from that of Kubler-Ross and is not concerned with revenge

Elizabeth Kubler-Ross goes on to suggest that maybe the purpose of the customs and rituals that have survived over the centuries, is to diminish the anger of the gods or of society. In many cultures the dead are objects of fear. Within Judaism there is a concept, perhaps a superstition, of *kein ayn hara* ("keeping off the evil eye") and there are many folk customs, some around the time of a death, whose purpose it is to protect a person from its destructive influence. Psychiatrist Dr. Joseph Berke has suggested that the evil eye can be understood as the "envious eye," or even the envious "I," that wants to destroy the object of its envy.[21] Perhaps the dead are envious of the living, and our customs and ceremonies might also be devices to protect ourselves from their destructive power. In some cultures there are traditions of self-inflicted injury, of cutting and mutilating the body at the time of death. Could this be anger and aggression turned inward? Or perhaps by punishing ourselves we can ward off the *eyin hara* and protect ourselves from its harm. Reflections of this type of behavior can be found in many cultures. In ancient Egypt the pharaohs were buried with vast amounts of treasure. Was this really because, as it states in the history books, they believed they would need it after death? Or was it the Egyptian's fear of the power of the dead and of their supposed desire for retribution that had to be propitiated? And then there is the English sentiment that one should not speak ill of the dead. Perhaps this is really less of a statement about respect for ancestors or politeness to those who can no longer answer back, and more a statement about the unconscious fear that the dead may retaliate if they are offended in any way.

The interactions between psychological processes and the religious traditions and customs surrounding death are clearly very complex. Nevertheless we can draw some conclusions:

- The impact of ceremonies and rituals is not automatic or inherent in the ceremonies themselves, but depends upon

---

or talion. The traditional understanding has been, rather, to see in the verse an ethic of limitation: no *more* than an eye, no *more* than a tooth. Kubler-Ross's psychological point, however, remains.

21. Berke (1988).

the meaning and relevance these rituals have for the mourners.

• Simply being religious does not always help someone to cope
with a bereavement. Certain types of belief are helpful; others
are not. Those people involved with a religious community
might receive more social and personal support. Religious
belief might influence the relationships between the person
dying and those who are left.

• Different cultures express and experience grief quite differently.
Some forms of ritualized grieving might facilitate the grieving process.

• There are recognizable patterns in the grieving process. This
process can be blocked when there were relationship problems
between the deceased and the bereaved. Sometimes these problems can result in anger, guilt, and fear.

• It seems possible that the religious traditions and ceremonies
have a latent function of enabling the mourners to work
through the stages of mourning and to cope better with a bereavement. This is what we shall explore next.

JEWISH CUSTOMS[22]

The Jewish customs surrounding death and mourning are precisely
laid down.[23] They are the result of a complex interaction between
halacha and *minhag*. Anyone choosing to follow the customs in de-

---

22. Anne Brenner, a psychotherapist and bereavement counselor, has shown
how sympathetic the mourning customs are to the bereavement process. Her book
Mourning and Mitzvah (1993) is a helpful guide assisting mourners to integrate
their own psychological processes with the requirements and customs of Jewish tradition.

23. *See*, for example, *Kitzur Shulchan Aruch* (Ganzfield 1961). The "laws"
outlined in this chapter are not a comprehensive guide. Advice about customs applicable in a particular case or in a particular community should be sought from
responsible and knowledgeable representatives from that community.

tail will find that their behavior is strictly governed by these rules for at least a year. The stages of this year that mourners travel through include: the immediate period after the death and before the funeral (known as *animut*), the week following the funeral *shivah*, which gives way to the *sheloshim* (or 30 days) and, finally, *Yahrzeit*, which occurs when the year ends.

In psychological terms the Jewish year of mourning seems to take us through all the stages of grief. At first, when we are still in shock, we take very little responsibility for ourselves and are guided through the period by our community and the prescribed rituals. This period is a liminal time[24] in which the boundary between life and death has been crossed and we need structure and support to help us through. Slowly we return to participate in society again, to adopt the role and habits of the mourner, and to begin the long process of reintegration following the dislocation resulting from our loss. The mourning period ends with a ceremony of remembrance and honoring of the deceased, and memorial becomes part of the annual cycle of our lives.

Jewish tradition prohibits "excessive" grief.[25] After the prescribed period of mourning is over, grieving is considered to be completed, and mourning customs after that time are forbidden. Paradoxically, it seems, even during the early intense days of mourning there are restrictions on the expression of grief. On *Shabbat*, for example, it is forbidden to mourn, as the tradition is very strict that one must take delight in *Shabbat* and celebrate. The hasidic groups take this very seriously, because for them *simchah* (joy) on *Shabbat* is a primary *mitzvah*. They relate tales of how their spiritual leaders and mentors have been able to overcome profound grief in order to inspire their followers. For example, Rabbi Joseph Isaac Schneerson, former spiritual leader of the Lubavitch sect, died on *Shabbat*. His son-in-law, Rabbi Menachim Mendel Schneerson, who was later to replace him as leader, reportedly showed no difference in his outward appearance or behavior on that *Shabbat* than on any other in the year. He ate, sang, and danced as usual. The moment *Shabbat* was over and

---

24. *See* earlier discussion of *Havdalah* (Chapter 4).
25. *Moed Katan* 27b.

Havdalah had been said, he broke down and wept uncontrollably for his father-in-law. Many years later when the same rabbi's wife died, he wept publicly. During *Shabbat*, however, he once again ate, sang, and danced as usual.

In behaving this way these rabbis were following an old custom. A most famous classical example is found in the *midrash*.[26] This is the extraordinary tale of the sage Bruriah who bore the loss of her two young children privately so as not to disturb the *Shabbat* peace of her husband who was spending the day with his colleagues. The text records it as follows: "When two of her sons died on *Shabbat* Bruriah did not inform Rabbi Meir (her husband) of their death upon his return from the academy in order not to grieve him on *Shabbat*. Only after the *Havdalah* prayer did she broach the matter."

These stories about mourning all show the way in which grief must not be allowed to disconnect the mourner from God. Not all of us will be able to achieve this degree of emotional control. However, the stories are clearly intended as role models to inspire us and as indicators of what may be possible.

We are now ready to take a detailed look at the customs. We will follow the traditions laid down in the *Kitzur Shulchan Aruch*. Some practices may vary in particular details from that which is described below, but the overall scheme is consistent throughout the Jewish world.

Watching and Purification of the Body

From the moment a person is in the throes of death he or she must not be left alone. Candles are lit and the person is surrounded by a *minyan* engaged in reciting prayers, saying psalms, and discussing Torah. As the soul departs, all present rend their garments. The eyes of the deceased are closed (sometimes by putting coins over the eyes).[27] There is a custom to pour out water stored in vessels in any of the

---

26. *Midrash* on the book of proverbs—*Mishlai Rabbah* 31.1.
27. Possibly following a Roman custom.

houses in the vicinity of the dead person.[28] The body is watched by relatives or by the *chevra kaddisha*,[29] who sit on the floor and recite psalms. The duty of watching the body is so strict that those who watch are instructed not to interrupt their watching by going away to say their regular prayers. No food should be eaten in the presence of the deceased.

What are we to make of such customs? The tradition offers us some clues. The rabbis believed that the soul left the body of the deceased sometime between the actual death and the burial. If that soul was unaccompanied then it might get confused and not leave properly, so the rabbis provided that the soul would not be alone at this point in its journey. Water, which might trap the departed soul on earth, had to be removed.[30] This type of explanation sounds very similar to rituals designed to protect the living from the influence of the dead.[31] Might not the custom of closing the eyes and weighing them down with coins be a response to the fear of the evil eye of the deceased? At certain times in Jewish history there was also a realistic fear of body snatchers who acted on libelous myths and persecuted the Jews.[32] In this context watching the body made sense. However, the recitation of psalms also suggests the watchers were concerned to ensure the safety of the soul in a metaphysical way, including, perhaps, protecting the body from being invaded by evil spirits.

Along with watching the body there are also customs concerning the purification of the body and dressing it in shrouds. This *mitzvah* is also usually carried out by the *Chevra Kaddisha* but may involve members of the family if they so wish.[33] Although there are

---

28. Rabbi Yochanan Ben Zakai, founder of the yeshiva at Yavneh, ordered his students to remove all water from the vicinity as his death approached (*Berachot* 28b).

29. Literally "the holy society" or "the holy companions." A group of adults, often from the local synagogue, who volunteer to watch the body and perform Tahara (see below) and other functions.

30. A superstitious view based on the reflective qualities of water.

31. This fear has also found expression in Jewish folk tales in the form of a spirit (a dybbuk) who might enter into the body of a living person.

32. Particularly because of the blood libels in medieval Europe.

33. In order to ensure modesty and respect for the deceased, the *Chevra Kaddishah* is male for a man and female for a woman.

some slight regional variations in how this is conducted, the main principles for how the purification is to be performed are recorded in the codes of law.[34] One such custom is for an egg with its shell to be beaten up with wine and used to wash the head of the corpse.

These customs also seem to have elements of a protection ritual about them, although the requirement to make the shrouds of fine white linen, and to wrap a man in his *tallit*[35] (which has been torn), is to indicate the mourner's belief in the resurrection of the dead.[36]

In a modern context we can see how watching and purifying the body can greatly help with the tasks of bereavement. We recall that at the early stages of bereavement there is a tendency toward numbing and denial. Sitting with the body confronts us with the reality of death and may help us to take it in. Perhaps, also, it is the last thing we are able to do for the dead person, our last gift to them.

Nowadays this practice of having direct contact with the body has regained wider acceptance. For example, it is now common practice for hospital staff to invite relatives to visit the body of the deceased in the mortuary if they wish to do so. Special facilities are provided. In the past, viewing the body was considered rather morbid and discouraged in case it upset people. In the Jewish community this led to the custom of relatives sitting with a closed coffin rather than with a body simply covered with a shroud. It was as if we were attempting to hide from death because it was too horrible or frightening. There is now, perhaps, a recognition that confronting the body

---

34. See *Kitzur Shulchan Aruch* (vol. 3, p. 98, Chapter 197).

35. Prayer shawl. In contemporary egalitarian communities a woman may also be wrapped in a *tallit* if she has one.

36. The exact meaning of the doctrine *T'chiyat Hamatim* (resurrection of the dead) is controversial in Judaism. According to the medieval commentator, Maimonides, it is one of the thirteen basic tenants of the Jewish faith (commentary on the Mishnah, Sanhedrin, Chapter 10) and is affirmed daily as part of regular prayers. Maimonides, however, preferred rationalistic explanations as far as possible and considered the doctrine to be partly metaphorical as only the soul is immortal. Later Nachmanides adopted a more mystical viewpoint and claimed that the resurrection would literally occur, but that bodies would become so spiritually refined that they did not require food and water to exist.

can assist the mourner in accepting the death and subsequently with the grieving process.

There may also be a more modern interpretation of the protection rituals. After a loss, relatives may be in a psychologically confused and vulnerable state. A death can be a threat to the sense of self and identity. Individuals may experience psychological changes in themselves that may be either temporary or long-lasting. These changes may simply be the result of a change in role or status in the family: for example, the oldest child becomes the senior member of the family when the last of the previous generation has passed on. Or it may be that relatives or loved ones unconsciously adopt qualities of the deceased person and make them part of themselves.[37] This might be unconsciously taking on certain personality characteristics of their relative or adopting some of their duties, concerns, responsibilities, ambitions, or worries. Although ordinarily this is a natural part of the process of life in a community, at times it can be a psychologically unhealthy adaptation to loss and, in a sense, an invasion of the living by the dead.

Rending of Garments—K'riah

The ritualized rending of garments is described in a minor tractate of the Talmud concerned with the laws of grieving.[38] The principal mourners cut a single garment while standing.[39] If it is for a parent who has died, the rent should be made opposite the heart and expose the heart (modesty permitting in women). The rent is usually made at home before the funeral, unless the rent has already been made at the time of the death. The rent must be made by hand although a

---

37. This possibility was suggested by Rabbi Zalman Schachter (personal communication).

38. *Evel Rabbatai* ("Great Mourning"), also known euphemistically as *Semahot* ("joyful occasions").

39. In a halachic context the mourners are defined as the immediate relatives, that is, children, parents, siblings, or spouse. The laws concerning the religious responsibilities of each mourner vary according to the type of familial relationship with the deceased.

knife can be used to start the tear. The mourner continues to wear the torn garment throughout the mourning period; however, if a festival intervenes, the "official" mourning is interrupted and suspended and the rent may be sewn up again.

The talmudic discussion of the laws of mourning provides a classic example of how the rabbis sought to modify preexisting practices. The tearing of one garment symbolically replaced the previous custom of rending all garments.[40] The Torah had already forbidden certain mourning practices that had been popular in Middle Eastern culture. These had included cutting or tearing the flesh and shaving the head. In talmudic times it seems likely that these customs had continued to some extent, and the rabbinic authorities replaced them with symbolic practices. In so doing, the rabbis demonstrated the psychohalachic principle. They recognized the psychological needs driving people to act destructively at a time of mourning and provided a means to express this need in a manner acceptable to the Jewish ethic and ethos of the time.[41]

From the perspective of psychology, we can infer still further meanings in *K'riah*. We recognize that the destructive urges may be hiding guilt or anger. The tearing of a garment can be useful as an expression of these feelings and as a cathartic act in itself. The instruction from the tradition to rend a garment so that the heart is exposed eloquently betrays the vulnerability felt at the time of a loss and signals to others our need to be protected. Rending a garment may express our own feeling of brokenness.

Between Worlds: Waiting for the Burial

From the time of the death until the time of the funeral the mourner is called an *Onan*. This is an exceptional status in Jewish law, as an

---

40. The tradition also suggests that cutting a garment symbolically represents the soul being torn from the body.

41. The Talmud also permitted other popular mourning customs such as wearing sackcloth, sitting on the ground, placing earth and dust on the head, weeping, and mourning by professional weepers (especially women). Most of these customs have not survived to modern times or continue mainly in symbolic form (e.g., sitting on low stools rather than sitting on the ground).

Onan is uniquely exempt from many of the precepts of the Torah, although they must follow all the prohibitions.[42] It is as if the rabbinic authorities have recognized that the mourner is temporarily not fully in this world but has entered an altered state and, therefore, the usual religious obligations are no longer applicable. As yet the *Onan* does not remove shoes (as later they will), but is forbidden from sitting in a chair (instead they sit on the floor or on low stools), sleeping in a bed, engaging in sex, or bathing. They are also prohibited from cutting the hair, participating in joyous occasions, and studying the Torah.

There is a further prohibition that is worthy of our consideration. For the time one is an *Onan* the tradition prohibits the mourner from greeting friends. The mourner becomes passive in all social interaction and has no social responsibilities toward other people. Later, through the process of shivah,[43] mourners slowly reintegrate with the people around them, but during this immediate period after the death, the mourner is encouraged to be alone. It seems as if, once again, the Jewish tradition has astutely anticipated the psychological needs of the bereaved individual. At the point where shock is normal and withdrawal natural, the tradition allows for this to happen and, in fact, encourages it. We do not carry on as before but give ourselves, wholeheartedly, to the business of grieving. Perhaps we can go even further. Social interaction at this stage, however well-intentioned, might encourage a person to "put on a front," distract them, and lead them to harden up psychological defenses against the eruption of feelings that loss brings. This could interfere with the "breaking down" that is sometimes an important part of the grieving process.

The problem, however, with the traditional prescriptions for mourning is that their rigidity just might not fit the individual too

---

42. In Jewish law women and men ordinarily have a different status from each other and different obligations. Women are not required to fulfill the positive time-bound *mitzvot* such as regular prayers. The traditional halachic discussion of the status of the *Onan* in this regard seems to assume that an *Onan* is male and, therefore, addresses only the exemptions that apply to men. The specific situation of women mourners in this regard is regrettably ignored by the *halacha*.

43. *See* discussion below.

well. We can recall our earlier discussion of different cultural patterns in the bereavement process. So too there are different individuals, with different needs, in different situations. Some people may benefit less from the type of social withdrawal that the tradition expects and more from the type of specialized talking with people that helps them to focus on their feelings; interactions of this type would not necessarily be detrimental.

In the modern world there are many distractions from the immediacy of a bereavement. Most of these are created by the consequences of the death itself, such as registering the death, making funeral arrangements, informing relatives, and so forth. These activities are sufficient in themselves to facilitate the avoidance of feelings. For some people this type of activity can be extremely helpful and adaptive; for others, less so. Unfortunately in some Jewish communities the officials who administer the Jewish burial societies are overworked and demoralized and may be less than polite or helpful to the bereaved families and friends. There may be arguments between the parties involved in making arrangements for the funeral. The feelings of anger and despair expressed at such times could, of course, be feelings of anger and despair associated with the loss and displaced onto a convenient target—the officials and administrators. This is not a good way to deal with the situation. Many enlightened Jewish communities today have responded by adapting the traditional mourning customs to fit their particular situation rather better. They have taken the central psychological insights of the status of the *Onan* and reworked it to fit today's needs. For example, a rabbi or trained religious pastoral counselor may visit the bereaved before the funeral. What makes their interventions particularly "Jewish," however, is the counselor's awareness of the special mourner's status and the encouragement to not "put on a face" or deal with their ordinary everyday affairs. In this way the community demonstrates the precept of *lifnim musharat hadin*[44] and has extended the halachic requirements to cover a new situation.

---

44. "Going beyond the letter of the law." *See* Chapter 3.

The Funeral

Perhaps the major identifying characteristics of Jewish funerals are their simplicity and the speed with which they happen—usually within one or two days of the death.[45] The body is placed in either a shroud or simple coffin and buried in the earth.[46]

The burial for the mourners, when they may carry the coffin and fill the grave, is a stark confrontation with physical mortality and death. Although the funeral is only one element of an extended grieving rite, it is often the point when feelings are at their most intense and most painful.

Prior to burying the body a few prayers and psalms are recited, often in a hall away from the graveside. It is at this point that the rabbi or other officiant will address the congregation.

In English this address is usually called the eulogy. The word eulogy derives from Greek, means "good words," and invariably consists of praising the deceased. In Hebrew the word used is *hesped* and, although the deceased may well be praised, this is not its primary function or meaning. *Hesped* derives from the Hebrew root *sapad*, which means to mourn, to wail, or to lament. And this is indeed one

---

45. Unless there is a postmortem or some other contingency delaying burial.

46. Burial of the body is the norm within Jewish communities and is the method required by *halacha*. This is partly a consequence of the belief in bodily resurrection of the dead. In some progressive communities cremations are conducted, although this is not common. Some communities and families abhor cremation because of its psychological associations with the Holocaust.

Most modern Jewish cemeteries arrange the graves so that they lie east-west. This is supposedly so that at the time of the resurrection the dead can walk directly toward Jerusalem without having to turn around. The literal way in which this custom has been regarded is quite extraordinary. For example, as there is no actual halachic requirement that the graves be laid out in this way, some communities have arranged the graves so that they are oriented according to the major trade routes and road systems that the dead are expected to take (*See* Lauterbach [1970] p. 252 who cites *Hatam Sofer, Yoreah Deah* No. 332). Additionally, some communities have the custom of placing small sticks of wood in the hands of the dead body. Lauterbach (p. 253) relates this again to the belief in resurrection and cites the Palestinian Talmud (*Yerushalmi, Kilayim* IX, 4, 32b) where it is related that Rabbi Jeremiah requested that a staff be put into his hand when placed in the grave, so that when the Messiah comes he will be ready to get up and march.

of the primary purposes of the address—the facilitation of the emotional grief work of the mourners. As usual, Jewish law states its psychological insight in the form of an explicit halachic requirement: "Lament the dead in words which break the heart . . . to cause much weeping." [47]

There is also a secondary function to the *hesped*, which is that of a "reckoning"—a weighing up of the person's life. The image evoked here is that just as the plea of the soul of the deceased will be heard in the heavenly court, so the soul's plea is to be heard on earth. It is as if the *hesped* given as the funeral oratory can play a role in the judgment that takes place on high: the *Bet Din* below participating in the *Bet Din* above. The role of the orator, then, is a little like a lawyer putting in a plea on behalf of a client, being careful to mention all the person's bad points, but more than balancing them with the good ones.

Psychologically the *Hesped* is fundamentally different from the eulogy. The eulogy that praises the deceased may encourage denial and discourage acceptance of the person's death. The *Hesped*, on the other hand, forces a confrontation, at a very early stage of the grieving process, with the reality of who the deceased person really was. [48]

Shortly after the *Hesped* the mourners make their way to the graveside for the interment. Often it is at this point that the reality and finality of the death hit home. What comfort or assistance can the tradition provide? Until now the emphasis in the psalms and prayers of the funeral service has been on the quality of judgment. [49] The opening words of the funeral service, for example, make this clear. The prayer book begins: "The Rock, [50] his work is perfect, for all his ways are judgment . . . just and right is he. . . . The Rock, perfect in every work, who can say to him, What workest thou? He ruleth be-

---

47. *Shulchan Aruch, Yoreah Deah* 344.1.

48. Of course a *Hesped* can be badly done or a eulogy well done, but the fundamental difference in purpose is clear.

49. The burial service is called in Hebrew *Tzodok HaDin*: "acceptance/justice of the judgment."

50. An allusion to God.

low and above; he causeth death and reviveth: he bringeth down to the grave and bringeth up again." [51] The traditional Jew on hearing of a death will pronounce the blessing *Dayan ha-Emet*: "Blessed is the true Judge." It is as if we, who have been left to mourn our loss, have to accept that we may never have an adequate explanation for why the person had died. It is for God to decide these things and we have to accept the judgment.

The description of God in the prayers up until now has been primarily that of the supreme judge over human destiny. After the actual burial, however, there is a perceptible shift in the tone of the prayers—a change from the harshness of divine judgment to the compassion of a nurturing and caring God. This finds its fullest expression in the memorial prayer itself, *El Moleh Rachamin* ("God who is full of compassion") with its haunting melody. The prayer portrays God as forgiving and merciful: ". . . slow to anger and abounding in loving kindness. . . . O shelter her/him for evermore under the cover of thy wings; and let his/her soul be bound up in the bond of eternal life. . . ." [52] Thus, in psychological terms, the choreography of the funeral service has taken the mourner from an enforced confrontation with the reality of death through to the place of consolation where there is sufficient emotional containment and support for working through of the grief to begin. The original poetry of these prayers suggests changes are occurring at an even deeper level. The portrayal of God as divine judge is generally considered to be a masculine image. *El Moleh Rachamin*, however, hints at a feminine image of God, as the Hebrew word for compassion, *rachamin*, has the root *rechem*, which means "womb."

Mourning

Immediately after the funeral the participants form two parallel lines and the mourners walk between them. They are greeted with a traditional formula: "May the Almighty comfort you among the other

---

51. Singer (1962).
52 Ibid.

mourners for Zion and Jerusalem." This immediately puts the personal loss into a larger context. The mourners are not alone; they join with all the others, throughout Jewish history, who have lost relatives and loved ones. And, along with their personal losses, they are reminded of a collective loss—the exile from Zion and Jerusalem.[53] In the United Kingdom, Ireland, Australia, and perhaps elsewhere the customs vary slightly and the comforters may wish the mourners "a long life." Surely this is more than simple well-wishing for the mourner, but has its roots in the irrational fear of retribution by the dead person discussed above.

Officially the mourning period begins as soon as the deceased is buried. The mourners remove their shoes and eat the "meal of condolence." This meal, cooked by friends or relatives, is a recognition that the mourners are not expected to look after or provide for themselves in any way, but are to devote themselves to the task or duty of mourning. The foods eaten are highly symbolic. Eggs are traditionally served on returning from the "grounds" and are representative of the cycle of life. Lentils are also common as, like eggs, they are round and have no mouth, just as the mourner has no mouth and doesn't speak (*see* below). Nowadays visitors may bring a variety of traditional foods to a house of mourning including bagels which, like eggs, are round and also represent the cycle of life.[54]

The *mitzvah* of comforting mourners is highly valued by Jewish tradition. In English there is a saying, "don't intrude on private grief." The Jewish view could not be more different. A shivah house[55] is usually full of people who come to visit the mourners, bring food, and offer practical help. The codes, however, specify the behavior that is appropriate for the occasion. They direct, for example, that consolers must not speak before the mourners speak and that they must withdraw if they perceive that the mourner wishes them to. A mourner is not required to rise from his or her seat or greet the consolers during

---

53. This is a figurative or spiritual exile.

54. From a mystical point of view the cycles of life are the *gilgulim*—the wheels of birth and rebirth.

55. Where the mourners sit and gather to say prayers each day for a week.

the first three days of mourning. From the fourth to the seventh day they can greet others, but not respond to their greetings. After the shivah period the mourner is encouraged to greet others, because "they have peace of mind but the mourner does not have peace of mind,"[56] and after thirty days normal greeting patterns are resumed. A delicate balance is maintained between providing support and allowing the mourner time and space to grieve and return to ordinary participation in the community. During the shivah period mourners sit on the ground or on low stools, a memorial candle burns, and all mirrors in the house are covered. The code does not explain this latter custom but we can speculate that, like emptying the vessels of water (which would also provide a reflection), it may have something to do with a superstitious fear of ghosts. Or it may be that seeing our appearance in the mirror at this stage would be frightening or would move us away from inward reflection to a concern with outward appearances.

The tradition advises that, whenever possible, the mourning rites should be observed "in the place where the deceased gave up their soul."[57] This makes good psychological sense in that it encourages the bereaved to face the reality of the death. The traditional sources, however, suggest another interpretation that shows as much concern for the deceased as for the bereaved. The soul of the deceased is considered to be in mourning also, and prayers held (preferably with a *minyan*) in its honor will provide comfort. This perspective illustrates how actively the belief in the afterlife has determined the mourning customs. The mourners are encouraged to do certain things for the sake of the dead person. From a psychological perspective it may be that having things to do that are of benefit to the deceased helps ameliorate any guilt felt by the mourners. Very often the bereaved feel that they have not adequately fulfilled their duties toward their loved one and will be grieving the lost opportunity to do so. This sense of guilt and unfulfilled responsibilities may be intangible and,

---

56. *Kitzur Shulchan Aruch* 210:7.
57. *Kitzur Shulchan Aruch* 207:5.

therefore, difficult to do anything about. The Tradition's focus on the well-being of the soul of the departed provides an immediate and practical way to help relieve the guilt.

The belief in the afterlife underlies several other customs. Mourners are encouraged to study holy texts in honor of the dead person in order to increase the merit of the deceased. Some may make a particular effort to study certain specified tractates of the Mishnah. They choose this text because the Hebrew letters that spell Mishnah also spell *neshama*, which is the Hebrew word for soul. The first tractate studied is the section on *Taharah* (ritual purity) because those who have been touched by death are considered, in some way, to require purification before reemerging into life. The second tractate selected may be one in which the first letters of the text spell out the name of the deceased. This is done as a remembrance of the dead person, but also to assist the dead person in his or her journey after death.

According to Jewish eschatology, after death the soul encounters the angel Dumah who asks the name of the deceased.[58] If unable to give it, the soul is prevented from progressing to the next stage of purification. As the soul is likely to be confused as a result of the death process, it may well forget its name. The prayers and the study undertaken by the living for the sake of the deceased are thought to assist the soul in recalling its identity. In anticipation of this during their lifetime, religious people may make a special study of biblical verses whose first letters form an acrostic of their own names, to help them recall their names more easily when the angel eventually requires this of them. Some traditional prayer books contain selections of appropriate verses to include in daily prayers to make this easier.

These metaphysical aspects of the mourning process point to an otherwise hidden psychological perspective. By saying that one is required to reveal one's name to an angel, the tradition is perhaps hinting at the importance of self-knowledge and identity. At the end of our life do we know who we really are, who we have become, and what we have done with the opportunities that life presented to us? Knowing our name, our true name, is knowing ourselves through and

---

58. I am grateful to Rabbi Zalman Schachter for these teachings.

through and having an in-depth understanding. If we believe that at the end of our lives we will be asked a question such as this, then surely this expectation will shape and direct our lives toward becoming more self-aware and self-conscious, which is, according to the Jewish mystical view, the ultimate goal of human existence. And if the dying person has this knowledge then it may facilitate the development of the type of healthy relationship with one's relatives that promotes an easier and less traumatic grief reaction.

The value placed by the Tradition on knowing one's name and on self-knowledge is illustrated in this well-known hasidic tale. Reb Zusia is reported to have said that after his death, when he comes before the heavenly court and his life is revealed before the throne of the Most High, he will not be afraid that he will be asked why during his life he had not been more like Moses. He will be afraid, however, that he will be asked why he had not been more like Zusia.

Kaddish[59]

The *Kaddish* is the most famous of all the Jewish memorial prayers. Written in Aramaic it dates from Temple times, and parts of the text can be found recorded in the Talmud.[60] The central theme of the prayer has nothing to do with death or loss whatsoever, but is an affirmation of the greatness and holiness of God. The various forms of the *Kaddish* are repeated throughout ordinary synagogue services to mark the changes between different sections of prayers. Mourners were often acknowledged by inviting them to recite the *Kaddish* during services, and from there the custom of reciting a special "mourner's *Kaddish*" developed in Germany around the year 1200.

Mourner's Kaddish

Mourner
> Magnified and sanctified be his great name in the world which he hath created according to his will. May he estab-

---

59. Literally, "sanctification"; however, the Hebrew root, *kadesh*, also means to separate (*see* also Chapter 6).

60. *Berachot* 3a.

lish his kingdom during your life and during your days, and during the life of all the house of Israel, even speedily and at a near time, and say ye, Amen.

Congregation and Mourner
Let his great name be blessed for ever and to all eternity.

Mourner
Blessed, praised and glorified, exalted, extolled and honored, magnified and lauded be the name of the Holy One, blessed be he; though he is high above all blessings and hymns, praises and consolations, which are uttered in the world; and say ye, Amen.

May there be abundant peace from heaven and life for us and for all Israel; and say ye, Amen.

He who maketh peace in his high places, may he make peace for us and for all Israel; and say ye, Amen

—Translation from *The Authorised Daily Prayer Book*,
by Rev S. Singer

The custom of saying the mourner's *Kaddish* has assumed a significant and central role in mourning rituals. Traditionally it is recited daily in the presence of a *minyan* for eleven months after the funeral, and then annually on the *Yahrzeit*[61] and certain holidays.[62] Jewish custom states that it is recited by relatives to add to the merit of the soul that has passed on and that no soul will remain in purgatory for longer than one year. No relative would want the community to think that the deceased was so sinful as to remain in purgatory for the maximum term of twelve months, so the practice has developed of reciting *Kaddish* for just eleven months so as not to shame the memory of the dead person. The psychological impact of this tradition is to equal-

---

61. Anniversary of the death, marked by saying *Kaddish* and lighting a memorial candle. In some communities there is the custom that anyone who "has *Yahrzeit*" may lead prayers and/or be called to the Torah. The anniversary may also be marked by special prayers being said in the synagogue.
62. Especially the *Yizkor* service on Yom Kippur.

ize the public expression of grieving, so that no mourner is seen, or sees him or herself, as abnormal.

The recitation of *Kaddish* seems to have a singularly powerful hold on the Jewish psyche. The beat poet Allen Ginsberg wrote a poem about his Jewish identity based on it. Many Jews, otherwise estranged from their tradition, make their way to synagogue in order to recite it.

The recitation of *Kaddish*, like so many Jewish practices, has traditionally been the preserve of the men. In progressive communities women have been able to say the prayer for many years, and in some Orthodox communities it is, nowadays, also permitted for women. In communities where women do not say *Kaddish* the prayer is recited by the closest male relative. This has been an arena where many Jewish women have felt angry at the injustice and inappropriateness of the patriarchal customs.

The intensity of the women's desire to say *Kaddish* is beautifully illustrated in the novel *Davita's Harp*:[63]

> There had been a brief discussion over the supper table about my mother reciting *Kaddish* for Jacob Daw. . . . She announced that for the next eleven months she intended to get up very early and go to the synagogue to say *Kaddish* for Jacob Daw and did we think we could make our own breakfasts?
> We all looked at her in a long moment of silence.
> "Why?" my Father asked quietly.
> "No one else will say it."
> "Ask one of the men to do it."
> "I want to say it."
> "You're not part of his family Channah. You were not related to him."
> "I want to say it anyway."
> "But you don't have to. You shouldn't. It falls into the category of a Commandment that doesn't need to be performed. It has no meaning in the eyes of God."
> "It has meaning in my eyes, Ezra. . . ."

---

63. Potock (1985).

"A woman is not supposed to say *Kaddish*," my father said very quietly to my mother. "You'll upset the *shul*.[64] Especially if you go to the daily *minyan*."
"Should I go to a Conservative or Reform synagogue?"
He gave that no consideration at all and shook his head.
"Then I'll go to our *shul*."
He shrugged. "All right. It will be awkward. There will be a fuss about it, that I promise you. But if that's what you want, go ahead. We'll manage with breakfast. . . . [65]

In this extract from Potock's novel it is clear that the woman's desire to say *Kaddish* was not based on halachic considerations, but on the meaning it had for her to say it. Reciting *Kaddish*, however, does not always provide the consolation or meaning that we might imagine. Mashey Bernstein wrote a piece in the London *Jewish Chronicle* revealing the conflicts the practice produced in him:[66]

It was not that I didn't love my mother. She was the most important person in my life. But she was concerned about my level of observance and once, in the middle of a conversation, she suddenly grew weepy and said, "Promise me that you'll say *Kaddish* for me. . . ."

So Bernstein decided to observe the daily recitation of *Kaddish* as scrupulously as he could:

. . . Part of the problem could have been finding a suitable environment in which to say the prayer. To my consternation, I discovered that the town where I live does not have a daily *minyan*.
    I made every effort to compensate for this. Whenever I found ten Jews together, I would ask to say *Kaddish*. When I heard of a *minyan* for a Shiva house, I would pop up even if I didn't know the family, say my *Kaddish* and sneak out quietly. When I went to a larger city finding a *minyan* was no problem— though that did not always bring satisfaction. . . .

---

64. Synagogue (Yiddish).
65. Potock (1985) pp. 378–379.
66. March 24, 1995.

. . . Maybe because I made so many compromises, I began to question the whole experience itself. Would the prayer lose its efficacy if there were fewer than ten people present? . . . I wondered if I would not be better off just looking at a picture of my mother, kissing it and saying, "I love you and have not forgotten you."

Eventually I gave up the manic behavior. I prayed with earnest devotion, wanting to feel the words resonate in my heart. They didn't.

Ironically, as soon as the final *Kaddish* of the first year had been said, I went into a deep depression, deeper than I had felt all year after her death. I had thought that after the year had passed, I would be over my loss at her death.

I sought the advice of a therapist. He argued that my concern over saying *Kaddish* and trying to do it "right" had actually prevented me from mourning my mother. It was only when the rituals were taken away and I could not hide behind them that I was finally able to confront my sorrow.

These two accounts of reciting *Kaddish* return us full circle to the hypothetical case studies outlined at the beginning of this chapter. The Silvers and the Rosens differed in the extent to which the customs and traditions had meaning for them and in their levels of involvement with the tradition. Our two examples of people saying *Kaddish* raise the same issues. Whatever theology or mythology underlies the customs, it seems that their ability to serve as psychological vehicles for transformation and growth depends, almost entirely, on the extent to which they fit with our preexisting psychological, cultural, and religious assumptions. The liturgy won't do it on its own. It needs to be sensitively translated and interpreted in the light of its inner meanings and psychological insights. In this way the *mitzvot* surrounding death and mourning remain valuable assets and aids in the bereavement process.

Coping with a bereavement is a process that all of us can expect to deal with at some point in our lives. Most of us anticipate it and try to imagine how well we will cope when the time comes. The Jewish tradition provides rites of passage, role models, and communal support to help us through. For some it is a path of initiation into a new life stage and social role.

In Jewish culture the bereaved are recognized and even honored. This happens through the medium of the liturgy associated with the various festivals in the Jewish year and the daily cycle of prayers and observances. The ritualized mourning begins at home with the week of *Shivah*. As the year progresses the mourner returns to full participation in synagogue and communal life. The liturgies of the festivals and life cycle ceremonies emphasize and help with this. The language of the prayers frequently merges personal losses with collective losses so that the grieving process becomes a shared experience engaging the entire community. For example, during the *Yizkor* service on Yom Kippur all Jewish martyrs (including the six million victims of the Holocaust) are memorialized. This is a very powerful and significant occasion during the Jewish year. Even Jews who are not normally observant or do not regularly attend synagogue find themselves making considerable effort to ensure that they are in the synagogue at the right time for *Yizkor*. This ensures that at least once a year they feel the support of the entire community grieving along with them. There are many other examples, although these are often less widely observed or understood. At Tisha b'Av,[67] grief at the destruction of the Temple is recalled, just as it is when the glass is ritually smashed during a wedding ceremony.[68] In some non-Jewish cultures mourners wear black for a year or longer as an outward sign of their loss. In Judaism we wear black throughout the year during our prayers in the form of a black stripe on the *tallit*,[69]—another sign of mourning for the Temple. Formal grieving ends eleven months after the death, often with the stone setting or unveiling ceremony. As our personal grief lessens and finds its place in the weave of our lives, it becomes merged with the collective loss experienced by the entire Jewish people. The individual mourner has moved slowly from isolation and aloneness and returned to full participation in the community.

---

67. A fast day.
68. *See* Chapter 6.
69. The traditional prayer shawl worn by men. Nowadays brighter colors with imaginative designs are customary among both men and women in progressive communities to symbolize a form of Judaism that is no longer fixated on mourning for the Temple.

have, perhaps, done so because of the financial and legal advantages that civil recognition affords. Marriage is no longer universally considered either obligatory or binding as the rise in divorce rates over the last century has testified. The increasing legal, financial, social, and psychological independence of women has facilitated the opportunity for both sexes to break away from the traditional gender roles of mother, father, wife, husband, housekeeper, breadwinner, and so forth.

Tragically for some individuals the family has not provided a safe, nurturing environment, and even where there has been no major trauma many people have found family life to be stultifying and an obstacle to personal development and growth. It may be for these reasons that as adults they have avoided marriage and chosen not to recreate the conditions of their own early lives. Furthermore, gays and lesbians have been excluded from the institution of marriage. And even when accepted or welcomed by a Jewish community, they have often rejected the heterosexual assumptions on which the traditional wedding ceremony is based.

Nevertheless, marriage remains popular and synagogue weddings occur fairly frequently. Are these ceremonies relics from a previous age, clung to through the forces of habit, social conformity, and inertia? Or do they retain a vital spiritual and psychological value in themselves? And within the traditional discussions and commentary, can we discern inner meanings to the marriage ceremony, which give us clues about how we might confront the challenge of establishing growthful and fulfilling relationships today?

PSYCHOLOGICAL PERSPECTIVES

Wedding ceremonies are among the grandest and most elaborate rituals marking life-cycle events. Most cultures have them in one form or another, and they are treated with considerable importance and significance. As with the ceremonies we discussed in the two previous chapters (*Havdalah* and funerals), weddings are at times of transition. In this case it is the moment when two individuals change their status in relation to each other, themselves, their families, the community and, in Western culture at least, the state. What marks the wedding ceremony as distinct is that couples can fix the date of their wedding themselves. This date setting is not, seemingly, entirely a matter of free choice. Apart from practical considerations, other psychological factors will often intervene. Experienced family therapists and premarital counselors have remarked on how often a marriage is decided upon within six months of another major change or life event within the family of one of the prospective partners.[6]

This observation sensitizes us to one of the vital psychological functions of a wedding. Wedding preparations provide a window into the psychodynamics of the families involved. The premarriage period may be a time when family relationships undergo profound change. This is not just true of the young couple who are embarking on an independent life for the first time. It can be equally significant for the established couple who have been happily living together for quite a while, the divorcée who is remarrying perhaps with children from a previous relationship, or the widow and widower who are forming new relationships, having lost their previous life partner. With the family dynamics exposed, a great deal of constructive change becomes possible at this time.

Such change is, of course, emotionally difficult and challenging, and there are plenty of opportunities to avoid the psychological issues that get raised. A family argument may ostensibly be about how many guests to invite, where the wedding will be held, or what the bridesmaid will wear. It may not be difficult to see that the underlying issues are around power and control; however, this insight (and opportunity) may be easily avoided by the early capitulation of one or more of the parties involved. It may seem easier, for example, to accept the guest list provided by one set of parents than to challenge the assumption that their particular family or friends have priority. Sometimes, however, the issues are too emotionally compelling to hold back in this way. A parent may object powerfully to a daughter's or son's choice of partner and may try to prevent the wedding from going ahead. Or they may exaggeratedly show their disapproval so as to spoil

---

6. Carter and McGoldrick (1989) p. 134.

the celebrations in some way. Such a powerful objection suggests that there is psychological work for the parents to do as part of their own preparation for their offspring's forthcoming marriage. Perhaps they are experiencing difficulties in letting go of, and separating from, their child, or in resolving difficulties in one of their own important relationships (perhaps with their own spouse or parents).[7] A wedding ceremony has the potential to provide a structure for this type of psychological processing to occur. The extent to which this potential is realized depends, of course, on the consciousness and openness of the parties involved, including those who are helping the couple and family prepare for the ceremony.

Unconscious factors may play an enormous role in the psychodynamics of the relationship between the couple. There is an extensive body of research emanating from institutions such as the Tavistock Clinic and the Institute of Marital Studies that illustrates the influence of early childhood and family experience on choice of partner.[8] While partners are selected for all sorts of conscious reasons, the hidden factors may be very important. For example, there may be a motivation to make reparation for damaging childhood relationships or a collusion between partners to keep unresolved intrapsychic con-

---

7. *See* Carter and McGoldrick (1989) pp. 136–139.

8. This research has been heavily influenced by the psychoanalytic school of object relations developed from the ideas of Melanie Klein and others. This theory states that early relationships within the family are internalized (object relations) and then projected onto close relationships as adults. The degree of intimacy experienced in a romantic encounter, and then in a sustained sexual relationship, recapitulates these early experiences, which are then acted out in the new setting. These early relationships will vary in the degree to which they have developed and matured. The earliest relationships are "paranoid/schizoid" where the parent (mother) is experienced only as a part object and can be manipulated as such. Development brings "ambivalence" where the infant is able to make a connection between the mother who feeds, the mother who picks the baby up when it cries, and the mother who is too busy or preoccupied to respond. In other words, the caregiver becomes a whole person. The infant may experience love and hate toward this person almost simultaneously. Eventually in healthy psychological development the child learns to accept the whole person, and this is the basis for the later development of healthy adult relationships where there is mutuality and respect for the needs and desires of the other.

flicts at bay. Or there may be the projection of internalized role models onto a partner. Some aspects of earlier relationships may be well understood by the partners themselves, and then their influence can be muted and incorporated consciously into the relationship. When the influences are unconscious, however, there is a greater risk that the relationship may flounder and contain unresolved and misunderstood conflicts that are destructively acted out or, alternatively, lead to a dull, lifeless, and unsatisfying marriage.

Marriage, however, is an act of hope. Robin Skynner put it this way: "Marriage is always an attempt at growth, at healing oneself and finding oneself again. . . ."[9] The partner selected may be exactly the person needed to correct for an earlier damaging relationship, and when this is conscious there is great potential for development. It is not something that can be faked and herein lies the danger. All too often once the decision to marry has been made, the behavior of one or both of the partners changes in ways that surprise both themselves and outsiders. It is one of the pitfalls of the modern approach to founding relationships. "During the wooing both people constantly attempt to be as attractive to each other as possible; each trying to exhibit only those parts of themselves which will please and capture the other."[10] Anything that may possibly be unacceptable to a prospective partner remains hidden until, that is, the intimacy of married life recapitulates early family experiences and all is unexpectedly, and uncomfortably, exposed.

A wedding ceremony and the processes surrounding it have the possibility of either colluding with the denial and avoidance of the unconscious process or confronting and incorporating them in a helpful and growthful manner. There is one more element, however, that we need to address: the myth of romantic love.

Jungian analyst Robert Johnson has identified two types of love in Western culture:[11] the ordinary human love of friends, family, and neighbors and the special, passionate love of romance. Romantic love

9. Skynner (1976) p. 127.
10. Lederer and Jackson (1968) p. 246.
11. Johnson (1983).

doesn't mean simply loving someone; rather, it is the act of "falling in love" with all the intensity and absolute devotion that implies. Johnson suggests that this type of love first entered into the consciousness of Western society in the Middle Ages in the form of the great myth of the courtly love of Tristan and Isuelt.[12] Since then, and especially today, it has become the type of love that we expect to find in our most enduring sexual relationships.

Over time romantic love has mistakenly and unconsciously become equated with, and has largely replaced, the religious quest of seeking completion and wholeness of the soul, something that we could be looking for within ourselves rather than pursuing in another person. The ecstasy of feeling we experience when we are in romantic love has become the yardstick by which we judge our relationships, and other forms of love seem cold in comparison. When "in love" we may experience both highs and lows, but when we are not "in love" many of us are left with lengthy periods of loneliness, alienation, boredom, and despair.

The wedding ceremonies of today greatly emphasize this notion of romantic love. The flowers, the clothes, and the music all conjure an image, perhaps a mirage, of otherworldly mystique. Of course, there is a very important role for myth and symbol in the wedding ceremony. The archetypes of bride and groom, the sacredness of the ceremony, the presence of elders, and the representations of the Divine all assist in the focusing and transformation of powerful emotions. However, the confusion arises when there is no acknowledgment of the other type of love—human love—on which a successful long-term relationship must surely be based.

> Human love necessarily includes friendship: friendship within relationship, within marriage, between husband and wife. When

---

12. Robert Johnson relates and then analyzes this myth in great detail. He shows through his analysis how men are seeking their inner feminine qualities (*anima*) through the aegis of romantic love. Johnson reminds us of Jung's observation that when a new symbol emerges into the culture a new stage in the evolution of consciousness is underway. Romantic love is a necessary stage in this evolution toward psychic wholeness, but it is not the endpoint.

a man and a woman are truly friends, they know each other's difficult points and weaknesses, but they are not inclined to stand in judgment on them. . . . They want to affirm rather than judge, they don't coddle, but neither do they dwell on our inadequacies. . . . They don't set impossible standards on each other, they don't ask for perfection.[13]

This type of friendship, which is so important for a relationship, differs from romantic love. There will be times of romance within a successful relationship, but they are not its sole basis. If the romance in a relationship fades, this need not be viewed as a disaster but perhaps a signal that another kind of love awaits.

A wedding ceremony and the preparations that surround it may risk unconsciously reinforcing the false importance of romantic love. Alternatively, the ceremony may be able to help the partners get to know each other and face the reality of who they each are.

THE JEWISH WEDDING

A search on the World Wide Web does not immediately reveal much information about the inner meaning of the Jewish wedding. There are some pages describing the structure of the ceremony and how it should be conducted according to the strictures of Jewish law, but other topics are more noticeable. As with local newspapers all over the globe, advertising broadsheets, and telephone directories, the main preoccupations are with caterers, florists, bridal gowns, and travel agents. The Jewish wedding, as featured on TV and in the movies, is an example *par excellence* of the romantic, lavish, often expensive "affair," where the dancing may be good and there is plenty of nostalgia for the old days, but little room for psychological growth or change.

This view of the Jewish wedding ceremonial does little justice to the depth inherent in the ceremony or to the variety of cultural forms that have developed throughout the centuries and across the world. The music and dress in a Jewish Yemenite or Moroccan wed-

---

13. Johnson (1983) p. 197.

ding, for example, may be totally different from those of the more familiar modern Ashkenazi ceremony. As we saw in Chapter 1, holding a wedding indoors is a relatively recent innovation. Nevertheless, the Jewish wedding as it exists today has had the same basic structure and form since the twelfth century, when two separate elements were brought together to form a single whole (*see* below). Many of the components of the wedding ceremony are even older and recorded and discussed in the Talmud.

The wedding ceremony, like most Jewish rituals, has a democratic structure at its core. There is no need for a rabbi to conduct the wedding as rabbis have no priestly function. Anyone with the appropriate knowledge can act as *m'sader kiddushin* (the director of proceedings). The wedding is made "official" by the presence of proper witnesses.

Purpose of the Ceremony

In the rabbinic perspective the primary purpose of a wedding ceremony is to bring a couple's relationship into the halachic framework. Marriage has a technical, legal status, and halacha carefully defines the status of the bride, groom and, most importantly, the children. Within traditional Judaism there are clear rules about who can and who cannot marry each other. Marriage between certain categories of person are forbidden and if they should occur, then the consequences for the children may be severe. Some of the restrictions are more obvious than others. For example, incestuous relationships and adulterous relationships are forbidden by biblical law. Any children born from such unions are called *mamzerim*, and they and their offspring, in turn, are forbidden from marrying another Jew for ten generations.[14] This is a harsh ruling and rabbis will usually go to great lengths (while remaining within the halachic framework) to prevent such a situation

---

14. It is advisable to seek the guidance of a competent rabbi if advice is required about any particular case. General information can be found in a number of books written by Orthodox rabbis about weddings. A useful starting point is Lamm (1982).

developing if possible. Many non-Orthodox communities have abandoned this halachic requirement because of its impact on the children. A less obvious restriction on marriage is the prohibition on *Kohenim* (priests) marrying a divorcée.[15] Should a *Kohen* enter such a marriage then any resultant children are not permitted to marry other *Kohenim* or carry out priestly duties in the synagogue.

The psychological implications of this halachic undertone to wedding celebrations are profound. Because the consequences of breaking the *halacha* are so severe, forbidden unions almost never occur within an Orthodox community. Were they to do so, then the couple would probably have to move away to a place where they are not known. It also means that, in modern times, getting married in an Orthodox synagogue has become the passport to Jewish status in the Orthodox world. Producing one's mother's marriage documents is usually the main requirement for proving Jewish status. For some couples, proving their legitimacy in the eyes of a rabbi is a degrading and dispiriting experience, whereas for others it is acceptance that they are part of the Jewish fold.

At a wider level, the public celebration of a marriage establishes and reinforces the community's expectations about gender roles and appropriate sexual behavior. This becomes obvious when one thinks about the issue of same-sex marriage. In Orthodox communities these relationships are forbidden, and no public celebrations of gay or lesbian relationships take place. Hence the relationships of gay and lesbian members of those communities remain hidden. Gender roles are also clearly defined as part of the wedding ceremony. In the Orthodox community, for example, the man gives the woman a ring, but it is not permitted for the woman to give a ring to the man as part of the ritual.[16] As we will see below, this act (*kinyan*) symbolizes the nature of the contract that they are entering and the different status of men and women in the Orthodox community.

---

15. A *Kohen* is a man who has a family tradition that he is descended from the Temple priests. In Orthodox communities they continue to carry out certain duties in the synagogue. By and large, progressive communities have abandoned this category.

16. In egalitarian communities an exchange of rings is possible.

The wedding ceremony provides a microcosm of the *halacha* at work. The central status of marriage in the life of an individual, a family, and a community publicly establishes the *halacha's* categories and requirements. Hence, in one way, the traditional wedding ceremony functions as a means of establishing compliance with the rabbinic framework. Any change to the traditional manner in which a wedding is conducted is at one and the same time a challenge to the legal and mental categories of the *halacha*. We saw in Chapter 4 how, during the *Havdalah* ceremony, halachic categories were reinforced at a moment of vulnerability, when we make the transition from sacred time to ordinary, secular time. Now we see that once again halachic categories become important at another time of change, this time at a wedding when there is a breakdown of the previous order of relationships and a new order begins.

Kedushah and Covenant

The legal aspects of a wedding are only part of the story. At the core of a marriage is *Kedushah* (holiness) and the relationship between human beings and God. In Judaism, sex is considered sacred, and sexual union a path to the holy. The marriage ceremony itself is a reflection of the relationship between ourselves and the Divine, between God and the people of Israel. A *midrash* describes it eloquently: when Israel encountered God on Mount Sinai, and Moses spoke with God "face to face" on the mountain top,[17] this was the enactment of the marriage between God and Israel. The written Torah was the wedding contract.

There are numerous references throughout Jewish literature to the sexual metaphor for the relationship between Israel and God. The "Song of Songs," which Rabbi Akiva considered to be the holiest book in the Bible, is an exquisite and explicit love poem. Rabbinic tradition understands it as an allegory of the relationship between God and Israel. On Friday nights, when it is customary for a married couple to make love, the liturgy refers to the "Sabbath Bride." The act of

---

17. Exodus 33:11.

union between a couple similarly reflects the union of the Creator and the *shechinah*.[18] This relationship does not exist in a vacuum.[19] God's covenant with Abraham promised that his descendants would be "like the stars in the heavens,"[20] and it is through marriage that this promise can be fulfilled.

There is a famous *drash* that many rabbis like to include as part of their address during a wedding ceremony.[21] The Hebrew word for a man is *Ish* (spelled *aleph yud shin*) and the Hebrew word for woman is *Isha* (spelled *aleph yud shin hey*). If the *yud* is removed from *Ish* and the *yud* and *hey* from *Isha*, then the remaining letters in each word (in both cases *aleph* and *shin*) spell the word *Aish*, which means fire. The *yud* and the *hey* together, however, spell one of the names for God. Thus, runs the sermon, when a man and woman are brought together and God's name is absent we are left only with fire and its possibility of burning and destruction. But when God's name is present, there is harmony between the sexes. The contract made at a wedding needs to be a three-way contract, with God as the ever-present third party.

The wedding ceremony itself should inject *Kedushah* (holiness) into a marriage. Beautiful music, flowers, and clothes, the sense of occasion, and the preparation beforehand all contribute. In rabbinic parlance a wedding is called *kiddushin*, which carries the connotation of holiness and of each partner being set aside for the other.[22]

---

18. The *shechinah* is the indwelling "feminine" aspect of God that is conceived of as estranged and in exile and seeks unification with her "masculine" counterpart.

19. For a fuller discussion *see* D. H. Gordis's "Judaism's 'other' covenental relationship" in Geffen (1993) pp. 90–131.

20. Genesis 22:17.

21. Attributed to Rabbi Joshua ben Korno.

22. Both *kedushah* and *kiddushin* derive from the Hebrew root word *kdsh*, which is usually translated as "holy" or "sanctify." It also means "separate." There is a strong theme within Jewish tradition that something is made holy by separating it. Interestingly, there is also a sexual connotation as the word *kadesha* is used in the Bible to refer to prostitute or harlot (Genesis 38:14) and is possibly connected with some early cultic practices.

Development of the Ceremony

The basic principle of marriage is stated starkly in the Torah as "when a man takes a wife."[23] The patriarchs, it seems, did just this, and they often took more than one wife as with Abraham and Sarah, Hagar, and Keturah.[24] Abraham instructed his servant to seek out a wife for his son Isaac, and Isaac made Rebekah his wife simply by taking her into his mother's tent.[25] This seems to have been the approved method for the biblical characters, although there are hints of a more elaborate ceremony in the reference to the "bridal week" of Jacob and Leah.[26]

In talmudic times marriage by the biblical version of "taking," that is sleeping together after having recited the appropriate vows, was no longer considered appropriate. And even though it was halachically allowable, anyone who followed this route risked a public flogging.[27] Instead the Talmud mentions two separate ceremonies that together constitute a marriage: the betrothal (*erusin*) in which the couple are set aside for each other and, usually a year later, the marriage proper (*nissuin* or *chuppah*) when they set up home together. We will consider these elements in detail later.

Around the twelfth century *erusin* and *nissuin* were brought together into one ceremony. This was a change born of practical necessity. The times were perilous and there was a real danger that a man promised to a woman at the *erusin* ceremony might for some unforeseen reason disappear without trace during the ensuing twelve months.

---

23. Deuteronomy 24:1.

24. Today monogamy is the norm throughout the Jewish world. The principle of monogamy was formally established by Rabbenu Gershom in the tenth century and, strictly speaking, holds only for the Ashkenazi community. However, it seems clear that polygamy was always the exception, and it has not been practiced in modern times.

25. Abraham's servant was charged with the responsibility of selecting a wife for Isaac. He did so with the help of an angel and from his observation of the considerate behavior of Rebekah when he asked her to draw water for him from the well (Genesis 24).

26. Genesis 29:27.

27. *Kiddushin* 12b.

As well as being an emotional trauma, this state of affairs could also cause great halachic problems. The woman would be unable to marry anyone else until the situation of the man could be established. If he was dead, although unfortunate, the woman was better off, as she was now free from her betrothal vows. If he had been captured, or there was no reliable information about him, then she was considered "chained" and unable to marry anyone else.[28] The easiest practical solution to this problem was to bring the two ceremonies together.

The fourteenth century brought another innovation, again for practical reasons. Although there were precedents as far back as the Mishnah for the man giving the woman a formal contract of marriage (*ketubah*), setting out his financial obligations to her if he should divorce or predecease her, it was not always required. The *ketubah* was, in effect, a financial safeguard for the wife during a historical period when it was difficult, if not impossible, for her to support herself. In 1306 the Jews were expelled from France and a great many were robbed of their possessions, including their documents. The rabbinic authority of the day, the *Rashba*, ordered that no couple should live together until each man had issued his wife with a *ketubah*. In so doing *Rashba* established a precedent that is still followed today.

There is, however, an exception to marriage with a *ketubah*. This is the *Pilagesh* relationship. Although the rabbis have not generally been in favor of it, it exists as a separate halachic category and has no negative status implications for any of the parties or for the children. The *Pilagesh* is a "half marriage" and describes the status of a couple who are permitted to each other in Jewish law and who openly live together without a *ketubah*. This situation, common today, apparently has been known and accepted throughout Jewish history. Maimonides ruled against such relationships, but he seems to have been in the minority. Nachmanides accepted the legitimacy of the *Pilagesh* and,

---

28. The problem of "the chained wife" or *agunah* exists today but for a different reason. In an acrimonious divorce case a husband will sometimes refuse to give his wife a formal bill of religious divorce (a *get*). In such circumstances a woman cannot, according to Jewish law, remarry, as this would constitute adultery.

so it seems, did many of those who came after him. Rabbi Yaakov Emden (eighteenth century) published a responsum on the issue and dealt with all the related *halacha* in detail.[29] Rabbi Schneur Zalman of Liadi (the founder of Habad hasidism) ruled that a special form of a bill of divorcement[30] is required if such a relationship ends, implying that he took it seriously as a form of marriage. The significance of the *Pilagesh* relationship for us is its psychological impact. Those couples who might previously have appeared to be outside the framework of *halacha* can be included within it and recognized.

Preparation

Although wedding preparations may take many months and, in enlightened circles, include pastoral talks with the rabbi about the relationship, the ceremony, and family life,[31] the actual ceremonial begins a day or even a week before the wedding day itself.

The marriage will take place in a community, and the community has the opportunity to acknowledge the couple before the wedding at an occasion known as the *aufruf*. At the *aufruf* the groom, and in progressive circles both the bride and the groom, are honored in the synagogue by being called to the Torah.[32] This is usually followed by a brief reception hosted by the couple for the entire community. The *aufruf* may be held either the day before or the week before the marriage. This depends upon whether the *aufruf* is held at the groom's home synagogue, the bride's home synagogue, or even in both synagogues, in which case there will be two celebrations.

The significance of the *aufruf*, in the light of our earlier comments about family issues, is obvious. Here the family dramas of letting go and redefining relationships can begin to be played out, but

---

29. *Sheylot Ya'avetz*, Vol. 2, No. 15. Translated by Rabbi Gershon Winkler in *Pumbedissa* (1995) Vol 3, No. 6 and (1996) Vol. 4, No. 2.

30. A *get M'safek*.

31. In some communities this may include a separate discussion between the bride and the *rebbetzin* (rabbi's wife) about following the laws of *taharat mishpacha* (family purity) and about attending the *mikvah* (ritual bath) each month.

32. A central moment in the *Shabbat* morning service.

in a safe context. The influence of the community softens and dilutes the intensity of difficult emotions and, because it is held in a public space, everyone is invited and no one should be offended. Throughout the whole wedding ritual the community plays an important role in witnessing the joining together of two lives and two fates. This is the first of many opportunities for public involvement.

There is also another level to the *aufruf*, a subtext. The couple are honored by being called to the Torah and in so doing the connection is made between them and the *Kedushah* of the Torah. Sometimes the couple will be invited to give a brief *devar Torah* (teaching) explicating the meaning of the particular passage selected for that week's reading and possibly connecting its theme to their own lives. They will often be blessed by the community and in some synagogues showered with nuts and raisins (*bevarfen*), a custom that may have originated as a fertility blessing. These elements all help set the tone for the ceremony itself.

The mood prior to a wedding, although full of joy and excited anticipation, is also one of purification and self-examination. It is customary for the woman to go to the *mikvah* (ritual bath) shortly before the wedding day and for the man to add prayers of confession and repentance to his normal daily prayers on the day of the wedding. Both bride and groom fast from sunrise on their wedding day until the moment of *yihud* (see below) at the end of the ceremony.

The visit to the *mikvah* can be understood according to its plain meaning (*pshat*) as fulfillment of the halachic requirement that a woman should immerse herself after her menstrual period and before having sexual intercourse. For some women this explanation is sufficient, but it has been rejected by many feminists as degrading and dishonoring to women. They argue that the laws of *taharat mishpacha* (family purity) are based on a male fear of women's natural bodily functions and reflect a patriarchal and misogynist attitude. Nevertheless, many women still choose to visit a *mikvah* before their wedding and use it as a tool in their psychological preparations. These women make use of another level of interpretation of the *mikvah* (*drash*) which understands the ritual as a rebirthing ceremony. The women immerse in the "living waters" and emerge as though reborn from the waters of the womb and ready to begin a new life. Their visit to the *mikvah* can be an opportunity for the ritual letting go of their former lives, of the old way of having relationships, their connection with previous lovers, old relationships with members of the family, and so forth in order to be free to enter the new.

The groom has a different way of engaging in a similar process, a symbolic encounter with death. There is a tradition that on the day of the wedding he will fast and wear the white robe (*kittel*[33]) that he wears on Yom Kippur (the Day of Atonement) and in which he will be buried. He recites the same confessional prayers that are said on Yom Kippur and at a death bed. The confrontation with mortality, as existential psychotherapists know well, returns us to our core values and enables us to perceive ourselves more deeply.[34] In this way the man comes to the wedding ceremony divested of his previous life and ready to begin the new.

One further custom should be mentioned, even though it is not universally observed, because it is a custom that is difficult to explain without referring to psychological ideas. In the days immediately prior to the wedding some couples make time to visit the graves of close relatives, even relatives who have died many years before. We encounter this frequently in Jewish folklore. In Ansky's classic Yiddish play "The Dybbuk,"[35] for example, Leah, the bride, goes to the cemetery not only to visit the ancestors, but also to invite them to her wedding. In the famous Broadway musical and motion picture *Fiddler on the Roof*, the ancestors (purportedly) come in a dream and interfere with the wedding plans. Can we simply dismiss these ideas as old-world superstition or do they have a resonance for us in today's rationalist world?

Let us hazard an explanation. The wedding is an example of a liminal time and, as we have seen in Chapters 4 and 5, such periods may be times of great anxiety. Perhaps these are times when it seems

---

33. There is a German custom that this should be given to him by his bride. Nowadays the bride will often buy him a new *tallit* (prayer shawl) instead.

34. *See*, for example, Yalom (1980).

35. Ansky (1992).

as though demons are active and it is necessary to placate them so we summon all the help we can get in the form of our dead ancestors.[36] Or perhaps we unconsciously expect the dead to be envious of the living, and it is actually our own deceased relatives whom we need to placate and be protected from. In this case it is our memories of the demands and expectations of these absent, but psychologically still alive, players that we now need to exorcise. In so doing we can be freed of their undue influence as we make our own way in the world of relationships, which they have left behind. Perhaps, then, these visits to the graveside are a kind of ghostly family therapy.

THE WEDDING DAY

From the previous evening at least, and sometimes from the previous week, the couple will not see each other until the ceremony begins. This adds to the tension and freshness of the ceremony and emphasizes the sexual component of the ritual. Two separate beings are joining together, and they enter as distinct individuals with much left to discover about each other. In a traditional setting, where there has perhaps been an arranged marriage or the couple have not yet been sexually intimate with each other, this separateness is self-evident. In a modern setting, however, where the couple may be living together already, the separation serves an even more valuable function. In any relationship there is a danger of the individual identities of a couple becoming merged and lost. Here, at the beginning of this new stage in their relationship the couple start out, willingly and consciously, as two separate people who are choosing to unite.

In the period immediately before the wedding the couple usually spend time separately with their families and friends. This enforced separation pushes them into a family situation that they may not have encountered for quite some time. The symbolism of leaving the family of origin to form a new family unit is significant and valuable,

---

36. Among the Afghan and Yemenite communities there was the custom of holding a secret wedding the night before the announced day in order to fool the spirits or demons that might wish to interfere or cast spells on the couple.

both for the couple and for the family who are letting them go. In the modern world it would be unusual for the bride to be provided with a dowry (at least formally). However, the opportunity for the parents of both bride and groom to release their offspring, having discharged their parental responsibilities, need not be lost. The psychological inheritance is at least as significant as the material one. In the past the couple were free to make use of the dowry in any way they pleased; the parents had no say in the matter, although they might offer advice. So too with the values, beliefs, attitudes, and experiences that they have freely given to the new couple. The newlyweds take what they have been given and are free to use it how they will, without parental consent or, hopefully, undue interference.

The Ketubah

The first part of the actual wedding ceremony is the writing, signing, and witnessing of the *ketubah*. Traditionally this is a document given by the groom to the bride, but in an egalitarian wedding both partners are likely to sign it. The language of the traditional *ketubah* is Aramaic and has a fixed form. Many couples nowadays choose to vary the wording and add additional promises and intentions (in their own language) to the original financial and material clauses. From a halachic perspective many of these innovations invalidate the document (as it changes the nature of the contract) and any additions need to be done outside of the actual ceremony. However, this has not been acceptable to the many couples who wish to personalize their wedding ceremony and are uncomfortable with excluding their personal feelings in this way.[37]

In practice the *ketubah* is likely to be prepared before the actual wedding day with only the signing and witnessing taking place as part of the ceremony. The *ketubah* has for centuries been a focus of artwork, and many Jewish artists weave significant symbols and addi-

---

37. *See* Anita Diamant's book *The New Jewish Wedding* (1985) for alternative wordings for the *ketubah* and many other suggestions about designing the ceremony to make it more personally meaningful.

tional meanings into their designs. The preparation of *ketubot* is far more than illustration and can be compared to the high level of intention and concentration given by the scribe who writes other sacred documents such as a Torah scroll, *tephillin*, or *mezuzot*. Even when only the traditional text has been selected, the artist may work with the couple to help them focus on their intentions prior to their wedding, which can then be given expressive form in the art.[38]

The *ketubah* may be signed either before or after the wedding, but it must be completed before the betrothal blessings. Completion requires that the signatories symbolically acquire the document beforehand by lifting a handkerchief, or by holding the scribe's jacket, or by some other action, in front of two valid witnesses.[39] This act takes place at a ceremony immediately before the main wedding ceremony begins. It is customary for the men and women to gather separately before the wedding for this purpose.

The men's gathering is not required by Jewish law, but in some communities it has become a strong *minhag* and adds to the atmosphere of separation and tension between the sexes. The ceremony is called variously in Yiddish *chosens tish* ("groom's table") or, in Hebrew, *kabbalat panim* ("receiving the faces"). The groom sits at a table and is toasted by the other men. He may give a *drash* based on the week's Torah portion, but he is also likely to receive some words of advice from the men (usually the married men) present. It is unlikely that the groom can take in much of what is said to him at this stage, but the atmosphere tends to be one of support and encouragement. In hasidic circles there may be lively singing of spiritual songs, dancing, and the imbibing of schnapps. The groom signs the *ketubah* and

---

38. The Jewish artist Shonna Husbands-Hankin (in Eugene, Oregon) has worked with many couples in this way.

39. The issue of who can be a valid witness is complex and discussed at length in the Talmud. In modern times a witness is usually considered valid in Orthodox circles if the person is not related, male, adult, and observant of the *Shabbat* laws. As the rabbi and cantor are usually assumed to fulfill these requirements, they very often act as the witnesses. In non-Orthodox circles more attention is usually given to personal and spiritual qualities, and the honor of being a witness may be given to valued friends or family members.

is then accompanied by the men to where the bride is sitting with her entourage for the next stage of the proceedings (the *Bedeken*, *see* below). On occasion, especially in hasidic communities, this accompanying can be rather overenthusiastic and the groom may look more like a prisoner under escort than a man on his way to meet his bride.

The *mitzvah* of attending or entertaining the bride (*hakhnassat Kallah*) is ancient and recorded in the Talmud. The talmudic injunction calls for her to be set upon a throne (*kisei ha-Kallah*) to give her honor, to praise her, and to do whatever is necessary to make her happy. If she has no money the community is commanded to provide her with everything she needs for her wedding (even as far as selling valuable items from the synagogue, including a Torah scroll, if necessary).

There is a fascinating dispute recorded in the Mishnah about the exact manner in which the bride should be praised. One school of thought, the school of Shammai, held that one should always tell the truth and not exaggerate. This means that if the bride is not beautiful then one should not say that she is beautiful, but should find some other characteristic or quality to praise, as there is no one without some positive virtue. The school of Hillel, on the other hand, argued that the bride should always be praised and told she is beautiful because, if mention is made of specific virtues, then the impression might be given that she lacks other virtues.

The Talmud decided in favor of Hillel, but this does not end the matter. In modern times we might well argue with the emphasis that these scholars placed on physical characteristics. In fact, Judaism does not as a rule emphasize the value of physical beauty and in this way has always differed from, for example, the culture of the ancient Greeks.[40] It is also clear that both Shammai and Hillel were concerned with personal and spiritual qualities as well as physical ones, and Hillel recommended that each bride should be praised as having "a thread of kindness drawn around her."[41] The dispute between these two

---

40. This is brought out very specifically at various points in the Talmud and is also an important aspect of the festival of Chanukah in which Judaism is specifically contrasted with the Greek culture.

41. *Ketubot* 16b–17a.

schools, however, brings out a psychological factor. Social psychologists have shown how the manner in which someone is treated influences the way in which that person perceives and conducts himself. Our image of ourselves is formed, to a significant extent, out of the reflections of the way people see and respond to us.[42] This affects our behavior. When we are treated as if we are clever, then we feel more intelligent and our performance improves. The same goes for physical attractiveness and personal qualities. What better way to send a bride into her wedding ceremony and into her marriage than full of her beauty, self-confidence, and power.

The Veiling (Bedeken)

It is customary for the face of the bride to be covered by a veil. The rabbis derive this tradition from the biblical story of Isaac and Rebekah. Rebekah veiled herself when she was told that Isaac was approaching,[43] and the rabbinic conclusion from this account is that it is proper for brides to be veiled. The rabbis interpreted her action as an act of modesty. From a psychological perspective, however, we can see that it is also, and perhaps primarily, an act of separation. It is a continuation of the separation and tension between the bride and groom that have been building throughout the preparations for the wedding.

The biblical account relates how Rebekah veiled herself. In the only other account of veiling in the Hebrew Bible we find that Tamar also veiled herself when Judah approached (although for different reasons).[44] In both cases it was an act of volition and initiated by the woman. The symbolism of veiling is closely connected with Kedushah. All the sacred objects in the temple were veiled, and the Bible relates that there was a veil over Moses's face when he ascended Mount Sinai to encounter the presence of God.[45] Once again we find the connec-

---

42. This concept of the "looking glass self" was first articulated by Cooley in 1902.
43. Genesis 24:64.
44. Genesis 38:14.
45. Exodus 34:33.

tion between holiness and separateness, only now the emphasis is on the woman's privacy. Behind the veil she is able to create her own space, and the veil can be symbolic of her self-possession.

Not all the symbolism of the veil is so positive. In many cultures the veil has a different resonance. Sometimes, especially after marriage, the veil is designed to prevent men other than the husband from seeing a woman's face. It indicates not that the wife is self-possessed, but rather that she is now possessed by another, her husband. The purpose and value of veiling are highly dependent on the values of the culture as a whole. If the culture is misogynist, then veiling is likely to be a tool of that misogyny.

The symbolism of the *Bedeken* (veiling) ceremony is ambiguous. It is a custom primarily of the Orthodox Ashkenazi community and occurs immediately before the public wedding ceremony begins. The groom, accompanied by his entourage, visits the bride and either places the veil over her head or lifts her veil and then replaces it. Significantly, the veiling is done by him and not by her.

The origins of the ceremony are obscure, but it is often associated with the biblical account of the wedding of Jacob.[46] The story is well known: Jacob was tricked by his father-in-law, Laban, into marrying Laban's elder daughter Leah, rather than the younger daughter Rachel, whom he preferred. The trick was possible because, presumably, Leah came to the wedding ceremony covered by a veil and Jacob couldn't see who it was he was actually marrying.[47] Because of this, it is claimed, bridegrooms now need to check that they have the right bride.

Although one may enjoy the humor of this folksy custom, it is possible that the veiling ceremony is also associated with a fertility blessing. In the *Bedeken* ceremony the groom lifts the bride's veil and recites the biblical verse "our sister, may you be the mother of thou-

---

46. Genesis 29:20–25.

47. The biblical narrative actually makes no reference to a veil. Rashi's comment on this section complicates the matter further. Rashi is bothered by the verse that states "in the morning it was Leah" (Genesis 29:25). Rashi concludes that Rachel and Jacob had a secret signaling system in operation and that it actually was Rachel that Jacob spent his wedding night with. At some point Rachel and Leah swapped places, and in the morning it was Leah who was in his bed.

sands of myriads."[48] This is often enacted before the immediate family who offer their own blessings. The groom may be accompanied by musicians who turn the event into a celebration. The lifting of the veil surely symbolizes the sexual act and sexual initiation. The *Bedeken* ceremony is held only if it is the bride's first marriage. The veil of a widow or divorcée has, no doubt, been lifted previously.

There are, inherent within the veiling customs, assumptions and values that do not sit comfortably with the egalitarian ethos of progressive communities and couples. Many simply ignore the custom and proceed without it. Others have tried to reframe it in such a way as to restore some of the psychological nuances that may have been lost. One such example is for the bride to go back to the biblical precedent and veil herself before her partner or lift the veil herself to indicate how she is choosing to reveal herself to him. Another is for each of the partners to place a *tallit* over the other's head and then lift the *tallit* again so that their faces are revealed. This then becomes a brief moment of coming together after the period of separation, but before the main ceremony begins. At my own wedding ceremony my partner and I incorporated this approach into *kabbalat panim*. We each lifted our *tallit* and took a moment to look at each other's faces, as if for the first time, to take in more deeply the countenance of the person we were marrying, so that when it came to the betrothal section of the ceremony we could more fully make our vows.

Chuppah

The wedding ceremony itself is conducted under a canopy (*chuppah*). This may be a large and ornate *chuppah* decorated with flowers and belonging to the synagogue. Or it may be a simple *tallit* held over the heads of the couple. The *chuppah* might be supported on four wooden poles cut, perhaps, from a tree planted at the time of the bride's birth and nurtured in anticipation of this day. And it might be held aloft by four specially chosen and valued relatives or friends.

---

48. Genesis 24:60.

The *chuppah* represents a room, the groom's chamber. The bride processes to the *chuppah* where the groom stands alone, waiting for her. She may process to music, perhaps a psalm set to an ancient melody, and she may carry flowers or a plaited *Havdalah* candle. The bride might be supported by her parents or sisters and accompanied by bridesmaids. But when the bridal party arrives at the edge of the canopy, these others remain outside. The bride leaves her family and enters the chamber alone to join her future husband.

This action of the bride is the central act of a marriage and is possibly the most powerful emotional moment of the ceremony. Symbolically the bride has left her old life to start a new one. The members of her family of origin have brought her to this point, but they are now left behind (literally). Although they may be invited to participate in parts of the ceremony that are to follow, they are no longer actually needed. The ceremony can proceed without them. Of course these symbols assume that this is a first wedding, that the bride is still bound up with her family, and so forth. However, we need not concern ourselves over with these difficulties. We are dealing with archetypes, and consciously or unconsciously each participant plays his or her role in the drama. The act of walking into a new life is always powerful; each bride will be able to specify exactly what and whom she is walking away from and what she is walking toward.

On entering the *chuppah* there is an ancient custom that the bride circles her groom seven times.[49] This tradition is derived by the rabbis from the verse in the book of Jeremiah "a woman encompasses a man,"[50] but it seems unlikely that this is the actual origin of the tradition. There are many other possibilities. The woman may be surrounding her lover with light, or casting a spell of protection around him, or invoking seven attributes of God,[51] or she is creating invis-

---

49. Seven is a mystical number because it represents the seven days of the week, the *sephirot*, and so forth. It is also significant in this case because the phrase "and when a man takes a wife" appears in seven different biblical verses (*see* Geffen [1993] p. 108).

50. Jeremiah 31:22.

51. These are the seven lower *sephirot* of the "Tree of Life." In approximate translation these are: loving kindness, justice, beauty, eternity, splendor, foundation, and kingdom.

ible walls around him to create a private space into which she then enters. Perhaps, also, she is enacting a psychodrama in front of her parents (who are now standing outside the *chuppah*). She is placing her husband at the center of the circle of her life, and her parents are now separated by an invisible wall. Thus, in another way, the wedding ceremony subtly signals the changes that are occurring in the family configuration. Throughout the circling, the husband remains passive, unless the couple have chosen to change the customs and he also circles her or they circle together.

The *chuppah* itself has accrued many symbolic associations over the centuries. The Talmud records that fathers built the *chuppah* for their sons, often using very valuable materials in its construction.[52] It most obviously resembles a room without walls and is said to be like Abraham's tent, a construction open on all sides indicating hospitality and a warm welcome to guests. The *chuppah* is usually (although not essentially) made of cloth, which represents the covering on the bridal bed. And it floats above the heads of the couple, just as the *shechinah* also hovers above them.

Erusin (Betrothal)

The arrival of the bride under the *chuppah* brings to an end the drama of separation and individuation. From now on the focus of the ceremony is on the unification of the couple and their establishment in a new relationship and a new home. The betrothal ceremony begins, as with most Jewish rituals, with the blessing over a cup of wine. Wine is symbolic of the fullness of life and transformation. It has, through the process of fermentation, been changed from a sour to a sweet taste and has the power to uplift the soul. A toast with wine brings holiness to the occasion.

The betrothal blessing is concerned with the legalistic aspects of the marriage service. The wording runs " . . . and has commanded us concerning forbidden marriages; who has disallowed unto us those that are betrothed, but has sanctioned unto us such as are wedded to

---

52. *Sotah* 49b.

us by the rite of the canopy and the sacred covenant of wedlock. . . ."[53] It is this blessing that, from an Orthodox point of view, rules out same-sex marriages along with the union of any couple that are prohibited from marrying according to *halacha*. Progressive communities normally abbreviate the blessing to something like " . . . the ceremony of *chuppah* and the sanctity of marriage" and omit the legal categories. Thus it is possible for them to allow weddings that the Orthodox community finds unacceptable.[54] Nevertheless, the intention is clear. The purpose of this part of the ceremony is clearly and publicly to state that the couple are committed to each other and to no one else. Both the bride and the groom then drink the wine from the same cup, symbolizing their togetherness. It is often customary for the parents of the couple to offer the wine to them, indicating that they too accept their new status and offer their support.

The betrothal is formalized by *kinyan*. The groom places a ring on his bride's finger and addresses her with the required formula in front of the witnesses: "Behold, by this ring you are consecrated (reserved) to (for) me as my wife according to the laws (ways) of Moses and Israel." In egalitarian weddings the bride also addresses her husband with a similar formula and gives him a ring. It has not always been a ring that is used for this ceremony; in the past it may have been a written contract, fruit, or a prayer book. Today a simple ring of ascertainable value is almost universally used.

The *erusin* ceremony is concluded by the public reading of the *ketubah*. The *ketubah* is written in Aramaic so it is recited in Aramaic, but in most communities a translation in the vernacular is also read.

Sheva Berachot (The Seven Blessings)

The second part of the ceremony establishes the couple in their new home. Seven blessings are recited as part of the wedding ceremony

---

53. Singer (1962) p. 396.
54. Not all progressive communities permit same-sex wedding ceremonies. Some communities prefer to hold commitment ceremonies and, thereby, avoid these technical problems.

and are then repeated at the reception that follows. In some communities the couple are invited as guests to seven different homes during the week following the wedding. On each occasion they are given a festive meal, and the blessings are recited. We can see how this custom helps to integrate the couple into the community. For this reason the blessings must be said in the presence of a *minyan*.[55] We can also see how this custom stands as equal and opposite to the seven days of *shivah*.[56]

The themes of the seven blessings are simple enough. Sometimes guests are invited to recite them and even to improvise additional blessings based on interpretations of the originals. The first blessing is over wine and signifies *Kedusha*. It is followed by blessings for creation, for the Jewish people, for the people of Israel, and for fertility. That there are seven blessings hints at their connection with the seven divine attributes. The blessings reiterate, as so often in Jewish ceremonies, the primary concerns of creation, covenant, and the historical direction of the Jewish people. It is as if the couple are being reminded, once again, that their relationship has a sacred purpose and that human beings alone are not responsible for creation in the world.

The language of the blessings is both poetic and precise. For example, the sixth blessing includes, "O make these loving companions greatly to rejoice even as Thou didst rejoice Thy creation in the Garden of Eden as of old." The blessing is teaching the couple about the importance of joy and companionship in loving relationships—not just romantic love but also human love. And it is this companionship that is known even at the beginning of all relationships, in the Garden of Eden.

The final blessing lists ten synonyms of joy and is a petition to God

> . . . who has created joy and gladness, bridegroom and bride, mirth and exultation, pleasure and delight, love, brotherhood, peace and fellowship. Soon may there be heard in the cities of Judah and in the streets of Jerusalem, the voice of joy and the

---

55. The exception is the final blessing, which needs only three people to be present.

56. *See* Chapter 5.

voice of gladness, the voice of the bridegroom and the voice of the bride, the jubilant voice of bridegrooms from their canopies, and of youths from their feasts of song. . . .

The *Sheva Berachot* provide a high point to the ceremony. Here all the concerns, emotions, and prayers are woven together and expressed in the Hebrew poetry. There are beautiful musical settings for the blessings, and one can often feel the joy and expectation build as they are recited. The energy raised and gathered by the preceding ceremonial finds containment and then expression in the declaration of hopes and intentions for the future. The tension is released in the final public act of the ceremony.

Breaking the Glass

As the music fades away there is a silent hush. Someone quietly places a small cloth bag on the ground in front of the groom. The bag contains a glass. The groom raises his foot and stamps down hard on the bag, smashing the glass to smithereens. Everyone shouts *mazel tov, mazel tov*[57] and the band, when there is one, starts playing lively, joyful music. The celebrations begin.

This custom is almost universally observed at Jewish weddings, but the participants usually have little notion of its origins or significance. The most popular explanation of the ritual is as follows: the glass is smashed as a reminder of the destruction of the holy Temple in Jerusalem. Joy at the wedding is to be tempered with sadness and mourning. There is another custom, observed by Sephardim, that carries the same interpretation. The groom places ashes on his forehead and recites the verse, "if I forget Thee, O Jerusalem, may my right hand lose its cunning."[58] Both of these traditions remind us of the custom of spilling wine as the ten plagues are named at the Passover Seder, because the joy of freedom is to be balanced with compassion for the suffering of the Egyptians.

---

57. Usually translated as "congratulations," but literally means "a good star" referring, presumably, to astrological beliefs.
58. Psalms 137:5.

But what is so bad about unrestrained joy at a wedding? The rabbis of the Talmud clearly feared it.

> Mar, son of Rabina, made the wedding feast for his son. When he noticed that the rabbis were very gay, he brought a precious cup, worth four hundred Zuz, and broke it before them, and they immediately became sad. R. Ashi made the wedding feast for his son. When he noticed that the rabbis were very gay, he brought a cup of white glass and broke it before them and immediately they became sad.[59]

These references to a method of sobering up the rabbinate are usually taken to be the source of the custom. However, Jacob Lauterbach has argued that the practice of smashing the glass is actually much older and is based on preexisting rituals of protection against demons.[60] According to Lauterbach, the rabbis, being unable to stop a popular custom, incorporated it instead and explained it in their own terms.[61] The connection with the mourning for the Temple came only very much later (in the fourteenth century).[62]

We recall that in our previous discussion of the mourning rituals (*see* Chapter 5) we interpreted some customs in terms of their value in warding off the evil eye (*eyin hara*). Demons and evil spirits are purportedly jealous of the living, so how much more so are they jealous when the living are having a good time. By making himself appear mournful, the groom can fool or appease the "other side" (*sitra achra*[63]),

---

59. *Berachot* 30b–31a.

60. Demons could be fought and driven away by throwing a glass at the wall in which they were thought to be hiding (a wedding custom of medieval Eastern Europe and Germany), or bribed with gifts (the offering of pouring the wine from the *erusin* cup onto the ground), or deceived by pretending that the groom was not happy at all, but weighed down with grief. Smashing the glass incorporates all three of these methods.

61. Lauterbach (1970) pp. 1–29a.

62. According to Lauterbach, the first mention of this custom is in *Kolbo, Halchot T'aseh B'Av* (Venice, 1547), but it did not gain wide acceptance until at least the eighteenth century.

63. This is the traditional designation for evil spirits or demons.

and he will be safe from their evil intent. In a modern psychological language we could suggest, as Joseph Berke has done in regard to the *eyin hara*,[64] that we might really be unconsciously protecting ourselves from the envy of other people. The demons are projections of our own fears.

The superstitious element continues in a reduced form in the modern version of the ceremony. It is generally considered to mean bad luck if the groom is unfortunate enough to fail to break the glass at the first attempt. For this reason the glass is placed within a small bag to make the groom's task easier. One might think that the bag is also provided in order to prevent splinters of glass flying around and injuring the other participants. However, Lauterbach reports that some believe the glass should be contained within a bag so that the shards cannot be collected by those skilled in witchcraft and made use of to bewitch the groom.[65]

The custom of breaking the glass lends itself well to homiletic interpretation. The connection with mourning provides an opportunity to acknowledge, in a symbolic form, that the world is not yet perfected and that one task of a marriage is to heal, as Robin Skynner suggested, the brokenness that many have experienced in family relationships. For this reason care is taken not to smash the cup used in the nuptials (*nissuin*) ceremony as this might create the wrong impression about the future of the relationship.[66]

The ceremony also provides a symbolic expression of a more personal aspect of mourning. At most weddings there is an awareness that various relatives or friends have not lived long enough to witness the event. The absence of parents, grandparents, aunts, uncles, or old friends, who may have known one or other of the couple since childhood, is strongly felt. The ceremony of breaking the glass in-

---

64. Berke (1988) pp. 35–56.
65. Ibid p. 29A.
66. Which of the two wedding cups to use has been argued back and forth over the centuries. The custom nowadays is for neither cup to be used; they are replaced by a small glass bulb. This substitution arose because of the biblical prohibition against wanton waste and destruction (*Bal Tashit*, Deuteronomy 20:19).

cludes their memory and may give expression to the poignant feelings prompted in those present by the wedding ceremony.[67]

Finally we can consider this aspect of the ceremony from a mythological or Jungian perspective. Something has to be broken before the new can emerge. The breaking of the waters before birth and the cutting of the umbilical cord are the paradigmatic examples. The cords of the old relationships have to be cut so that the new relationship can develop.

Yihud

The wedding ceremony is concluded with a moment of privacy, a moment of intimacy. The couple are conducted to a private room where they spend time alone together.[68] This is a requirement of the *halacha* and has to be observed by two witnesses who stand guard outside. No one else is allowed to enter. The bride and groom usually spend about ten minutes together and may eat something as they have been fasting up to this point. When they emerge from the room the marriage is complete. They have symbolically set up home together.

Yihud provides a brief moment of contemplation and integration. *Yihud* can be translated as "unity" or "unification," the couple whose separateness was paramount at the beginning of the ceremony are now united. It seems a pity that this aspect of the ceremony tends to be rushed in many modern weddings. The demands of anxious and excited guests, relatives, photographers, and caterers can easily overwhelm. After any powerful ceremony there is a need for stillness, a time to experience and ground the powerful emotions invoked and provoked by the ritual. Without such a moment its transformative power may be weakened.

---

67. A growing custom is for the names of such people to be included in a specially prepared explanatory wedding booklet given to the guests.

68. Presumably this was originally the moment when the marriage was consummated.

7

Prayer

From the perspective of Jewish tradition praying is obligatory for both women and men. Men must pray on at least three occasions each day (sometimes more), and what they say and when they say it are fully prescribed by the *halacha* and recorded in the codes. Women generally do not participate in these prescribed prayers, but have composed many beautiful freeform prayers (*Techinas*) often in vernacular languages such as Yiddish and Ladino, some of which have found their way into the liturgy. The position of women in Jewish tradition has already been discussed in Chapter 2. In regard to prayer, the obligations of women are rather different from those of men. Generally it is thought that women are not obligated to pray although, as Blu Greenberg makes clear, they are actually obligated to pray but fulfill their obligations in a way different than men.[1] In particular they pray in private and do not have to participate in public prayer. Of course progressive Jews see this situation entirely differently. Even in some Orthodox circles the advent of women's *Tefillah* groups has changed the situation radically.

1. Greenberg (1981) p. 82–87.

Some required prayers fall outside of the rigid framework of prescribed prayers, but even these involve the recitation of established formulae. Certain blessings, for example, are to be made before and after eating, and there are those that are to be recited on special occasions such as observing a rainbow, hearing thunder, meeting a sage, wearing new clothes, seeing the blossom in spring, and on hearing bad news. There is a custom that a person should ideally recite one hundred blessings each day. And there is even a tale of a Hasidic *rebbe* who wished his coffin to be made from the wood of his kitchen table, so that in death he could be surrounded by the countless blessings that he and others had made at that table during his lifetime.

The prayers themselves are read from the *siddur* (daily prayer book). The *siddur* itself is filled to capacity with inspired poetry and prose, along with selections of the finest biblical and rabbinic literature. When read in its original language (Hebrew or Aramaic) and savored and meditated upon, the words of the *siddur* have the quality to uplift the spirit and feed the soul. Unfortunately, all too often, it is not read in this way. In a typical traditional synagogue, on a typical weekday morning, it is recited at high speed, in a low mumble, with little comprehension. The intention of the congregants is obvious, to finish as quickly as possible and, having fulfilled their religious obligations, to be on their way. This type of prayer experience is not for beginners, for without a guide and personal trainer, they will quickly be lost and left far behind. That is not to say that in some places and at some times there isn't a deeper quality to the experience, but these are the exceptions that prove the rule. No wonder, then, that from the time of the early German reformers, changes have been made to shorten and simplify the synagogue services. Some prayers and sections of prayers have been omitted and replaced with modern selections of prose.

This technical aspect of prayer is not, of course, the whole story. *Shabbat* and festivals provide ample opportunities for both showpieces of musical virtuosity in the synagogue and for quiet leisurely devotion. Furthermore, daily familiarity with the *siddur* facilitates a deepening relationship with the prayers as they enter into consciousness by virtue of constant repetition. The words of the *siddur* may become vehicles of emotional expression and personal meaning. Prayer can play an important role in one's emotional life.

Abraham Joshua Heschel[2] (1907–1972), an inheritor of the Hasidic legacy, understood personal prayer in this manner. How, he asks, could one bear the aloneness of a world in which there is so much misery and evil, without an "Other" to turn to? Prayer is one of the ways in which an individual can become known to and known by God. The purpose of religious discipline is to become worthy of God's attention.[3]

> To disclose the self we must learn how to cast off the shells of ambition, of vanity, of infatuation with success. We are all very poor, very naked, and rather absurd in our misery and in our success. We are constantly dying alive. From the point of view of temporality we are all dead except for a moment. There is only one bridge over the abyss of despair: prayer.[4]

However, Heschel warns against equating prayer with emotion. "Emotion is an important component of prayer, but the primary presupposition is conviction. If such conviction is lacking, if the presence of God is a myth, then prayer to God is a delusion. If God is unable to listen to us, then we are insane in talking to him."[5] How many of us, therefore, are insane? The studies of belief and practice

---

2. Descendant of many Hasidic dynasties including, most famously, that of Reb Joshua Heschel of Apt. Heschel was raised in a traditional Hasidic family in Poland and was groomed to become a *rebbe* himself. He later studied in Germany but was then forcibly returned to Poland by Hitler. He escaped to the United States and held positions at the Hebrew Union College in Cincinnati (Reform) and then later at the Jewish Theological Seminary in New York (Conservative). The author of countless scholarly articles, he has written significant books discussing philosophy and theology. He was both a passionate educator and a political activist for civil rights.

3. Elsewhere in Hasidic literature we find the notion that God is aware of us at all times and that there is no way in which we can fall outside the knowledge and awareness of God. In this discussion Heschel is emphasizing the importance of self-refinement and purification in order to become even closer to and more identified with God.

4. Heschel (1959), p. 257.

5. Ibid p. 258.

referred to earlier suggest that while religious practices may be maintained, belief in God is very low.[6]

Heschel also suggested another view of prayer, as an authentic response to the experience of "radical amazement," the sense of wonder and mystery that is the prelude to any religious experience.[7] People pray because they are stirred in their hearts to give expression to their sense of awe. The experience of wonder is the necessary prerequisite for supplication,[8] but the experience of wonder is itself given form by the words of the prayers, which then act to transform the individual. Prayer without words is possible but rare. For Heschel, as for William James,[9] the virtue of prayer resides in its transformative effects upon the individual and their consequent engagement in right actions.

Heschel had little time for the type of "religious behaviorism" that is preoccupied with fulfillment of obligations and unconcerned with meaning, right action, and the relationship with God.[10] The concern about empty prayers, however, has a long and illustrious history in Jewish thought and can be found in the early discussions of the Talmudists.[11]

The rabbis of the Talmud discussed the question of whether it is permissible to say a prayer without proper concentration. And, furthermore, they wished to determine whether, if one reaches the end of a prayer and then realizes that the mind had wandered, one is required to repeat the prayer. The concept they were discussing was *kavvana*, which can best be described as intentionality during prayer. Nevertheless it is not, as Buber has pointed out, the type of intention

---

6. *See* Introduction.

7. *See*, for example, Heschel (1955) p. 45.

8. The form of the main daily prayer, the *Amidah*, follows this format. The three initial blessings are concerned with the legacy of our ancestors, the wonder of creation, and the holiness of God. Only then do the prayers turn to supplication and requests. The final blessings express gratitude.

9. *See* Chapter 3.

10. *See* Heschel (1955) p. 320–332.

11. This area has been excellently discussed in a recent comprehensive study of the topic by Seth Kadish (1997).

associated with will or desire as when one is trying to achieve a purpose. Rather it is engagement with the Source of all existence during
prayer that vivifies the pray-er.[12]

The Talmudists formulated their conclusions in the form of Rabbi
Eliezer's law, which insisted that *kavvana* is required for prayer. If
one cannot pray with concentration, then one should not pray at all.
However a contradictory opinion ruled that while the mind should
be concentrated for all the blessings (of the *Amidah*), if this cannot
be achieved then it is permissible to pray provided concentration is
maintained at least during the first blessing. This apparent contradic-
tion is resolved by a later authority who explained that when one
begins to pray one should have the clear intention of concentrating
throughout. However, if after prayer one becomes aware of lapses of
concentration, then one has still fulfilled the obligation if concentration was held for at least the first of the blessings (and the first line
of the *Shema*).[13]

The rabbis, therefore, had made a concession to human limitations for they had not wished to make prayer requirements so difficult that they could never be fulfilled. *Kavvana* is central for prayer,
but it cannot be insisted upon. They preferred that believers should
be *lifnim mushurat hadin* and pray with *kavvana*, but had no way of
guaranteeing this for the majority, so they allowed second best.[14] The
concern with *kavvana* continued into the Middle Ages and the halachic
codes. Maimonides understood concentration to be essential, that one
should ". . . empty (the) mind of all thought and see (oneself) as standing in the presence of the *shechinah*." [15] However, the *Tur* ruled that
prayers should not be repeated because of a lack of kavvana, as a failure to concentrate the first time around was unlikely to be improved
on the second reading.[16] It seems a pity that as prayer practices evolved
over the centuries the importance of kavvana in prayer diminished. It

---

12. *See* Buber (1955) p. 33–50.
13. *See* Kadish (1997).
14. *See* Chapter 3 for an explanation of the concept of *lifnim mushurat hadin*.
15. *Yad, Tefilah* 4:15–16. Translation by Jacobs (1972).
16. *Orah Hayim* 101. *See* Jacobs (1972) p. 73.

was left to the hasidim and their descendants, such as Heschel and, as we shall see, Rabbi Zalman Schachter, to revitalize it.

But what of today when many people find prayer difficult, if not impossible? When so many, in Heschel's understanding, would be considered insane if they were to recite the words of a prayer, because they do not believe that there is anyone to listen to their prayers. As with the previous chapters we will first consider psychological viewpoints before going on to explore the Jewish traditions.

PSYCHOLOGY AND PRAYER

The most obvious question facing psychologists can be put bluntly. Are people who pray different from those who don't? The next question is also straightforward. What do people experience when they pray? We will look at each question in turn.

Beit-Hallahmi and Argyle have reviewed the psychological research into religious behavior, belief, and experience.[17] A great deal of religious behavior can, of course, be explained in terms of conformity to the normal behavior expected by the group. And we have already looked at some of the suggestions about intrapsychic causes in Chapter 3. One of their other suggestions, however, is that religious people are different from nonreligious people in their responsiveness to ritual. During some forms of prayer and religious ceremonies, music, dance, and drumming are commonly used. These might lead to a hypnotic trance or states of increased suggestibility. In such states the right hemisphere of the brain is activated, and it is possible that religious people are more prone to be right-hemisphere dominant.[18]

Religious experiences are quite common and so is prayer.[19] In Britain over 40 percent of people claim to pray daily, and in the United

---

17. Beit-Hallahmi and Argyle (1997).

18. There is some neuropsychological evidence from studies of the effects of drugs on the brain, response to brain lesions, and EEG recordings that the right cerebral hemisphere is associated with spatial, aesthetic, and nonverbal activities and the left hemisphere is associated with verbal and cognitive abilities.

19. *See* the work of William James and the postscript at the end of this book for a brief discussion of the frequency of religious experiences.

States more than 60 percent say they do so, with 19 percent praying three times a day or more.[20] There are different types of prayer: colloquial prayer (conversations with God), meditative prayer, petitionary prayer, and ritual or set prayer. Meditative prayer is similar to meditation and more likely to lead to a religious experience than the other types of prayer.

Techniques of meditation vary a great deal among religious traditions. What they share, however, is that they all reduce heart rate, blood pressure, and other physiological indices of stress/arousal. This is also true of secular techniques of meditation such as progressive muscle relaxation or techniques taught without reference to the underlying belief system (such as Transcendental Meditation). Unusual experiences can arise during all of these practices, and they are interpreted according to the beliefs of the religious tradition.

The nature of the prayer experience has been discussed in detail by two clinical psychologists who have a great interest in religion. Fraser Watts and Mark Williams, both researchers in Cambridge, England, have been involved for many years with the development of new forms of treatment for people who suffer from depression. They have utilized their approach, that of cognitive psychology, better to understand "religious knowing," that is, the inner experiences of religiously committed people. Although they have been mainly concerned with the traditions of prayer in Christianity, they have reviewed much of the available psychological literature and research.[21]

Prayer is one of the ways in which individuals come to a religious understanding of the world. In many ways this is a radical departure from the widely held popular view that religion is mainly about faith. In fact, according to Watts and Williams, religious knowing involves the same psychological processes as many other forms of knowing. Although religious knowledge is a special kind of knowledge, it is not unique. They give three examples of kinds of knowing that throw light on religion and prayer.

---

20. Beit-Hallahmi and Argyle (1997) p. 82.
21. Watts and Williams (1988).

The first example is *psychotherapy*. A person who engages seriously in psychotherapy expects to be changed by the experience. It is not simply that one gains new information about oneself, although this may be important, but also that this information is connected with one's feelings. Watts and Williams use Gendlin's term "felt meanings" to convey the idea that it is only when some internal, perhaps symbolic, event is articulated and accompanied by emotion, that it can really be considered as an insight.[22] In psychotherapy, as with a religious understanding, true insight leads to changes in the person and in his or her behavior.[23]

Aesthetic knowing is the second example. Appreciation of a work of art involves, initially, a kind of distancing between ourselves and the object. Personal needs and beliefs are put aside so that they do not interfere with perception. We hold back our thoughts about the work, and our other preoccupations, so that we can allow ourselves to become fully absorbed in it. We are focused only on the "now." This type of contemplation enables us to have an emotional response to the object. However, it is then necessary to restrain this response also, so that the "... web of associations at the fringes of consciousness ... elaborate themselves."[24] Not everyone is immediately capable of this type of perception, and repeated attention to a work of art is often necessary. When the work is finally, often suddenly, "seen," the object may appear entirely different from before, perhaps sharper, more vivid, and with greater detail. It may seem entirely new. The development of aesthetic perception shares much with contemplative prayer. The contemplative tradition in religious communities (especially Christian monastic communities) teaches much about the need for emotional restraint, sustained attention, and openness to experience.

---

22. Ibid p. 72.

23. In Chapter 3 we discussed some of the important differences and similarities between religion, spirituality, and psychotherapy. It is important to realize that while there may be similar processes involved in both, they are not substitutes for each other and that self-knowledge may be the bedrock for religious and spiritual growth.

24. Ibid p. 60–61.

The third analogy is *empathic knowing*. As with psychotherapy and aesthetic knowing, empathy may be easier for some than others, but can be developed by training and is often unpredictable. Empathy requires that a person share something of the other's emotional experience. This is a necessary part of seeing the world from another person's point of view. Empathy also requires a degree of intuition entailing perception that is nonanalytical, in which the person makes use of subtle cues that they would not normally utilize when acting more consciously or rationally. Freud recommended that analysts employ an attitude of "evenly suspended attention" in which they do not search too hard for meanings or interpretations.[25]

Emotions play an important role in religious experience. Some religious practices deliberately induce excited emotional states using aggression, hyperventilation, pain, or dance (e.g., Hasidic dance, whirling dervishes).[26] Conversely, others try to reduce arousal by techniques of meditation and contemplation. Religious experiences tend to occur at both ends of this spectrum. Historically, some religions have developed ascetic traditions to deliberately try to quell or control emotions. Asceticism has never been part of normative Jewish practice, although there were occasional exceptions in small mystical groups.[27] According to Watts and Williams, such approaches are unlikely to be successful for most people, as they tend to induce psychological conflicts that interfere with religious experience. They commend a more

---

25. Ibid p. 64.

26. *See*, for example, the study by Wavell and colleagues (1966) who describe the use of needle piercing, fire walking, blood letting, as well as vigorous and exhausting dance in trance induction as part of religious and shamanistic ceremonies.

27. For the most part Jewish asceticism took the form of regular fasting and extended periods of Torah study (*see* Chapter 2 for discussion of the practices of the Vilna Gaon). Although there are occasional stories of Hasidic masters immersing themselves in icy waters for the purpose of purification, this was not typical. There are, however, documented rules of piety that were adopted by the kabbalists of Safed, and these vary in their degree of severity (*see* Fine [1984]). It is reported, for example, that at times Luria would refrain from eating meat, except on *Shabbat*, and that during the week he would live in isolation and not cohabit with his wife. Many of those associated with him would also adopt strict rules about what they would eat and drink, practice regular vigils, and impose strict rules of conduct upon themselves (*see Reishit Hochma* by Elijah de Vidas).

balanced approach in which sensitivity to emotional states is developed. Expression of emotions may be of value because they help to produce a state of calmness that is conducive to spirituality. In fact, becoming aware of one's emotions may play an important role in the development of the self-knowledge that is a vital aspect of the spiritual path.

"Prayer is, among other things, the medium through which the religious person engages in the interpretation of experience."[28] Wishes and desires are expressed in petitionary prayer. In the course of regular daily prayer, events and actions are reviewed. Young children's prayers (ages 7 to 9) tend to be about very concrete requests, and if their hopes are not realized they attribute the failure to their own "naughty" behavior. Later (ages 9 to 12) God is understood less as a magical figure and more as a supernatural concept. God can bestow feelings of peace, happiness, and confidence; if prayer fails, this is because the pray-er asked for the wrong things. In adolescence, prayers are more likely to be either on behalf of another person or for confession or forgiveness.[29]

Adult prayer incorporates all these early levels of prayer in much the same way as Wilber described the incorporation of earlier stages of consciousness in spiritual development (see Chapter 3). Early stages of prayer are assimilated into later stages of prayer and at times of stress the early stages may reappear. Hence, in an emergency situation, people who do not normally expect prayer to produce concrete results find themselves asking God to rescue them and promising that they will be "good" in the future. However, in adulthood, the main value of prayer is understood by the religious person to be its beneficial effects on the one who prays, rather than its ability to influence external events.

This latter point of view is rather easier to understand for prayers of confession than for prayers of petition. If one feels guilty, then it makes sense that prayer can provide some relief. This is especially the

---

28. Watts and Williams (1988) p. 109.
29. These descriptions of children's prayer are based on research conducted by Goldman. See Beit-Hallahmi and Argyle (1997) p. 110.

case if the pray-er believes that forgiveness is possible. In a prayer of confession a person will identify the role they have played in some misdeed and accept responsibility for their part. Forgiving other people clears the path to forgive oneself. The confessional prayer may also involve the pray-er in running through the events concerned in the mind. This is a little like psychotherapy in which clients are encouraged to go over events and accept their part in them. In psychotherapy, as in prayer, they are encouraged to identify thoughts and feelings (such as sexual, aggressive, or envious thoughts) that may be unacceptable to them and normally unconscious. Jung referred to this aspect of our personality as the "shadow." The confessional prayer provides an opportunity for this kind of "working through" facilitated by the subjective presence of God who, in most religious traditions, is considered benign, understanding, and accepting.

In petitionary prayer one's hopes and desires are exposed. They are then vulnerable to transformation. Once again the comparison with psychotherapy is helpful. At first a person comes to therapy with a series of demands and complaints. They don't like this or that aspect of themselves or others, life is not working out the way they would like or think it should. It is the therapist's task to help the person see that these concerns actually reflect deeper personal issues, often emotional needs, that are not being met. In psychoanalysis this is achieved by the analyst interpreting symbols of unconscious motivation. In cognitive therapy a series of questions are posed taking the individual on a voyage of "guided discovery." In prayer the individual is encouraged to align his or her will with that of the Divine power, and in so doing personal desires are challenged and redirected.

JEWISH PRAYER

> When R. Eliezer fell ill, his disciples went in to visit him. They said to him: Master, teach us the paths of life so that we may through them win the life of the future world. He said to them . . . when you pray know before whom you are standing and in this way you will win the future world.[30]

---

30. *Berachot* 28b.

Formal Jewish prayer is, first and foremost, a rabbinic invention. Although there are plenty of biblical precedents for prayer, it wasn't a regular practice until after the dispersion consequent on the destruction of the Temple in 70 C.E. The Temple itself had been the focus of the sacrificial rites performed by the priestly caste. The ordinary people had taken almost no active part in the service. Their role was to provide the offerings and occasionally prostrate themselves at the prescribed times. The Priests acted as intermediaries and the Levites assisted. The recorded accounts of the Temple services convey an impression of an extremely impressive and elaborate rite that must have been spiritually uplifting and nourishing for those present. It is surely no coincidence that the Hebrew word for "offering" is *korban*, which has the same Hebrew root as *kerev*, which means "to draw near." Presumably the offerings were a means of drawing near to God.

The most famous precedent for personal prayer took place in the Temple. It is the story of Hannah who was observed by Eli, the priest, to be praying silently, but praying so intently that her lips moved.[31] Eli mistook her for being drunk, but she replied that she was not drunk; rather, she was praying that she would give birth to a child. Her outpouring of spirit was so powerful that she has become the model of prayer for all generations. The traditional manner of reciting the *Amidah* as laid down in the *Shulchan Aruch*, vocalizing the words so that they cannot be heard by a neighbor, is derived from Hannah's prayer.[32]

Legend tells us that the *shechinah* dwelt in the Temple and that when the Temple was destroyed she beat her wings and departed. Yochannan Ben Zakai escaped from the Temple, hidden in a coffin, and negotiated with the Romans to establish an academy at Yavneh. The rabbis who followed him established the pattern of daily prayers that is still followed today. Services in the morning and afternoon both reflect the mood of the corresponding service in the Temple.[33] Hence the pattern of daily services was maintained after the Temple was

---

31. Samuel 1.
32. *Kitzur Shulchan Aruch*, Ganzfield (1961) vol. 1, Chapter 18:6.
33. The evening service (*maariv*) was added later.

destroyed. The standing prayer (*Amidah*), in particular, replaced the actual sacrifice in the Temple.

The English word "pray" is not really an adequate translation of the variety of Hebrew words relating to religious devotion. One Hebrew term often used is *avodah*. This can readily be translated as "service" and immediately conveys the multiple meanings of "service to God" and the "service in the Temple" on which the liturgy was originally based. The rabbis of the Talmud referred to prayer as "service of the heart." [34] Another word in use is *davennen*, which has an uncertain etymology and is originally Yiddish rather than Hebrew. *Davennen* is also understood to mean prayer, but generally refers to participation in the liturgical cycle. Hence, when one goes to the synagogue in order to *davven*, this usually means taking part in the synagogue service on a regular basis.

The most common Hebrew word for prayer is Tephillah, which is the term adopted in modern Hebrew. Tephillah, however, has strong biblical roots and appears in the book of Isaiah.[35] It also appears in its root form of *hitpallel* in the Book of Kings.[36] This grammatical form of the verb suggests that its meaning is reflexive; hence, a better translation might be "to pray oneself." The verb stem is *Pll*, which means "to intercede." There is also an older meaning of "to cut oneself," which perhaps refers to an ancient pagan custom of slashing oneself in a frenzy during worship. This latter practice was associated with idol worshippers in the Bible and was made the subject of a specific biblical prohibition.[37]

The rabbis of the Talmud were rather ambivalent about the importance of prayer; they certainly did not set it up as the highest virtue. Overall they preferred Torah study and understood prayer as involvement with this world, whereas study was a focus on the world to come. Excessive personal prayer was frowned upon. They considered that the conditions of this world were better dealt with by prac-

---

34. *Ta'anit* 2a.
35. Isaiah 1:15.
36. Kings (I) 8:42.
37. Deuteronomy 14:1.

tical means such as charity. Prayers, when said, should be recited as part of a community. "The Holy One, blessed be He, says: if a man occupies himself with the study of Torah and with works of charity and prayer with the congregation, I account it to him as if he had redeemed Me and My children. . . ."[38]

Nevertheless, over the course of centuries the custom of three daily prayer times has prevailed. Among observant male Jews this custom is very strong. Less strictly observant Jews may not pray as often but the pattern is the same. Prayers are said soon after dawn (*shaharit*), in the afternoon (*mincha*), and in the evening (*maariv*). One British Orthodox rabbi, Rabbi Jeffrey Cohen, has written about the spiritual and psychological value of such regular prayer. His focus was not so much on the words of the prayers themselves, rather on the practice of taking time out from one's everyday activities in order to pray.

> By means of our thrice-daily prayers we invest our workaday activity with a mantle of spirituality. *Shaharit* lays a sacred foundation for the daily tasks ahead; *mincha* interrupts them in full swing, in early afternoon, cautioning us against total absorption with our material objectives. *Maariv* serves to climax the day's activity, emphasizing that we do not live to work, but rather work to live a happy and dignified life in the service of God.
>
> Viewed in this light, daily prayer can also constitute a safety valve, to ensure that we do not lose our individuality in the face of the monotonous regimen of a working routine to which so many of us are subjected.[39]

I do not know whether Rabbi Cohen would feel comfortable with the analogy, but his pragmatic approach to prayer sounds very much like a technique for developing the state that Buddhists call "mindfulness." The purpose of blessing food along with gifts of nature and other daily occurrences is similar. The act of blessing raises aware-

---

38. *Berachot* 8a.
39. Cohen (1986) p. 124.

ness of the source of creation and can change one's spiritual and psychological consciousness.

Jewish prayer has been, since Temple times, primarily a verbal activity. The exception is the practice of swaying back and forth while reciting certain prayers, such as the *Amidah*. This custom is known as *shockling*. In addition, there is the instruction to take three steps forward at the beginning of the prayer, bend the knees and bow at prescribed points, and take three steps back at the end.

The origin of *shockling* is obscure. The codes recommend that the swaying is minimized, but no explanation of its purpose is given. Biblical support for the practice was found by the Ashkenazim in the Book of Psalms where it says, "All my bones shall say, Eternal, who is like unto Thee," but this does not constitute an explanation.[40] One suggestion is based on a passage in the *Zohar* (and also in the Book of Proverbs[41]), which describes the soul's relation to the body as like that of a flame to the wick of a candle. The swaying back and forth while *shockling* is reminiscent of a flickering flame and symbolizes this relationship well. More practically the swaying reminds us of the repetitive bodily movements made by students learning in a *yeshiva*. These movements are an aide to memorizing (along with using specific melodies for particular categories of literature), and it is possible that these movements were carried over by students into the *davennen*.

Music is also an important aspect of Jewish prayer—not only the set pieces of the synagogue service, but more importantly the specific melodies and rhythms that tradition has allocated to each service. These are known as *nusach*. Each service has its own *nusach* that conveys the atmosphere of the sacred time along with the words of the prayers. Hence the same words on Friday night are experienced differently on Saturday morning and differently again on an ordinary weekday or on a festival day.

Taken together the body movements and the melodies add an additional dimension to prayer. As Rabbi Zalman Schachter has pointed out they create a prayer dance, a "body Hebrew," that even

---

40. Psalms 35:10.
41. Proverbs 20:27.

the unlearned and unlettered can respond to.[42] The meaning is not carried only in the words.

Blessings and prayer require *kavvana*. The Talmudists understood that if one is tired or distracted (for example, after a long journey) then it is not possible properly to focus one's attention. In these circumstances prayers can be postponed until a more suitable time. Centuries later *kavvana* took on a more mystical meaning. The kabbalists of Safed, under the guidance of Rabbi Isaac Luria, developed a highly complex system of *kavvanot*, intentions for particular prayers. These required intense concentration and spiritual preparation. These *kavvanot* were not suitable for ordinary practice or everyday use. In comparatively modern times the followers of the *Musar* movement (*see* Chapter 2) emphasized the need for ethical and spiritual development alongside prayer, so that prayer could have the transformative effects that they intended. It was the hasidim, however, who developed prayer into its most advanced form, and it is to them that we now turn.

THE HASIDIC APPROACH TO PRAYER

The hasidic attitude toward prayer turned the rabbinic priorities on their head. Meaningful prayer was placed higher than scholarship, and prayer became the focus of the life of the Hasid. In hasidic communities prayer was injected with a new vitality, and their elevation of prayer, as opposed to scholarship, was one of the chief causes of their bitter feud with the Mitnagdim (*see* Chapter 2).

Prayer presented the hasidim with new theological difficulties that greatly affected their relationship with the *Siddur*. The purpose of prayer for the Hasid was to achieve a higher level of *devekut*, that is, cleaving to God. In prayer the Hasid strives to become as close to the Divine as possible. This requires *bitul hayesh*, the abnegation of self, so that nothing stands between the pray-er, the prayer, and the prayed to. Contemplative prayer and prayers of praise are suitable vehicles for exercises in developing such transparency and transcen-

---

42. Schachter (1993).

dence, but prayers of petition are problematic. Petitionary prayers strengthen the ego and demand that human needs be addressed rather than simply focusing on the presence of God.

Rabbi Louis Jacobs discussed the difficulty of petitionary prayer in his classic study of hasidic prayer.[43] He concluded that the ultimate purpose of petitionary prayer was not to satisfy human needs at all, but to satisfy God's needs. But what needs can God have, especially as the hasidic, indeed the Jewish, doctrine is that God is complete and perfect? The answer lies in the teachings of the Kabbalah. The human being was created as a microcosm of the universe. During creation God's essence was unchanged, nothing was added or taken away, but in the manifestation of the vital creative power a lack in the world was revealed. This lack is an aspect of the Divine itself. It is the receptive element through which the purpose of creation can be fulfilled; it is the capacity for God to bestow goodness upon the creatures of the universe. The receptive quality of this aspect of God led the kabbalists and the hasidim to name this aspect as feminine, and she is known in rabbinic and hasidic tradition as the *Shechinah*. If a person has needs then so does God and, therefore, petitionary prayer is a means of returning spiritual energy to the upper realms and reuniting God with the *Shechinah*. So even petitionary prayer can have the quality of *bitul hayesh*. Although it initially appears as outwardly directed, its influence is inward, transforming those who pray so as to align their needs and desires with something outside of themselves. Hence the psychological effects of petitionary prayer receive a metaphysical rationale.

Prayer, in the hasidic tradition, is not entered into casually. Preparation is crucial if prayer is to be effective. There were hasidic masters who, before prayer, would pray that they would be able to pray. Preparations for prayer range from taking care of physical needs, such as visiting the toilet before beginning and putting a silk girdle around the waist, to spending time in deep meditation before reciting the *Shema*. The *Habad* school developed the art of intellectual con-

---

43. *See* Jacobs (1972) Chapter 1.

templation on the mysteries of the cosmos before reciting the *Shema*, as a gateway to mystical prayer.[44]

Rabbi Louis Jacobs has provided a summary of the *Habad* system of contemplation.[45] It is of interest to us because the *Habad* approach makes great use of the intellectual capacities of the mind to arouse the sense of wonder (similar to Heschel's radical amazement) that is the prerequisite for contemplation of the mystery. It is such contemplation that reduces the ego to nothingness (*bitul hayesh*).

Reb Dov Ber of Lubavitch set out the system of contemplation in detail.[46] Contemplation is "powerful reflection on the profundity of a subject, pondering over it until it is understood perfectly in all the details of its various parts." The subject of contemplation is the system of the Kabbalah. Dov Ber's guide directs his followers to consider an idea's "depth," "length," and "breadth." Reflection on breadth reveals all the implications and the extensions of the idea. Length enables the subject to be conveyed to another who does not understand it. Attempts to understand the depth of an idea relate to trying to grasp its essential point, its source.

This type of contemplation before or during prayer directs one to the concept that God fills and sustains the world. All creation is from "nothing," and this idea is to be explored in great detail with many illustrations. An intellectual understanding of these concepts and mysteries alone is insufficient. They must be incorporated into prayer in order to arouse the fear and love of God.

---

44. The most well-known example is the tract *Sha'ar HaYichud v'Emunah* ("The gate of Unity and Faith"; *see* second section of *Tanya*) by the founder of *Habad*, Rabbi Schneur Zalman of Liadi (1747–1813).

At this point it is also worth briefly mentioning the Habad movement and their philosophy. *Habad*, also known as Lubavitch after the Russian town in which they became established, are the single largest contemporary hasidic group. They have been hugely successful in modern times and have emissaries all over the globe. The name *Habad* is an acronym of the names of three of the *sephirot*. These are *Hochma* (wisdom), *Binah* (understanding), and *Da'at* (knowledge). All three are concerned with the intellectual capacities. It is the desire to consciously activate these capacities that, among other factors, sets *Habad* apart from the other Hasidic groups.

45. Jacobs (1972) Chapter 7.

46. It is his *Kunteros Ha-Hithonanut* that has been summarized by Rabbi Louis Jacobs.

Dov Ber's description of the method of contemplation of ideas is remarkably similar to the manner in which a child, and then an adult, develops cognitive concepts and categories. A child learns about the qualities of objects by manipulating them. Weight, density, coarseness, and so forth are discovered in manipulative play. The child learns about categories by experimenting, or being shown, how different items or objects share similarities. Eventually the child grasps what it is that the different objects have in common and will then have learned a new concept. In cognitive psychology abstract concepts are generally referred to as schemas. Schemas are developed through experience in much the same way as categories of objects are developed, only the manipulation involved is the mental manipulation of ideas rather than the physical manipulation of objects.

Perhaps *Habad* has developed a system for establishing schemas for nonphysical realities.[47] This idea is consistent with the concept of the evolution of consciousness described in Chapter 3. Ken Wilber suggested that consciousness develops in stages and that each stage incorporates, and does not jettison, the previous stage. Progression depends upon the ability to move from *fusion* to *differentiation* and thence to *integration*. Perhaps in *Habad* contemplation there is just this process. The manipulation of objects in childhood has become the manipulation of ideas in adult prayer, so that the self can be increasingly differentiated from its thoughts. Wilber warns us that this process can fail if the individual is unable to integrate the new concepts and there is a consequent *dissociation*: a fragmentation of the mind and body rather than a fusion into a new stage of development. And we can find this concern in Dov Ber as well. Dov Ber describes two submethods of contemplation: the general method, which is to dwell on God's immanence, and the detailed method, which is to explore the way immanence is revealed in each detail of creation. Dov Ber suggests that beginners start with the general method. Too much differentiation at an early stage may be difficult to contain.

---

47. Perhaps the origin of the *Habad* technique can be found in the *Mishnah* ("Ben Bag Bag said: turn it and turn it over again, for everything is in it, and contemplate it. . . ." *Avot* VI:25) and in the traditional style of yeshiva learning.

During all contemplative prayer, not just that of *Habad*, the Hasid was instructed to focus his mind and concentrate entirely on the words of the prayer. This was particularly important if the individual was practicing Lurianic *kavvanot*, but applied throughout. The early hasidim recognized how difficult this is to do and were aware that during prayer all sorts of inappropriate and disturbing thoughts would arise.[48] They referred to them as strange or alien thoughts and developed techniques to deal with them. The thoughts were of three kinds: "Strange love" were sexual thoughts or images, "pride" were egotistical thoughts about the individual's spiritual attainments, and "idolatry" were blasphemous thoughts or attraction to Christianity.[49]

Concerns about strange thoughts are well known in psychiatry and psychology. Usually referred to as "intrusive thoughts," they are a feature of obsessive compulsive disorder. Intrusive thoughts are those that enter into the mind unbidden and are frequently ideas or images of violence or sexual acts that the individual finds abhorrent and distressing. Researchers have shown, however, that such thoughts are actually not uncommon, and many people experience them regularly even if they do not have a psychological disorder.[50] The key difference is in the interpretation of the meaning of the thought. Those who develop obsessive compulsive disorder are unable to accept the thought and try to get rid of it. Others find that although the thought is distasteful, they do not feel guilty about having had the thought and are able to discount it.[51]

The approach of the early hasidic masters to strange thoughts was to "elevate" them. They rejected the notion that the thoughts could simply be pushed out of the mind. Instead they explained that the origin of these thoughts was, according to the kabbalistic doctrine, holy energy (sparks) that had fallen into the evil side (*Sitra ach'ra*)

---

48. *See* Jacobs (1972) Chapter IX.
49. *See* Raphael Patai (1977) pp. 182–191 for an account of the relationship between hasidic practices and those of some contemporaneous Orthodox Christian cults and the latter's influence on the development of the early hasidic movement.
50. Rachman and de Silva (1978).
51. Salkovskis (1989).

and needed to be redeemed. The elevation of thoughts was achieved by tracing a thought in the mind back to its source in God. For example, if an individual was distracted by sexual thoughts concerning a beautiful woman, his task was to recall that her beauty is a pale reflection of the source of all beauty and that physical beauty is only a manifestation of the spiritual world where real beauty resides.

The hasidic approach makes good psychological sense. Strange thoughts were not to be rejected or suppressed, thereby reducing the risk of them becoming dissociated or split off and experienced as external. Instead, an interpretive framework was offered that enabled the contemplator to accept them, but to differentiate them from himself.

Hasidism also recognized that the existence of strange thoughts was only possible because something of that thought already existed within the person. It is told, for example, that the Seer of Lublin rebuked a follower who complained of having impure, alien thoughts. He said, "Alien? They are not alien—they are yours."[52] Hence, because of this personal involvement, there may be an emotional attachment to the thought that makes it very difficult to elevate. Intense contemplation during prayer may in fact awaken these feelings. This is, again, reminiscent of psychological ideas. Emotions arise from the unconscious and the ego finds them unacceptable, so they are experienced as external influences that need to be rejected.

The later hasidic teachers, however, found that the practice of elevation was too difficult for many of their followers to achieve. Practitioners were discovering that the more intensely they tried to concentrate on the thoughts in order to elevate them, the more powerful the alien thoughts became.[53] Instead of elevation, the practice of rejecting some thoughts but not others was recommended. The technique adopted was to direct one's mind away from the thought onto a more suitable topic. In cognitive therapy, techniques of distraction are utilized to help an individual manage intolerable feelings or

---

52. Weisel (1978) p. 86.
53. This is a well-known phenomenon in psychology. The harder one tries to reject or change a thought, the more likely it is to persist (*see* Linke 1989).

thoughts. The hasidic approach is similar. Recommendations were made to focus on a particular name of God. One *rebbe*, Nachman of Bratzlav, provided his followers with a special selection of Psalms to be recited.

Intrusive thoughts during prayer are not peculiar to the Jewish tradition; much has been written about them in the Christian contemplative tradition and by teachers of meditation. Practitioners of Transcendental Meditation are, for example, encouraged to see that thoughts arise quite naturally during meditation. When the mind becomes quiet and begins to relax, it releases stress in the form of thoughts. While meditating one is instructed not to become engaged with the content of the thought, nor resist it, but to return attention to the recitation of the mantra. In Buddhism there is a similar instruction. When intrusions arise, one is first to try and think of a different, incompatible thought. If this is unsuccessful, one is to ponder the effects of the troublesome thought. If this fails, one should attempt to ignore the thought and finally one can reflect on the source of the thought and try to remove it.[54]

Before we consider modern developments in Jewish prayer, it will be useful to take stock of where we have got to so far. It seems that in the general community spiritual experiences are common and that around half of the population of the United States and the United Kingdom pray each day. However, the level of daily traditional Jewish observance is low along with the Orthodox belief in God. It is likely that apart from special occasions, prayer services, at least in traditional synagogues, are poorly understood and inaccessible to most people. No doubt people attend synagogue for a variety of reasons, but probably few attend in order to have a deep experience of prayer. Heschel's experience of "radical amazement" and existential solitude, however, may be familiar to many, but they do not know that prayer may hold some of the clues to their situation.

The psychological studies of prayer suggest that traditional faith in God may not be necessary for effective prayer. This is a rather

---

54. *See* de Silva (1984).

counterintuitive conclusion. It is based on the manner in which prayer can influence individuals for the better and help them change the way they experience themselves and the world. The value of prayer lies in its effect on the pray-er.

Judaism provides a rich storehouse of the experience of prayer. Jews have been praying for two thousand years and grappling with its difficulties. It is hard to pray with attention and intention and the tradition makes allowances. It recognizes that daily prayer has profound spiritual, psychological, and practical benefits, but so does regular study and charity. Prayer, although required, is not elevated above these. Some people, however, may have a greater need, or desire, for prayer. The hasidic tradition has taught how prayer can be a bridge to the infinite.

The modern situation calls upon the deep resources of Jewish tradition to provide a response to the spiritual needs of contemporary Jews. There are many in the community today who, as ever, have been touched (like Heschel) by existential loneliness or have had experiences of wonder and awe at creation. Yet often they have found that the meditative traditions of the East, or the native traditions of North America, speak more deeply to them than does the traditional davennen of the synagogue. Also there are many women and men who feel alienated by the traditional *Siddur* because of its patriarchal language and imagery. The central synagogue organizations have responded in many different ways. Their *Siddurim* have introduced more contemplative and philosophical material, provided accessible *kabbalistic* commentaries on the central prayers, and changed the language so that it is more sensitive and gender-inclusive. Perhaps the most innovative response has been the Four Worlds approach of the movement for Jewish Spiritual Renewal founded by Rabbi Zalman Schachter-Shalomi.

DAVENNEN IN FOUR WORLDS

The Four Worlds approach integrates the spiritual perspective with the psychological and the physical. Much of traditional Jewish prayer in the past has been concerned with the intellect. It has been an exercise of the mind, the body and emotions having been largely neglected. However, unless the body is prepared, and the heart open, there is little opportunity for an experience of the realm of the spirit. Attention to the physical body and to the world of feelings should also be part of prayer. Psychological development is a necessary aspect of spiritual development. There is no need for the kind of split between the psychological and spiritual that we discussed in Chapter 3. Psychological development can be engaged in the service of the spiritual. These considerations have been the founding principles of the Four Worlds approach.

The four worlds are those of the Kabbalah.[55] Rabbi Schachter has taught how the service in the *siddur*, especially the morning service, is a model of these worlds. The hasidim developed their own *siddur* from the traditional *siddur* of the *Sephardim* and the mystically inspired *siddur* of Isaac Luria. Encoded within their *siddur* is a structure that takes the *davven-er* on a journey of ascent through these worlds. Each section of the service represents one of these worlds. In a kabbalistic *Siddur* such as *Siddur Kol Ya'acov*,[56] one can see the sections of the service marked, not with their usual exoteric title such as "morning blessings" (*Birkhat haShachar*) or "verses of song" (*Pesukey d'Zimra*), but with the names of the four worlds.

The service begins with the morning blessings. These blessings are mostly inspired by the daily activities of getting out of bed and preparing for the day. This is the world of *Assiyah* and the blessings, Rabbi Schachter wrote, "call on conscious focusing in the body, asking for its messages and responses."[57] The second world, that of *Yetzirah*, is evoked by the *Pesukey d'Zimra*. It consists largely of psalms and other poetry,

---

55. The worlds of *Atzilut* (Spirit), *Briah* (Creation), *Yetzirah* (Formation), and *Assiyah* (Action/Making/Doing). *See* Chapter 3.

56. Attributed to R. Lipshitz Jacob Koppel of Mezeritch. Printed in 1859 in Lemberg and still available, it represents one of the most elaborate and detailed kabbalistic texts. On each page, and for each passage, there are numerous diagrams and commentaries relating the words and concepts to *sephirot* and holy names.

57. Schachter (1993) p. 200.

". . . with its emphasis on the affective, attitudinal, and emotional (to) bring your body awareness with you and periodically attune it in order to use it as a *merkavah*, a vehicle for the feelings to which you will now want to direct your attention.

Moving then to the third phase (*Briah*), the *Shema* and its blessings, the intellective level, you will want to maintain your awareness of the sensory and the affective-feeling levels in order to give the intellect and its way of being with God a good base.[58]

The level of *Atzilut* is called both the "Standing Prayer" (*Amidah*) and the "Eighteen Blessings" (*Sh'mona Esreh*). Here ". . . you maintain the equipoise of body, heart and mind to give the higher self—the ever-connected God spirit— . . . the opportunity to reach the rest of your awareness and to express your wholeness and needs to the cosmos. . . ."[59]

Zalman Schachter's work has not been restricted to the psychological and spiritual dimensions of only the morning service. He has also shown how many of the prayers in the *Siddur* can be utilized in the service of psychological development and spiritual growth. For example, the prayers said before retiring at night are considered in the hasidic tradition as an opportunity to perform a *Cheshbon HaNefesh*, an accounting or self-examination of the soul. Rabbi Schachter recommends that it can also be an opportunity to review one's day and take stock of one's activities, life direction, and relationships. What patterns are we stuck in that we need to change? Perhaps this is also the right time to make entries in a personal journal. These are all recommendations that any psychotherapist can endorse.

The Four Worlds approach to Jewish prayer is avowedly holistic. It does not see the psychological world as an obstacle to be overcome, but rather as part of creation, an aspect of a spiritual path. Psychological blocks, rigid emotional patterns, developmental fixations are as much the province of prayer as are traditional petitionary, con-

---

58. Ibid p. 200.
59. Ibid p. 200.

templative, or celebratory themes. This approach has inspired many creative artists, poets, musicians, and writers to elaborate on the words of the traditional *siddur*. Now that the underlying purpose and meaning of the prayers have been made clear and rendered into a modern psychological language, it has become possible to revitalize their meaning and restore them to their place as vehicles for psychological and spiritual growth.

8

Dreams

A dream is one sixtieth of prophecy.

—Berachot 55b

Dreams are the royal road to the unconscious.

—Freud (1900)

The biblical narrative contains numerous accounts of dreams and visions. Jacob dreamed first of a ladder that reached from heaven to earth and then of a dramatic encounter with an angel. Joseph, as a young man, had prophetic dreams and was later able to interpret the dreams of others. The pages of the Hebrew bible, and most especially those concerned with the lives of the Prophets, are filled with such stories, as is the Talmud. Many rabbis gave accounts of both mundane and spectacular dreams and discussed their possible meanings. The kabbalists and mystics invoked trances and visions. The hasidic *rebbes* described mystical journeying and the stories of their exploits, particularly those of the Baal Shem Tov himself, read as if they were constructed from dreams.

How is it, though, that a chapter on dreams finds its way into a book on Jewish tradition? On the one hand it is self-evident that the Jewish people have dreamed and, just as others have done, striven to discover the meanings of their dreams. Yet dreaming is not a part of

Jewish tradition in the same way as customs such as attending the synagogue, lighting candles on a Friday night, or eating kosher food. The psychologist, however, can reply that dreams may teach us a great deal about consciousness.

The customs of a people play a major role in shaping the way they experience the world. We have seen in previous chapters how, for example, traditions establish categories for experience, mediate between the conscious and the nonconscious realms, and provide vehicles for the transformation of emotional states. The Jewish traditions concerning the dream world provide a further gateway into the depths of the inner world.

PSYCHOLOGICAL PERSPECTIVES

The psychological interest in dreams can be divided, more or less, into two broad streams. There is the concern with the content of dreams and then there is an interest in the process of dreaming itself. The first of these areas is most well known and is closely associated with the work of Freud, Jung, and other well-known psychologists. We will return to this field later. The second area is somewhat different, occupying the complex disciplines of neuropsychology and cognitive science, the area of crossover between psychology and biology. Another way of putting this would be to say that the process of dreaming radically challenges the dualist distinction between the body and the mind.

Why, however, is it important to study the biological basis of dreaming? Surely our interest is in the psychological aspects. This is a question asked by Brian Lancaster, a researcher in the field of consciousness and a student of Jewish mysticism. He uses categories similar to those offered by the kabbalists and says that explanations are needed at all levels. Although Lancaster does not use the actual Hebrew terms, he refers to three worlds or spheres: the biological, the psychological, and the spiritual.[1] Each of these spheres, he writes,

---

1. These correspond to *Assiyah*, *Yetzirah*, and *Briah*. The world of *Atzilut* (emanation) is considered, in kabbalistic terms, to be the realm that is the source of the dreams and, therefore, beyond a psychological analysis.

... bears meaning in its own terms. Whilst they are undoubtedly interdependent, each may be said to constitute a separate "world" which comprises properties irreducible to the world below it. ... A knowledge of the biology of dreaming should offer a foundation from which to approach certainly the psychological world and possibly also the spiritual world.[2]

Research into dreaming took a leap forward with the discovery of a specific brain state that reliably occurs during sleep and is thought to be associated with dreaming. This state, known as REM sleep, refers to periods in which the sleeper's eyes move very rapidly (hence Rapid Eye Movement sleep). If sleepers are woken during this stage of sleep they are more likely to report that they had been dreaming than if they had been woken during non-REM sleep. The state of the nervous system during REM sleep provides fascinating clues to the nature and function of dreaming.

During REM sleep the nervous system is extremely active which, as Lancaster points out, accurately reflects the intense nature of dreaming.[3] We frequently awaken from a dream feeling as though our senses were fully active and as though we had been busy actors in a drama. Dreaming is not like watching television. While watching television, even if we become excited or sad, we know we are passive observers of events. In a dream we are participants and the brain mirrors this. The brain sends signals to all the sensory systems and generates commands to the parts of the brain that control the muscles. In other words, during REM sleep the brain behaves as if we were fully awake and active. During non-REM sleep the physiological picture is quite different. The entire nervous system is much more quiet. This correspondence between the brain and experience during dreaming is a marvelous example of the Kabbalah's maxim "as above so below."

The actions of the nervous system during REM sleep are controlled by the brain stem.[4] This part of the brain is developmentally

---

2. Lancaster (1991) p. 134.
3. Ibid Chapter 6.
4. Specifically the pons and the thalamus.

much older than the cortex, which is the brain structure that controls the higher functions such as perception, thinking, and language. During REM sleep the visual cortex is stimulated by the brain stem in much the same way as it is when the person is awake. Recordings show characteristic bursts of electrical activity. This may account for the almost hallucinatory nature of dreams. The motor cortex shows a similar pattern; the electrical activity in this region reveals that it is just as busy as when movement commands are issued during wakefulness. Simultaneously the brain stem also inhibits the motor nerves in the spinal cord so that we are temporarily unable to move. Hence, in a dream we may feel that we are running, our brain may be responding as if we are running, but the inhibition in the spinal cord stops us from actually running. Similarly, sensory nerves in our skin and muscles are inhibited. This means that in REM sleep we are less aware of our bodies. It is true to say, therefore, that while dreaming we occupy a world only of images.

REM sleep seems to serve a useful function. If individuals are deprived of REM sleep (by waking them every time they enter it), then they will have a greater than normal amount of REM sleep the next time they have the opportunity for uninterrupted sleep. Babies in the womb spend most of their time asleep, and a great proportion of this time (up to 100 percent at some points) is spent in REM sleep. Infants may sleep up to fourteen hours a day and about 50 percent of this time may be spent in REM sleep. The 1-year-old's sleep consists of 20 to 25 percent REM sleep, a pattern that will continue throughout life.

There are several different theories about what the function of REM sleep might be. One purely biological theory suggests that REM sleep protects the brain from slipping into a dangerous state of unconsciousness during the night. Because, during REM sleep, our nervous system is activated, it prevents us from slipping into permanent unconsciousness. Another biological theory is that REM sleep provides an opportunity for animals (animals dream also) to integrate experiences that they have had during the day. They can safely "rehearse" predatory or mating behavior, for example, while asleep.

Cognitive psychologists have postulated that REM sleep assists with information processing. During REM sleep new information absorbed during the previous day is sorted and coded so that it can be stored in memory. Current experiences are thus integrated with past memories so that learning is optimized. Brian Lancaster has developed this idea even further and has suggested that this coding process is an important part of the way in which we form our identity. By identity he means experiencing ourselves in a unified way, as an "I." It is because of this "I" that our present activities and our memories of past activities have a subjective sense of continuity and coherence. Tagging memories so that they are connected with these other previous memories gives us this sense of "I." On the other hand, if we detach our memories from this "I," such as during meditation, then we are left only with memory itself, which is closer to an experience of pure consciousness and resembles Jung's idea of the "Self." [5]

Lancaster also speculates about the nature of lucid dreaming. During lucid dreaming the dreamer is aware that he or she is dreaming and may even be able to influence the course of the events in the dream. It is as though a part of oneself is detached from the dream and is able to watch the experience. Lancaster refers to this aspect as the "watcher," and he relates it to those parts of the brain that are responsible for interpreting images received and integrating them. This aspect of the process may be responsible for creating the sense of "I."

During lucid dreams the sharp division between the dream state and the waking state breaks down. During a lucid dream the dreamer has "woken up" to the fact that he or she is dreaming. Similarly, a practitioner of meditation or contemplative prayer may "wake up" to the illusory nature of "reality" and become aware of the spiritual nature of the physical world. We are also reminded of the abilities of the shamanic healers who are able to construct and direct visionary experiences for their patients. From the Jewish tradition Lancaster draws on the *Hekalot* literature, which is a genre of writing that de-

---

5. It would probably be better to refer, as phenomenologists do, to "remembering" rather than memory. Remembering is closer to consciousness than the mental structure of memory.

scribes the experiences of the "riders of the Chariot."[6] These riders memorized complex formulae to be chanted as they contemplated Ezekiel's vision of the Chariot. By this means they created for themselves an etheric body (the chariot) through which they were able to experience the "heavenly palaces."

The biological basis of the lucid dream is the same as that of the ordinary dream. It seems as though the higher functions are grafted onto the same brain structures as the lower functions ("as above so below"). It also seems that visual imagery, which seems to be the most salient feature of dreams both psychologically and physiologically, plays a vitally important role in brain functioning at all levels. Visual imagery may have an important survival function, may assist cognitive function, and may also serve in the creation of visionary experiences.

There is an *Aggadic* passage in the Talmud that hints at the connections between the physical, psychological, and spiritual levels. The passage relates how in the womb a light is held above the child's head enabling it to see from one end of the world to another and that while in the womb it is taught the entire Torah.[7] The Talmud is, perhaps, teaching us about both a cognitive and a spiritual role for dreaming. The cognitive Torah that the child is learning may be early forms of pattern development that lay down the basis for future cognitive structures and schemas. The spiritual Torah may be the deep pattern of life goals, the archetypal patterns recognized in Jungian psychology.

We now turn our attention to the content of dreams. There is no universally accepted system of dream interpretation and, in fact, empirically oriented psychologists have tended to reject the notion that a codex of dream symbolism is at all possible. It seems self-evident that personal life experiences and social and cultural factors will all influence the content of dreams and that any serious attempt at dream interpretation must first consider the individual's unique life circumstances.

---

6. Attributed largely to Rabbi Ishmael ben Elisha, the *HeKalot* literature, consist largely of ecstatic poetry composed between 0 and 500 c.e. Some of this poetry is preserved in the Ashkenazi High Holiday liturgy.

7. *Niddah* 30b.

Freud was probably not the first to see in dreams the key to an individual's psychic life. He was, however, the first to systematically present a view of how such material could be used in the treatment of patients with psychological or psychiatric illnesses. It was some time after publication of *The Interpretation of Dreams* (1900) that his work gained public recognition. However, he had considered it to be his most important work from the outset. Freud's proposition was that in a dream repressed material from the unconscious emerges in symbolic form. This led him to distinguish between the *latent* content of a dream and the *manifest* content. The latent content was, for Freud, the real meaning of the dream and presented to the analyst the means to interpret the dreamer's unconscious wishes and desires. It was for this reason that he, famously, referred to dreams as "the royal road to the unconscious."

According to Freud, dreams play an important role in protecting the dreamer's sleep. Dreams disguise unconscious wishes and desires that would otherwise be unacceptable to the individual and would disturb the person while sleeping. Dreams are constructed by the unconscious in order to fulfill the wishes of the dreamer so that the person does not have to act out these wishes in real life. The unconscious has its own mechanisms for achieving this. Wishes, for example, are condensed and combined into an abbreviated form so that a single word or image has multiple meanings. The material is further disguised by displacement, that is, having one thing stand for another. In particular, the ideas, objects, and events appear in symbolic form. Freud was working primarily, at that time, with individuals who had symptoms of hysteria and hysterical paralysis. Hysteria, he believed, was largely associated with the repression of sexual impulses and, therefore, many of the symbols he identified were associated with the sexual organs and the sexual act. His examples of phallic symbols are, nowadays, very well known even if many psychologists do not accept that they mean exactly what Freud said they mean.

Jung's approach took Freud's notions one step further. He too saw the images that arise in dreams as symbolic. However, his interest was not in symbolic "wish fulfillment" or the details of intrapsychic conflict, but in the archetypal qualities of the symbols. These, he held, arose not from the personal unconscious of the individual, but from the collective unconscious of the human race.[8] In this respect the content of dreams reflects a big picture, that of the myths that permeate the culture. When a new symbol has manifested in a dream, an aspect of the collective unconscious has emerged. This may represent a significant stage both in the psychological development of an individual and in the civilization.

Jung spoke of "big dreams" or "numinous" dreams. He was also interested in repetitive dreams and dream series. In these he felt he could discern how an individual's psychological life is aligned with the lines of the myths of the culture. Jung's studies of symbolism, mythology, and alchemy provided him with a rich vocabulary with which to analyze and describe meanings in the dream world. His tendency, and that of his students after him, was to offer the interpretations of these symbols in a fixed and sometimes quite rigid way.[9] He would sometimes, for example, interpret the meaning of a dream after only very brief contact with the dreamer. Even today it is possible to receive an interpretation of a dream by mail, without the dream analyst having any contact with, or knowing anything about, the person who had the dream. This approach is quite at odds with later developments in the use of dreams in therapy. Jung's great contribution, however, was to link the personal dream with the great themes of culture and with the spiritual world. It is easy to see why his approach has been so influential in the realms of psychology, spirituality, and religion.

Following on from the pioneering work of Freud and Jung there have been numerous other psychological theories of dream interpretation. Adler, for example, understood dreams as a kind of coded dress rehearsal. Something that was about to happen is unconsciously worked through in advance. The "third force" psychotherapies of the

---

8. *See* Chapter 3 for a summary of Jung's ideas.

9. There are significant variations between different schools of Jungian thought. Perhaps the strictest approach is that of the Zurich school (Jung was Swiss), which has developed the art of dream symbol interpretation to the greatest extent.

existential and humanistic schools adopted a more transparent viewpoint. Gestalt therapy, for example, sets the individual at the center of the dream and suggests that all the characters in a dream are different aspects of the individual's personality.[10] This enables the therapist to work with a dream directly in the therapy session. In Gestalt therapy the client may be encouraged to talk directly to the dream, as if it were an entity in itself, or to adopt the role of one of the protagonists or characters in the dream. In this way the personal meaning of the dream may become clearer and the various layers of meaning, including the archetypal, may be discerned. This technique allows the role of the "watcher" to develop, and one can begin to have some influence over the drama as in a lucid dream. It seems as though this is yet another area where the insights of psychotherapy, cognitive psychology, and spirituality may meet.

JUDAISM AND DREAMS

> A dream that has not had its interpretation is like an unopened letter.[11]

> Dumplings in a dream are not dumplings, but a dream!
> —Yiddish proverb

The traditional Jewish perspective is rather ambivalent about dreams. It is certainly clear that the epic dreams of the biblical characters were revered by the rabbis, but the consensus seems to have been that dreams should be treated with some suspicion. This is based on two principles. First there is the biblical warning against listening to the words of dreamers and prophets.[12] This was because of the presumed danger that they might turn the people away from the one true God and become idol worshipers. It seems reasonable to assume that this prohibition was focused primarily on the declarations of visionaries outside of the Mosaic tradition. The second principle is that,

---

10. For examples, *see* accounts by the founder of Gestalt therapy, Fritz Perls (1969) pp. 237–245.

11. *Berachot* 55a.

12. Deuteronomy 13:12–16.

according to the teachings of the rabbis, the age of prophecy ended with the destruction of the Temple in 70 c.e. Dreams and prophecies subsequent to this were not to be trusted or relied upon.

It is somewhat inconsistent, therefore, to find that there are a number of detailed discussions about dreams in the Talmud. No doubt, as people continued to have dreams and tried to understand them, there was a need for a rabbinic response. Indeed the rabbis themselves discussed the meanings of their own dreams. At one point there was an established profession of dream interpreters, with twenty-four practitioners based in Jerusalem.

There is a vast literature on dreams spread throughout Jewish texts. Dreams were widely regarded as a form of prophecy, and the rabbis were concerned to establish their status in *halacha*. Was an individual required to respond to a message or instruction received in a dream? And what if a dream provided evidence about an important legal matter? Should this be accepted as evidence by a *Bet Din* or rejected? Rabbi Shmuel Boteach has reviewed the halachic literature and drawn some conclusions.[13] As an Orthodox rabbi he was interested in determining the Torah view of dreams. Boteach's finding was that the expressed concern of the Talmud and the codes is that it is not always possible to distinguish between a dream that comes from a high source and one that emanates from the ordinary life and concerns of an individual. In rabbinic parlance dreams may be said to be "true" or "false." Dreams may be determined by such prosaic factors as the condition of one's stomach or, and here the rabbis anticipated today's cognitive psychologists, preoccupations and thoughts from the day. It is for these reasons that the rabbis were both fascinated by and wary of dreams.

Shmuel Boteach also set himself the task of contrasting the Torah view of dreams with the Freudian one. Overall Boteach finds that he has little sympathy with Freud's view. The interpretations made by psychoanalysts of symbolic communication in dreams often seemed to him to be too far-fetched to be taken seriously. Furthermore, the pious Jew should take care to ensure that his thoughts each day are

---

13. Boteach (1991).

pure. Therefore, as far as Boteach is concerned, dreams cannot function as wish fulfillment, as there should be no repressed wishes for sexual or other gratification to be fulfilled. Boteach's view of the rabbinic texts, while thorough, seems to be more concerned with an ethical perspective than a psychological one. He does not appear to give much credit to the role of the unconscious. As we shall see below, however, he does recognize that there is also a far deeper level to dreaming.

The Jewish religious view of dreams is that, as they are potentially a source of prophecy, they must be treated with considerable respect. After all, a dream may be a direct communication from God. If one has a bad dream, therefore, there is also considerable concern. The Talmud records a procedure for dealing with bad dreams.[14] The dreamer is instructed to take the dream to a *Bet Din* who will "turn" the dream so that good comes out of the dream and an evil prophecy will not be fulfilled. The dream is "turned" by the performance of a ritual, the utterance of a formulaic prayer, and the recitation of biblical verses. These verses are the key to the procedure. The dreamer should quote a verse emphasizing the positive aspect of an experience in order to counteract any negative consequences that might accrue if a more negative verse was thought of first.[15] The Talmud provides some examples. "Rabbi Yehoshua ben Levi said: if one sees a river in his dream, he should rise early and say, 'Behold I will extend peace to her like a river' before another verse occurs such as 'For distress will come in like a river' (Isaiah 66:12). . . . "[16]

This approach to disturbing dreams is strikingly similar to the techniques advocated by cognitive therapists for dealing with negative thoughts. As it is negative thoughts that result in negative moods, changing the thoughts should have some beneficial effects on mood. Changing thoughts takes training and dedication, as anyone who practices meditation will know. The assistance of an affirmative ritual along with support from others who are attempting the same thing may make all the difference between success and failure.

14. *Berachot* 55b.
15. *Berachot* 56b.
16. Ibid.

The interpretation of a dream was considered to be as vital as the dream itself. The Talmud advises that if a dream makes one miserable it should be taken to a dream interpreter.[17] From a religious standpoint this makes complete sense. Although dreams will include some wasteful and nonsensical material, all dreams also include some element of the truth.[18] If a dream has been sent by God then it must be understood (correctly) so that the revelation of God's will may be achieved. This is not so different from psychoanalytic practice if the theological assumptions are ignored. An analyst will consider the timing of a dream to be important. Some aspect of the unconscious is now ready to become known because the relationship between the therapist and the client has developed to the extent that the dream is sure to be interpreted.

Dream interpretation in talmudic times was a precarious business. Two rabbis, Abaye and Rabbah, had the same dream, and they each took it to Bar Hedya for an interpretation.[19] Abaye paid Bar Hedya the sum of one *zuz*, but Rabbah paid nothing. Now Bar Hedya was a talented dream interpreter and able to perceive all the possible meanings and implications in a dream (he may also have been an astrologer). To those who paid a fee he would interpret the good omens and to those who didn't pay he interpreted only the bad omens. Hence Abaye was told that his business would prosper and that he would not eat because of the extreme joy that he would experience. Rabbah, on the other hand, was told that his business would fail and that he would become so distressed that he would have no appetite to eat. A second dream brought a similar bias in interpretation. It would seem that Bar Hedya had a good eye for business. Rabbah, however, eventually caught on to what was happening and paid Bar Hedya a fee. Rabbah then brought five further dreams for interpretation and received five favorable predictions. Interestingly, at least one of these dreams calls out for a challenging psychoanalytic interpretation. "I dreamt that Abaye's villa collapsed and I was covered by its dust."

---

17. *Berachot* 55b.
18. *See Berachot* 55a.
19. *Berachot* 56a and 56b.

Bar Hedya, however, missed the opportunity and flattered Rabbah instead. His interpretation, "Abaye will die and his position as head of the academy will fall to you," makes no reference to the possibility of unconscious envy or wish fulfillment. Bar Hedya's interpretation of Rabbah's final dream also appears to lack psychological sophistication. "I dreamt that my head split open and my brains fell out" received the reply, "the stuffing will fall out of your pillow. . . ."

The medieval attitude to dreams by the Jewish commentators was essentially rationalistic. Maimonides discussed dreaming in his *Guide to the Perplexed*. He considered dreams to be the "seeing of resemblances during sleep" and he believed that they consisted of images and experiences from the day. He paid little attention to the contents of a dream and thought this aspect insignificant. Nevertheless, he recognized different levels of dreams and categorized them. The highest-level dreams are prophetic dreams. Examples in the Bible are the dreams of Jacob, Daniel, and Solomon. It is these dreams that are the "one-sixtieth of prophecy" referred to in the Talmud. These dreams derive directly from the will of God, but the spiritual impulses are mixed with the imaginative faculties of the individual and, therefore, the message often appears in a coded or symbolic form that needs interpretation by a divinely inspired prophet. The second-level dreams are the ordinary dreams, such as those of Joseph and Pharaoh. These are dreams that do not require symbolic interpretation but clearly state what they mean in simple terms. The final category comprises the wicked dreams of sorcerers and demons. These result from the deliberate invocation of dreams such as those outlawed in the Deuteronomic text mentioned above. Such invocations provide opportunities for evil powers to influence the symbolism of dreams and to confound the message. As we shall see below, this is not the same as dream incubation, which has a more positive role in Jewish thought.

In keeping with his rationalist bias, however, Maimonides was keen to explain the position of the Talmudists who had gone to some lengths to interpret dreams. He even condoned the practice of *Ta'anit Cholemot* (dream fasts) undertaken in the event of having had a bad dream. *Ta'anit Cholemot* were the customary fasts after a bad dream in order to purify oneself and reverse any harsh judgment that might be implied. Some even fasted on Shabbat, a day when fasting is not normally allowed. Maimonides accepted the practice because it provided an opportunity for repentance and self-examination. The customs surrounding dream fasts were later codified by Joseph Caro in Safed. Caro's approach provides us with a good example of the mixing of the legalistic and mystical approaches to dreams. He reviewed the rabbinic literature on dream fasts and concluded that it was only permissible to fast on Shabbat if one had dreamed of a Torah scroll being burned, or the concluding prayers of the Day of Atonement (*Neilah*), or the beams of one's house, or one's teeth falling out. Later Caro reported that the correctness of his conclusions had been confirmed by his *Maggid* whom he regularly encountered in a trance.[20]

In 1515, some time after Maimonides, a rather different approach was published by Solomon Alimoli in Salonica. His book, originally entitled *Mefasher Chelin* ("Dream Mediator"), proved to be an extremely popular work. This was, perhaps, because Alimoli's purpose was to provide an accessible system of dream interpretation for ordinary people. The book was republished in Constantinople almost immediately, but under the new title *Piron Cholomit* ("The Interpretation of Dreams"), anticipating Freud's volume by nearly four hundred years. *Piron Cholomit* was printed in 1518, in 1551, and in Cracow in 1576. There have been many subsequent publications and it was issued in Yiddish in Brooklyn in 1902. In 1990 an English translation and commentary was published by Joel Covitz, a rabbi and Jungian psychotherapist.

Alimoli's book was written in the traditional style of rabbinic texts. It is full of scriptural citations and references to standard rabbinic works that he assumed his readers would have been familiar with and understand. He also made frequent reference to mystical literature, most especially *The Zohar*.[21] Joel Covitz has provided many of the sources for this material in his translation, so that Alimoli's work is now far more accessible to the modern reader.

---

20. *See* Chapter 1.
21. "The Book of Splendor"—a mystical commentary on the Bible attributed to *Shimeon Bar Yochai*.

The purpose of dreams, according to *Piron Cholomit*, is communication. People desire to know the essence of reality, but are unable to achieve this without divine help. This help may come as prophecy or in the form of a dream. Anything that happens in this world is first announced from on high. However, we are not usually able to understand the meaning of a dream without assistance; hence, we need dream interpreters. The source of dreams, for Alimoli, is unquestionably God. But as Covitz points out, it is not clear which aspect or quality of God is involved.[22] Alimoli often refers, not directly to God, but to the "Master of Dreams" or the "Spinner of Dreams." Covitz explains that in the Talmud the "Master of Dreams" is described as an angel[23] and that in *The Zohar* this angel is identified as Gabriel.

Gabriel has many of the qualities of the Greek Hermes and, in Jungian terms, represents an aspect of the self that mediates between the conscious and unconscious and is in communication with archetypal realms. Dreams are a communication from the highest aspects of the self to the ordinary mind. By identifying Gabriel in this way, Covitz makes an important connection between the spiritual and psychological realms. He put it like this: "Angels, like Gabriel, represent the whisperings of our minds that we commonly refer to as intuition. Intuitions can come to us through dream work and it is the task of the dream interpreter to help uncover these hidden meanings and allusions."[24]

The psychological parallels between Alimoli's approach and modern psychology become even more apparent when the issue of distinguishing between "true" and "untrue" dreams is considered. The majority of dreams consist of representations of a dreamer's everyday thoughts and mundane concerns. It is the responsibility of a dreamer to realize that such dreams are insignificant and that their source may not be as high as the level of prophecy. Similarly, not every dream needs to be brought to a therapist for an interpretation, nor should a therapist interpret every dream that is presented. Aspects of the

---

22. *See* Postscript for a brief discussion about the names and aspects of God.
23. *Berachot* 10b.
24. Covitz (1990) p. 62.

dreamer's personality can also be expected to enter into a dream. Alimoli relates how in one of Pharaoh's dreams, Pharaoh pictures himself standing by a river (Genesis 41:17). Alimoli suggests that Pharaoh had a thought in the dream that he could walk on water.[25] This thought arose because earlier in the day he had been walking by the river contemplating his own status as an Egyptian God and believed that he had created the river and owned it. In modern psychological language we might say that Alimoli is suggesting that Pharaoh's unconscious narcissism found expression in the dream.

There are other similarities. Alimoli based much of his discussion of dreams on a text from the Book of Job. One of Job's "comforters," Elihu, says, "For God speaks in one way and then two, though man does not perceive it. In a dream, in a vision of the night, when deep sleep falls upon men, while they slumber in their beds . . ." (Job 33:14–15). Alimoli suggests that Elihu is obliquely referring to the three levels of dreams. The ordinary dreams occur "when deep sleep falls," that is, when one is sleeping deeply. This accords with the laboratory sleep studies that show that periods of REM sleep do not occur immediately but later and are associated with other physiological markers of deep sleep. The "Slumber in their beds," conversely, are "wicked" dreams. These occur during the early part of the night, which is most closely associated with deliberate invocations. Clinical psychologists are aware of sleep disturbances related to stress, anxiety, and preoccupations that occur at this time. Individuals with sleep-onset insomnia (a persistent difficulty in falling asleep) often experience disturbing intrusive thoughts and compulsive ruminations while trying to fall asleep.[26] Furthermore, there is a common form of hallucination, known as hypnagogic imagery, that may occur while falling asleep. This imagery is often disturbing and, although not psychotic, may be reported by people experiencing extreme stress.

Alimoli also suggested a rubric for distinguishing between true and false dreams based on the individual's psychophysiological response. He says that if the images in a dream are so intense that they

---

25. Ibid, p. 28.
26 See Morin (1994).

cause excitement, anger, or fear, then this is a sign that it is a true dream. If, however, the images are insipid and arouse no strong feelings, then the dream is not true. Most schools of psychotherapy would recognize this pattern and employ a similar system to evaluate the power of an experience. Psychoanalysts, for example, might look for catharsis in response to an interpretation. Gestalt therapists might prompt their clients to pay attention to their body's responses while describing or reenacting a dream. Cognitive therapists seek to identify "hot cognitions," and body psychotherapists may speak of "discharge" or "streaming." Even within Judaism there are other parallels. We saw in Chapter 2 that the advocates of the *Musar* school utilized emotional excitement in their training methods (*hitpa'alut*) and that, for the hasidim, ecstasy in prayer was a means of attaining contact with the higher worlds.

Alimoli's own explanation of the virtue of his system was somewhat different. His perspective no doubt reflects the point of view, widely held in his age, that the will and the body are separate and antagonistic to each other. Excitement in a dream occurs, he suggested, in order to diminish the bodily humors so that the intellect will be strengthened and only the will remains. The power of the body is, therefore, lessened and the will is free to receive divine inspiration. This assumption of an absolute split between the mind and the body would no longer find support in modern psychological, philosophical, or even religious circles. That the body is an aware receptacle of the divine is a cardinal feature of the principle of God's immanence.

The apparent conflict between these explanations can be resolved if we adopt a kabbalistic perspective. At the physical level, *Olam HaAssiyah*, there is a complete split between the spiritual, psychological, and physical levels. Yet there are parallels between them. As we have already seen, Brian Lancaster has described how precisely the experience of dreaming is reflected in the activity of the brain. As we move up the levels the division between these states, or between body and soul, diminishes. At the higher levels, the very source of dreams, there are still distinctions but they are not so apparent.

There are also hasidic teachings about the nature and source of dreams. An infinite spiritual energy or light surrounds the world. This is the *or makif*. There is also, within creation rather than surrounding it, the *or p'nimi*, the hidden light associated with the internal radiance, which is the light of the intellect. According to Shmuel Boteach dreams emanate from the *or makif*.[27] During the night while we sleep the *Or p'nimi* is diminished and, therefore, concealed. Hence revelation is available from the higher plane.

The purpose of a dream, according to Alimoli, is to communicate philosophical wisdom. This is not so very different from the modern psychological view that speaks of information processing occurring in dreams and of communication from the unconscious. The discovery of the chemical structure of benzene was such an example. This had been elusive until a dream of a snake eating its tail suggested that the structure of the hydrocarbon might be a ring. In order to ensure, however, that the philosophical wisdom obtained in a dream would be successfully communicated, Alimoli provided a "dream dictionary." It was this section that probably accounted for his book's popularity outside of the circle of scholars.

Jung considered dream dictionaries "vulgar." Providing ready-made interpretations of the symbols in dreams is a disservice to the power and individuality of a person's dream and the forces of the collective unconscious. Alimoli also understood this. He wrote, "It is impossible to enumerate the unlimited possibilities that can appear in dreams. . . . It is well known that . . . generalized interpretations are not meant to be used by everyone. All interpretations must be weighed against the particular dreamer's situation in life and his basic concerns, the context within which the dream occurred."[28] Alimoli's dictionary, therefore, provides a glimpse into aspects of the Jewish (or at least rabbinic) consciousness of his period. We will select a few examples to give a flavor of his ideas.

Alimoli cites a talmudic passage that says if a man dreams of having sexual intercourse with a married woman, and he does not know her or did not think of her the previous evening, then he is

---

27. Boteach (1991).
28. Covitz (1990) p. 79.

assured of a place in Paradise.[29] Apart from the fact that the Talmud makes no reference to women's sexual dreams (as they are not being addressed), this interpretation appears rather odd. The Talmud seems to be suggesting the possible role of sexual fantasies and wish fulfillment in determining the content of dreams, but is also hinting at the possibility of a disembodied, perhaps mystical, sexual imagery. Alimoli comments that "sexual pleasure is one sixtieth of the pleasure in paradise" and, as "stolen waters are sweeter" (Proverbs 9:17), the pleasure of sex with a married woman is even greater. The patriarchal assumptions here are obvious and are stated very clearly by Alimoli when he goes on to say, by way of further explaining the talmudic passage, that " . . . the dreamer is partaking of not only his own portion but also the portion of another, which is the case with a married woman [who also belongs to another]".[30] In other words the dreamer is experiencing double pleasure, his own and that of the woman's husband whom he has stolen from. The experience of the woman in this passage is considered irrelevant (she is an object), and the adulterous dream is elevated to a mystical level by the rabbis who, presumably, did not wish to conceive of themselves as having immoral dreams.

The sexual theme in the passage continues and takes up the problem of incestuous dreams. If a man dreams of intercourse with his mother, "he may expect to obtain understanding, since it says, Yea thou wilt call understanding 'mother' (Proverbs 2:3)." And if he dreams of intercourse with his sister, "he may expect to obtain wisdom, since it says, say to wisdom, thou art my sister" (Proverbs 7:2). These passages are interesting because they are evidence of explicitly sexual dreams in an age well before Freud, who was so heavily criticized for having brought this type of material into the public arena. They also call into question the remarks of Freud's Orthodox rabbinic critics, such as Shmuel Boteach, who claim that Freud's emphasis on the sexual content of dreams is irreconcilable with the talmudic view.

---

29. Covitz (1990) p. 81. The talmudic passage is from *Berachot* 57a.
30. Ibid.

Alimoli's method of dream interpretation utilizes techniques very similar to those of the authors of the *midrash*. There is extensive use of word play and allusions to folklore, mythology, and literature that the users of his dictionary would have been aware of. Hence, for example, a dream of finding a corpse in the house is interpreted as a sign of peace (*shalom*). The Hebrew word *shalom* means both "peace" and "wholeness"; therefore, according to Covitz's interpretation, dreaming of a dead person in the house is a good sign because, having fully observed the mourning customs of sitting *shivah* (*see* Chapter 5), one has not repressed the memory of a dead loved one and is at peace and feeling whole.[31] There are numerous other examples in Alimoli's text.

Before concluding this section it is worthwhile to consider a revelation about dreams from Joseph Caro's *Maggid*. Caro recorded this extract of automatic speech in his diary around the beginning of the sixteenth century and it probably predates Alimoli's work by only a few years. In any case it is well known that there were communications between a mystical group in Salonica and the kabbalistic circle in Safed.

> Know that if you see your garments torn in a dream there is something wrong with our deeds. It is a dream that Gabriel brings about. He extends throughout the world, even among the nations. If you will ask: Why is it that a man grieves over a calamity in a dream more than over one which befalls him while he is awake? It is because in man's waking life the soul is clothed by the body. No sense of urgency is experienced because the body acts as a shield. But the harm seen in a dream oppresses the naked soul so that it experiences far greater anguish.[32]

This passage summarizes a great deal of what we have said about dreams. Dreams are sent to warn us and they emanate from Gabriel. It is noteworthy that the *Maggid* identifies so closely with Caro when it says "our deeds" rather than saying "your deeds." The unification

---

31. Covitz (1990) pp. 82–84.
32. *Maggid Mesharim*, translated by Louis Jacobs (1976) p. 106.

between Caro's conscious self and his higher self (the *Maggid*) in the trance state seems complete. The *Maggid* also refers to the vividness of experience during a dream. It is almost as if the *Maggid* had knowledge of brain physiology: that while the sensory systems of the cortex are fully stimulated the motor response systems are inhibited.

DREAM INCUBATION

Before one retires to bed at night there are standard prayers in the *siddur* to be recited. These include the *Shema*, prayers for forgiveness and a prayer for protection. The prayer for protection invokes the presence, or energy, of the archangels: Michael on the right, Gabriel on the left, Uriel in front, Raphael behind, and the Shechinah above the head. Symbolically these represent the powers of mercy, strength, light, healing, and protection. Jewish tradition holds that sleep is one sixtieth of death and that at night the soul slips away from the body into another realm. The Kabbalah expresses this idea as the soul wandering while the body sleeps. The practice of dream incubation is an attempt to influence the soul on its journey and, thereby, receive guidance about some issue pertaining to the dreamer's current situation. Dream incubation techniques can be found in many spiritual traditions and are also, nowadays, a feature of many forms of psychotherapy.

The Jewish ritual for dream incubation is called *Sha'alot Cholem*. This literally means "dream question" and implies that just as one may take a question about *halacha* to a rabbi (a *sheilah*), one may also take a question about one's life to the "Master of Dreams." There are a variety of different techniques but they share common elements.[33] Detailed preparation is required so that the chance of receiving a significant dream is maximized. Attention is paid to the set-up of the room where the person will sleep. The individual may fast during the previous day and then eat only after sunset. They will avoid meat and wine, and drink other liquids and eat only raisins or figs in moderate quantities. Some versions require a visit to the *mikvah*; all involve the

---

33. *See* Covitz (1990) Chapter 6.

recitation of biblical verses. Many of the customs require the question to be written and placed under the pillow and a commitment by the dreamer to honor the dream that is received and to act in accordance with its interpretation.

Dream incubation techniques have been widely practiced among Jews. The Bible speaks of schools of prophets. These schools would no doubt have trained their students in techniques of dream incubation, meditation, ecstatic dance, and prayer in order to evoke dreams and visions. Many sections of the Jewish community would, at some time or other, have practiced variants of the dream incubation technique. Even the *Mitnagdim* were advised by the Vilna Gaon that the reason for the existence of sleep was so that the divine mysteries could be conveyed in dreams.[34] The foremost practitioners, however, were the hasidic *rebbes*. Their practice was to sleep for only a few hours in the early part of the night. They would then rise at midnight and sit on the floor, cover their heads in ashes, and weep over the destruction of the Temple and the exile of the Shechinah. As a result, many of them reported fantastic dreams and visions. In a rare document, attributed to the Baal Shem Tov himself, we have a first-hand account of a mystical ascent of the soul in which he encountered the Messiah as well as witnessed the activities of the heavenly court on Rosh Hashanah, which is the traditional annual day of judgment. Buber also records an account of the Baal Shem entering deep trance states during the night. These states were so deep that he almost stopped breathing, and his wife had difficulty in recalling him from sleep.[35]

The practice of dream incubation continues still in some sections of the Jewish community, most especially during a particular festival in northern Israel. The festival of Lag b'Omer is the occasion for a mass commemoration at the ancient tomb of Rabbi Shimeon Bar Yochai on Mount Meiron just outside of Safed.[36] Over 150,000 pil-

---

34. Hoffman (1981) p. 152.
35. Buber (1955).
36. Shimeon Bar Yochai (second century c.e., known in rabbinic texts as *Rashby*) was, according to tradition, the author of *The Zohar*. There are a great many legends about him, and he is credited with many mystical and supranormal powers. His *Yahrzeit* is on the day of a minor festival (Lag b'Omer) associated with

grims attend each year, the majority of whom are either Jewish immigrants from Morocco or their descendants. The commemoration
is known as the *Hillulah* and involves each pilgrim in making a personal visit to Shimeon Bar Yochai's tomb. Most of the available time,
however (often several days), is spent picnicking on the mountain and
celebrating with family and friends. Many of the participants expect
to receive guidance from Rabbi Shimeon during their stay and arrive
on the mountain prepared with their own specific concerns and requests. Often the responses come in the form of a visitational dream
from the rabbi.

A study of these dreams was conducted in the early 1980s in
which the details of one hundred dreams were collected and analyzed.[37]
Interestingly, 80 percent of the visitational dreams were dreamed by
women. In these dreams Rabbi Shimeon would be visualized in quite
some detail, although occasionally he would appear in symbolic form
(e.g., as a lion or as a horse) or in disguise (perhaps as a neighbor
who had the name of Shimeon). Often the Rabbi would appear as a
physician, which is unsurprising as this reflected one of the main
concerns of the dreamers who sought relief for physical ailments and
cures. Other common themes of the dreams were the naming of children, concerns about infertility, requests for divine protection, and
help with economic difficulties. The authors of the study point out
that the images in the dreams strongly reflected both the beliefs and
attitudes of mystical Judaism and the wider Moroccan custom of ven-
erating saints.

In modern Jewish life very little attention is paid to dreams. The
specific concerns and techniques that were once a key element of Jewish consciousness have now faded. Those who do pay attention to their
dreams are likely to be motivated by Jungian or other forms of psychotherapy and a desire for spiritual growth rather than Jewish belief. The language of dream interpretation is, nowadays, that of psy-

---

celebration and levity. Because this festival is also associated with fertility, weddings
are often held on this day.
37. Bilu and Abromovitch (1985).

chology, as the explicitly religious images and symbols no longer have as much significance. There are occasional exceptions such as the Moroccan Jews at Meiron and, perhaps, those Lubavitcher hasidim who visit the grave and shrine of their recently deceased *rebbe* and seek his help and intervention. Otherwise the distance between the rich interpretive language of the past and today's concerns is very great. There is no going back, but there may be a way forward.

The secularism that seems to pervade so much of the Jewish community today may be only skin deep. As I hope we have seen throughout this book, beneath the surface of many of the traditions and customs of Judaism there is often profound psychological and spiritual wisdom. Many people are dissatisfied with superficial customs and are anxious to explore these deeper levels of experience. Jewish people may take up meditation, study philosophy, or enter into psychotherapy in order to explore the inner reaches of their existence. They are, perhaps, on the same path as their Jewish ancestors who were sensitive to the *ta'amai mitzvot* (literally "taste of the *mitzvot*"), the inner meanings and purposes of the traditions. The integration of the religious insights of the past and the psychological language of today may create the opportunity for a richer Jewish identity than that of, simply, ethnic identification.

Postscript: A Note on God

Acentral theme of this work has been that Jewish practices are maintained in the absence of belief in God. However, nowhere have we considered what the tradition actually means by God, or quite what it is that people do not believe in. Space permits only a brief excursion into this complex arena.

In general use, God is an English noun referring to an all-powerful, supernatural deity that created and rules the world. In this sense God is often ascribed human, usually male, attributes, and is considered to be aware of the needs of individuals and groups and able to intervene in human history. God, in this general sense, is not particularly Jewish, but the product of the Western Judeo-Christian heritage. It is precisely this type of God figure that many people do not believe in.

This does not mean at all that the population is entirely secular. Far from it. Religious experiences are common and, in recent times, on the increase. Gallup polls in the United States found that, in 1962, 20 percent of the population reported having had a religious or mystical experience. By 1967 this figure had risen to 41 percent.[1] In Great

---

1. Back and Bourke (1970).

Britain surveys conducted on behalf of the Alistair Hardy Institute in 1982 found that 36 percent disclosed a spiritual or religious experience, and in 1987 48 percent did so.[2] Spiritual experiences, however, need not be equated with religious experiences, and neither category is necessarily related to religious belief or faith in a "prime mover." Experiences are interpreted psychologically, and if they happen in the concert hall or under the influence of drugs they may not be considered religious at all. If they occur in the synagogue or church, then a religious interpretation is more likely.

These experiences of inner peace, oneness, timelessness, and joy are the "peak experiences" that Maslow described (*see* Chapter 3) and are, in their very essence, ineffable. It is in the nature of religion, however, to attempt to put them into words. The language chosen is metaphor. And not any metaphor will do. The metaphor must be powerful enough to carry sufficient nuance of meaning to do justice to the experience and convey something of its quality to others. It is a limitation, therefore, that the common metaphors in Jewish liturgy are male. "Father," for example, conveys the sense of protectiveness that people describe during moments of religious awareness, but not the feeling of nurturance. "King" invokes the sense of awe and power that accompanies moments of "radical amazement," but probably not the intuition of divine guidance.[3]

Theologians might argue that the concept of God is beyond gender. However, as Jenny Goodman has shown, the common assumption of the maleness of God becomes apparent when we begin to use alternative pronouns. She wrote, "What happens when we say 'She' instead? The first thing to happen is that everyone sits up and takes notice. They notice that you've changed the gender, so they proceed to notice that there *is* a gender routinely attached to God."[4] The maleness of the image of God is, no doubt, a product of the image

---

2. Beit-Hallahmi and Argyle (1997) p. 74.

3. Marcia Falk has recently published *The Book of Blessings* (1996) in which she includes a range of feminine images for God. Many of these images are based on traditional, but little known, sources and are sensitive to the nuances of the Hebrew language.

4. Goodman (1991) p. 93.

we portray of ourselves. While we continue to refer to ourselves using such terms as "mankind," we will be limited in our descriptions of the source of our spiritual being.

The liturgy and philosophy of Jewish tradition are as influenced by patriarchy as anything else is. However, the Jewish texts contain numerous images and multifaceted references to spiritual experiences and these are not exclusively male. Perhaps this is why complex poetry, such as selections from the Book of Psalms, is retained in the liturgy. In Hebrew there is no single word that translates as "God." In fact, it seems impossible to enumerate all the different ways in which reference is made to a "Supreme Being," and these vary according to the type of literature in which they appear. The central prayer of Judaism, the *Shema*, states categorically that "God is One," but it is also true that there are many holy names, each of which describes a different attribute of God.

It beyond the scope of this book to categorize the images of God definitively, but the following should give some idea. The view of God that emerges from the halachic literature and Codes is that of the "law giver." In prayer we have the compassionate parent; in *Aggadah* the teacher, companion, and friend; and in *midrash* the lost and lonely Deity separated and in exile. The biblical characterizations are complex and various. They are of an angry, vengeful Lord who must be appeased with sacrifices, a nurturing mother bird hovering over her nest, a revolutionary, a rescuer, and a holy spirit who is the source of visions. In Kabbalah God is the highest mystery; in hasidism God is both a lover and a Judge and is present in all of creation. The name Elohim is the Creator, Shechinah is the indwelling feminine presence, and Tzev'ot the captain of hordes of angels. *Shaddai* refers to strength and is the name bound on to the arm each day by men when they tie the *tephillin*.[5]

One of the most revered names is the Tetragrammaton spelled by the Hebrew letters *yud, hey, vav*, and *hey*. This name is considered unpronounceable, usually rendered as Adonai and translated as "Lord."

---

5. Berke and Schneider (1994) point out the *Shaddai* is also closely connected with the Hebrew words for breast, demon, and robbery.

In fact, the name has no precise root translation and there are many variant interpretations of its meaning. One of the most compelling is that the letters spell out the three tenses of the Hebrew verb "to be" and, therefore, the word is not a noun at all. It could mean, "The One who was, is and will be." Thus some texts translate the Tetragrammaton as "Eternal" although "Eternal Being" might better connote the meaning. This understanding connects it with another name of God, the one that was given to Moses in his encounter with the burning bush in the Midianite desert.[6] According to the biblical text, God is identified to Moses as *Eheyeh Asher Eheyeh*, which has been translated both as "I am that I am" and as "I am that which I am becoming." Both of these names for God refer to God as a verb rather than as a noun. A third suggestion, offered by Rabbi Arthur Waskow, has even fewer anthropocentric associations. Rabbi Waskow has suggested that the Tetragrammaton represents the sound made when one breathes out and, therefore, conveys the sense of the "Breath of Life."[7]

Although all these renderings of the concept of God can be found in the texts of Jewish tradition, there is little doubt that the predominant view has been that of God as an authority figure. It is this notion that has been so overwhelmingly rejected in modern times. The authors of the traditional texts may have had a more complex and subtle picture as they labored to translate their visions into a practical religion, but today there has been a failure of translation.

Rabbi Schachter has spoken of an image of God being a *Partzuf*.[8] A *Partzuf* is a kabbalistic concept that helps us understand the relationship between the infinite world of the Source of All and the finite world of our own existence. Names of God are root metaphors that need to be updated to fit our own contemporary experience, which today includes pictures of reality far removed from those of the ancient and medieval worlds.

---

6. Exodus 3:14.

7. Rabbi Waskow is making an allusion to a section of the *Shabbat* morning liturgy where God is referred to as *Nishmat Kol Chai*, the "Breath of Life."

8. *See* Schachter (1993) Chapter 25.

The paradoxical notions of God as a verb, as both male and female, as the source and breath of life, as infinite energy, and as an aspect of our deepest selves may begin to provide us with contemporary *partzufim*. Not only are they far more attractive to the modern person but they may also be closer to the actual experience of the Halachists and codifiers than the feudal language of the past. At first they may seem foreign to the notions that we are generally accustomed to in the wider culture. They just take a little getting used to.

Glossary of Hebrew Terms

Aggadah : stories and other nonhalachic literature in rabbinic texts.

Amidah : prayer that is said while standing and is included in all the daily services, also known as the "Shmoneh Esreh" (the eighteen blessings).

Barachu : call to prayer.

Bet Din : rabbinic court.

Chanukah : midwinter festival of lights.

Chavurah : informal group who meet for study, prayer, social action, socializing, and so forth.

Davven : Yiddish term for prayer.

Dayan : senior rabbi who serves as judge in a rabbinic court.

Devekut : cleaving or attachment (to God).

Gemmatria : system of numerology based on the Hebrew alphabet.

Gemorah	:	commentary on the Mishnah.
Habad	:	Hasidic group originating from the town of Lubavitch.
Haggadah	:	volume containing the story of Passover.
Halacha	:	Jewish law.
Kabbalah	:	"received"—generic term for Jewish mysticism.
Kaddish	:	memorial prayer for the dead.
Kavvana	:	intention during prayer.
Kedushah	:	holiness.
Kiddush	:	sanctification; a blessing over wine.
Lag b'Omer	:	a minor festival occurring on the thirty-third day of the Omer.
Lulav	:	palm branch waved during Sukkot.
Maariv	:	evening service.
Masorti	:	"traditional" Judaism (in the United Kingdom the *Masorti* synagogues are similar to Conservative synagogues in the United States).
Mikvah	:	ritual bath.
Minchah	:	afternoon service.
Minhag	:	custom.
Minyan	:	quorum of ten adult males required before certain prayers can be recited.
Mishnah	:	Oral Law.
Pesach	:	spring festival of Passover.

Rebbe	:	Hasidic leader—"Grand Rabbi."
Rosh Hashanah	:	Jewish New Year.
Shaharit	:	morning service.
Seder	:	Passover meal at which the Haggadah is read.
Sephirot	:	qualities or attributes of God depicted in the kabbalistic Tree of Life.
Shabbat	:	Sabbath.
Shechinah	:	indwelling, feminine presence of God.
Shema	:	central prayer declaring the unity of God.
Siddur	:	daily prayer book.
Sukkot	:	autumn harvest festival of "Booths."
Talmud	:	Oral Law—the combined Mishnah and Gemorah with commentaries.
Tanya	:	collection of texts in a single volume discussing hasidic philosophy by the founder of *Habad*.
Tefillah	:	prayer.
Tenach	:	the Hebrew Bible; an acrostic of Torah, *Nevi'im* (the books of the prophets), and *Ketuvim* (the remaining books, usually referred to as the "Writings").
Tephillin	:	phylacteries—leather boxes containing extracts from scripture that are bound to the arm and head by observant Jewish men during morning services.
Torah	:	Jewish sacred writings.

Tzaddik : a righteous person; in hasidism also a *rebbe*.

Yiddishkeit : Yiddish term referring to Jewish tradition and culture.

Zohar : the "Book of Splendor," a key kabbalistic text.

References

Adler, R. (1983). The Jew who wasn't there: halakhah and the Jewish woman. In *On Being a Jewish Feminist: A Reader*, ed. S. Heschel. New York: Schocken.

Amsel, A. (1969). *Judaism and Psychology*. Jerusalem: Feldheim.

Ansky, S. (1992). *The Dybbuk and Other Writings*. New York: Schocken (Library of Yiddish Classics).

Bakan, D. (1958). *Sigmund Freud and the Jewish Mystical Tradition*. New York: Schocken.

Beit-Hallahmi, B., and Argyle, M. (1997). *The Psychology of Religious Behaviour, Belief and Experience*. London: Routledge.

Berke, J. H. (1988). *The Tyranny of Malice: Exploring the Dark Side of Character and Culture*. London: Simon and Schuster.

Berke, J. H., and Schneider, S. (1994). Antithetical meanings of 'the breast.' *International Journal of Psycho-Analysis* 75:491–498.

Bernstein, M. (1995). *Jewish Chronicle*, March 24, 1995.

Bettelheim, B. (1982). *Freud and Man's Soul*. London: Penguin.

Bilu, Y., and Abromovitch, H. (1985). In search of the Saddiq: visitational dreams among Moroccan Jews in Israel. *Psychiatry* 48(February):83–92.

Bilu, Y., and Witzum, E. (1993). Working with Jewish ultra-orthodox patients: guidelines for a culturally sensitive therapy. *Cultural and Medical Psychiatry* 17(2):197–233.

Boteach, S. (1991). *Dreams*. New York: Bash.

Bowlby, J. (1980). *Attachment and Loss*, vol. iii. The Tavistock Institute of Human Relations. London: Hogarth.

Brenner, A. (1993). *Mourning and Mitzvah: Walking The Jewish Path*. Woodstock, VT: Jewish Lights Publications.

Buber, M. (1955). *The Legend Of The Baal-Shem*. Edinburgh: Harper & Row.

—— (1988). *The Origin and Meaning of hasidism*. Atlantic Highlands, NJ: Humanities Press.

Carter, B., and McGoldrick, M. (1989). *The Changing Family Life Cycle: A Framework for Family Therapy*. Needham Heights, MA: Allyon and Bacon.

Cartwright, A. (1991). Is religion a help around the time of death? *Public Health* 105(1):79–87.

Cohen, J. M. (1986). *Horizons of Jewish Prayer*. London: United Synagogue.

Cooley, C. H. (1902). *Human Nature and the Social Order*. New York: Scribners.

Cooper, H., ed. (1988). *Soul Searching: Studies in Judaism and Psychotherapy*. London: SCM Press.

Covitz, J. (1990). *Visions of the Night: A Study of Jewish Dream Interpretation*. Boston and London: Shambhala.

de Silva, P. (1984). Buddhism and behaviour modification. *Behavior Research and Therapy* 22:661–678.

Diamant, A. (1985). *The New Jewish Wedding*. New York: Summit Books.

Etkes, I. (1993). *Rabbi Israel Salanter and the Musar Movement*, Philadelphia and Jerusalem: The Jewish Publication Society.

Falk, M. (1996). *The Book of Blessings*. New York: Harper Collins.

Fine, L. (1984). *Safed Spirituality*. New York: Paulist Press.

Freud, S. (1927). The future of an illusion. In *Sigmund Freud 12. Civilization, Society and Religion*, trans. J. Strachey. London: Penguin.

—— (1939). *Moses and Monotheism*. New York: Vintage.

Freud, S. (1900). The interpretation of dreams. *Standard Edition*. London: Hogarth Press.

Ganzfield, S. (1961). *Code of Jewish Law (Kitzur Shulchan Aruch)*. New York: Hebrew Publishing.

Geffen, R. M., ed. (1993). *Celebration and Renewal: Rites of Passage in Judaism*. Philadelphia and Jerusalem: The Jewish Publication Society.

Gold, N. (1995). Ima's not on the Bima: psychological barriers to women taking leadership in Jewish religious practice. In *Jewish Women Speak Out: Expanding the Boundaries of Psychology*, ed. K. Weiner and A. Moon. Seattle: Canopy.

Goldman. (1997). Beit-Hallahmi and Argyle.

Goldstein, S. (1992). Profile of American Jews: insights from the 1990 national Jewish population survey. In *The American Jewish Year Book*, ed. D. Singer and R. Seldin. New York: American Jewish Committee and Philadelphia: The Jewish Publication Society.

Goodman, J. (1991). Sex, symbols and the unity of God. In *The Absent Mother: Restoring the Goddess to Judaism and Christianity*, ed. A. Pirani. London: Mandala.

Green, A. (1992). *Seek My Face, Speak My Name*. Northvale, NJ: Jason Aronson.

Greenberg, B. (1981). *On Women and Judaism: A View From Tradition*. Philadelphia: The Jewish Publication Society of America.

Gross, J. J., Fredrickson, B. L., and Levenson, R. W. (1994). Psychophysiology of crying. *Psychophysiology* 31:460–468.

Halevi, Z. (1986). *Kabbalah and Psychology*. London: Gateway Books.

Hertz, J. H. (1967). *The Pentateuch and Haftorahs: Hebrew Text, English Translation and Commentary*, 2nd ed., London: Soncino.

Heschel, A. J. (1955). *God in Search of Man: A Philosophy of Judaism*. New York: Farrar, Straus and Giroux.

——— (1959). *The Insecurity of Freedom: Essays on Human Existence*. New York: Schocken.

Heschel, S., ed. (1983). *On Being A Jewish Feminist: A Reader*. New York: Schocken.

——— (1986). Current issues in Jewish feminist theology. *Christian–Jewish Relations*, 19(2):23–40.

Hoffman, E. (1981). *The Way of Splendour: Jewish Mysticism and Modern Psychology*. Boston and London: Shambhala.

Hoffman, L. (1987). *Beyond The Text: A Holistic Approach To Liturgy.* Woodstock, IN: Indiana University Press.

Idel, M. (1995). *Hasidism: Between Ecstasy and Magic.* Albany: State University of New York Press.

Jacobs, L. (1972). *Hassidic Prayer.* London: Routledge and Kegan Paul.

Jacobs, L. (1973). *A Jewish Theology.* London: Darton, Longman and Todd.

———— (1976). *Jewish Mystical Testimonies.* New York: Schocken.

———— (1984). *A Tree Of Life.* Oxford: Oxford University Press.

James, W. (1950). *The Principles of Psychology (Authorized Edition).* New York: Constable.

———— (1960). *The Varieties of Religious Experience.* London and Glasgow: Fontana.

Johnson, R. A. (1983). *The Psychology of Romantic Love.* Great Britain: Penguin.

Jung, C. G. (1954). *The Archetype and the Collective Unconscious, Collected Works,* vol. 9, part 1. Princeton, NJ: Princeton University Press. (original edition 1935).

———— (1983). *Memories, Dreams and Reflections,* Flamingo ed. New York: Random House.

Kadish, S. (1997). *Kavvana: Directing the Heart in Jewish Prayer.* Northvale, NJ: Jason Aronson.

Kahan, Y. M. (1976). (The *Chafetz Chayim*) *Ahavath Chesed,* 1967. Jerusalem: Feldheim Publishers.

Kaplan, A. (1982). *Meditation and Kabbalah.* York Beach, ME: Samuel Weiser.

Klein, D. B. (1981). *Jewish Origins of the Psychoanalytic Movement.* Chicago: The University of Chicago Press.

Kubler-Ross, E. (1969). *On Death and Dying,* London: Tavistock.

Lamm, M. (1982). *The Jewish Way In Love and Marriage.* New York: Harper and Row.

Lancaster, B. (1991). *Mind, Brain and Human Potential: The Quest for an Understanding of Self.* Great Britain and USA: Element Books.

Lauterbach, J. Z. (1970). *Studies in Jewish Law, Custom and Folklore.* New York: Ktav.

Lederer, W. J., and Jackson, D. D. (1968). *The Mirage of Marriage.* New York: Norton.

Levi, P. (1985). *If Not Now, When*, trans. W. Weaver. London: Abacus.

Lewis, C. S. (1961). *A Grief Observed.* London: Faber and Faber.

Linke, S. B. (1989). Resistance and restraint. *Behavioural Psychotherapy* 17:119–124.

Lovell, D. M., Hemmings, G., and Hill, A. B. (1993). Bereavement reactions of female Scots and Swazis: a preliminary comparison. *British Journal of Medical Psychology* 66(3):259–274.

Maslow, A. (1968). *Towards a Psychology of Being*, 2nd ed. New York: Litton Educational Publishing. (1st ed. 1962)

———— (1970). *Motivation and Personality*, 2nd ed. New York: Harper. (1st ed. 1954)

Meier, L. (1988). *Jewish Values in Psychotherapy: Essays on Vital Issues on The Search for Meaning.* Lanham, MD: University Press of America.

Meyer, M. A. (1988). *Response to Modernity: A History of the Reform Movement.* New York: Oxford University Press.

Morin, C. M. (1994). *Insomnia: Psychological Assessment and Management.* New York and London: Guilford.

Or Chadash (1988). *New Paths for Shabbat Morning.* P'nai Or Religious Fellowship.

Parkes, C. M. (1991). *Bereavement: Studies of Grief in Adult Life*, 2nd ed. London: Penguin.

Patai, R. (1997). *The Jewish Mind.* Detroit: Wayne State University Press.

Perls, F. S. (1969). *Gestalt Therapy Verbatim.* USA: Bantam.

Plaskow, J. (1990). *Standing Again at Sinai: Judaism from a Feminist Perspective.* New York: Harper Collins.

Potock, C. (1985). *Davita's Harp.* New York: Fawcett Crest.

Rachman, S., and de Silva, P. (1978). Normal and abnormal obsessions. *Behavior Research and Therapy* 32:311–314.

Rotenberg, M. (1994). PaRDeS and PaRDeS: Towards a Psychotherapeutic Theory. *Israeli Journal of Psychiatry and Related Sciences*. 31(3):162–9.

Salkovskis, P. M. (1989). Cognitive-behavioral factors and the persistence of intrusive thoughts in obsessional problems. *Behavior Research and Therapy* 27:677–682.

Schachter, S., and Singer, J. E. (1962). Cognitive, social and physiological determinants of emotional state. *Psychological Review* 69:379–399.

Schachter-Shalomi, Z. (1991). *Spiritual Intimacy: A Study of Counselling in Hasidism*. Northvale, NJ: Jason Aronson.

——— (1993). *The Paradigm Shift*. Northvale, NJ: Jason Aronson.

Schmool, M. (1997). We cannot stop inter-marriage. *Manna*, No. 54, (Winter).

Schmool, M., and Miller, S. (1994). *Women in the Jewish Community Survey Report*. London: Office of the Chief Rabbi.

Shorter, B. (1996). *Susceptible to the Sacred: The Psychological Experience of Ritual*. London: Routledge.

Shulman, S. (1996). Identifying politics with religion. *Women Against Fundamentalism* No 8:8.

Singer, Rev S. (1962). *The Authorised Daily Prayer Book*.

Skynner, R. (1976). *One Flesh: Separate Persons: Principles of Family and Psychotherapy*. London: Constable.

Soloveitchik, J. (1944). *Halachic Man*. Philadelphia and Jerusalem: The Jewish Publication Society.

——— (1965). The lonely man of faith. *Tradition* 7(2):

Spero, M. L. (1990). Parallel dimensions of experience in psychoanalytic psychotherapy of the religious patient. *Psychotherapy* 27(1):53–71.

Steinsaltz, A. (1980). *The Thirteen Petalled Rose*. New York: Basic Books.

Stroebe, W., and Stroebe, M. (1987). *Bereavement and Health: The Psychological and Physical Consequences of Partner Loss*. Cambridge: Cambridge University Press.

Watts, F., and Williams, M. (1988). *The Psychology of Religious Knowing*. Cambridge: Cambridge University Press.

Wavell, S., Butt, A., and Epton, N. (1966). *Trances*. London: George Allen & Unwin.

Wiesel, E. (1972). *Souls on Fire*. Penguin.

Weissman, M. (1980). *The Midrash Says: The Book of Sh'mos*. New York: Benei Yacov.

Welwood, J. (1983). *Awakening The Heart: East/West Approaches to Psychotherapy and the Healing Relationship*. Boston and London: Shambhala.

Wiener, A. (1978). *The Prophet Elijah in the Development of Judaism: A Depth-Psychological Study*. London: Routledge and Kegan Paul.

Wilber, K. (1977). *The Spectrum of Consciousness*. Wheaton, IL: Quest Books.

———— (1980). *The Atman Project: A Transpersonal View of Human Development*. Wheaton, IL: Quest Books.

———— (1981). *Up From Eden: A Transpersonal View Of Human Evolution*. London: Routledge and Kegan Paul.

Winnicott, D. W. (1989). *The Family and Individual Development*, London: Routledge.

Worden, J. (1991). *Grief Counselling and Grief Therapy: A Handbook for the Mental Health Practitioner* 2nd ed. Boston: Springer, Harvard Medical School.

Yalom, I. D. (1980). *Existential Psychotherapy*. New York: Basic Books.

Index

About the Author

Stuart Linke is a Consultant Clinical Psychologist in Islington's Adult Mental Health Service in London, England. He holds an Honorary Lectureship in Psychology at University College London and has taught at the Spiro Institute for Jewish History and Culture. Stuart Linke has studied with a wide range of teachers of Judaism and Jewish mysticism and is a longtime student of Rabbi Zalman Shacter-Shalomi. He has been an activist in the Jewish peace movement and is a co-founder of the *Ruach Chavurah* of London. For over ten years, Stuart Linke has been involved in the Alliance for Jewish Spiritual Renewal in the United Kingdom and regularly teaches and leads workshops in London and elsewhere. His previous publications have included articles in professional psychology journals on alcohol abuse, community mental health, suicide risk, and violence. He lives with his wife, Jenny Goodman, and their son on the outskirts of London.